IN THE WORLD, OF THE CHURCH

IN THE WORLD, OF THE CHURCH

A Paul Evdokimov Reader

edited and translated by
Michael Plekon and Alexis Vinogradov

ST VLADIMIR'S SEMINARY PRESS
2001

Library of Congress Cataloging-in-Publication Data

Evdokimov, Paul, 1901-1970.
    [Selections. English. 2000]
    In the world, of the Church: a Paul Evdokimov reader / Paul Evdokimov;
Alex Vinogradov, translator, Michael Plekon, translator.
       p. cm.
    Includes bibliographical references.
    ISBN 0-88141-215-5 (alk. paper)
    1. Orthodox Eastern Church—Doctrines.   I. Title.
BX597.E77 A25 2000
230'.19—dc21   00-051842

IN THE WORLD, OF THE CHURCH
A Paul Evdokimov Reader

Copyright © 2001

St Vladimir's Seminary Press
575 Scarsdale Road, Crestwood, New York 10707
1-800-204-2665

ISBN 0-88141-215-5

PRINTED IN THE UNITED STATES OF AMERICA

CONTENTS

ACKNOWLEDGMENTS

There are many to thank for help in producing this volume of Paul Evdokimov's essays: Father Michel Evdokimov, Paul Evdokimov's son, emeritus professor of the University at Poitiers and rector of the parish of Saints Peter and Paul, Châtenay-Malabry, and Marie-Claire, his wife, for friendship, thoughtful suggestions, conversation and for hospitality beyond imagination; Mrs Tomoko Faerber-Evdokimoff, Paul Evdokimov's widow, likewise for support and for permission to translate and publish these essays; Ms Catherine Roulin of Editions du Seuil for permission to translate and publish essays gathered in *L'amour fou de Dieu;* the editors of *Contacts* and the Abbey of Bellefontaine for permission to use essays they published; Dean Alexandra Logue of the Weissman School of Arts and Science, Baruch College of the City University of New York and the Committee on Reassigned Time for released time to work on this project, similarly to Joyce M. Mullan and the Research Foundation of CUNY for PSC-CUNY Faculty Research Awards 667121, 668132, 669124 and 61140-00-30, which enabled the work and publication; our spouses and children and the people of the parish of St Gregory the Theologian Orthodox Church, Wappingers Falls, New York, for support. To these and those whom we have omitted "through ignorance, forgetfulness and multitude of names," as we say in the preparatory rite of the Liturgy, our thanks, prayers and love.

Michael Plekon
Alexis Vinogradov

INTRODUCTION

While searchers for spirituality have some acquaintance with the tradition of the Eastern Church through such treasured collections as the *Philokalia* or the *Sayings* and *Lives of the Desert Fathers*, from here on recognition becomes uneven. Some know the writings of such nineteenth-century figures as Ss Ignatius Brianchaninov and Tikhon of Zadonsk. Others have come to love the saint who much resembles St Francis of Assisi, St Seraphim of Sarov, only canonized in 1903 and also a nineteenth-century priest and monk in Russia. Perhaps the most widely known character, one with a significant teaching to impart even though he appears within a densely populated novel, is Fr Zossima of *The Brothers Karamazov*. This monk was drawn by Dostoevsky from his own relationship with the elders of Optino monastery, several of whom, such as Ambrose and Macarius, have now been glorified as saints by the Church of Russia. Likewise, *The Way of a Pilgrim,* whose actual author Archimandrite Mikail Kozlov has recently been identified, has enjoyed broad popularity.

Here and there other names have become familiar. First in France and then among English-speaking readers familiar is "The Monk of the Eastern Church," the literary name of Fr Lev Gillet, a Benedictine monk-priest who entered the Orthodox Church in the late 1920s in Paris and then served in many capacities: chaplain to student associations and at Mother Maria Skobtsova's settlement-house in the rue Lourmel, pastor, teacher, ecumenical representative, retreat master, spiritual father in addition to his work as an author. Lay theologian Elisabeth Behr-Sigel, a lifelong friend of Fr Lev's, has now given us a rich biographical account of his life, even more fascinating than many suspected. Due to the efforts of his disciple, Fr Sophrony Sakharov, both the life and the sayings of a contemporary canonized elder

St Silouan of Mount Athos have become known both in Europe and here.

And there surely are other holy ones whose lives and writings have made some impression in recent years: the dynamic and yet eccentric parish priest (and some would say ecclesiastical entrepreneur) St John (Sergeiv) of Kronstadt, even the bishop of San Francisco in the Russian Church Abroad, St John Maximovitch, who died in 1966. There is a strong bond with those glorified by the Church as saints who lived and worked here in America—the elder Herman, missionaries such as Innocent who later was Metropolitan of Moscow, Peter and Juvenaly, Tikhon, archbishop here and later Patriarch of Moscow, priests Alexander Hotovitsky and John Kochurov who worked here and were martyred during the Revolution in Russia. The talks, homilies and numerous publications of the recently assassinated Fr Alexander Men, an enormously loved educator and priest of the greater Moscow area, have now begun to enrich readers outside Russia. Quite differently, the radical and confrontational version of Orthodox tradition disseminated by the recently deceased Fr Seraphim Rose is attractive for some, and yet most troubling for others.

This is not to ignore a formidable corpus of work, ordinarily identified more with mainstream theology, produced by some of the most brilliant minds of the Russian emigration, the lights of what Nicholas Zernov called the "Russian religious renaissance" that preceded the Revolution. Both within the Eastern Church and in that of the West there is still much to "receive" from Frs Sergius Bulgakov and Pavel Florensky, from Frs Nicholas Afanasiev and Mother Maria Skobtsova, from philosophers Nicholas Berdiaev and S.L. Frank, historians Kartashev and Feodotov, and from the generation that followed them, working here in America: the immensely significant work of theologians such as Frs Georges Florovsky, John Meyendorff and Alexander Schmemann.

Very much a part of this second generation and well-known in France, where he settled upon emigration from Russia, known even among Catholics and Protestants, is a most compelling and lively figure, the lay theologian Paul Evdokimov. There are many intriguing aspects to his life and his work. His biographer, also a lay theologian,

Olivier Clément, identifies several. One is that very although much a man of the Spirit, in his own words, a "liturgical being," a person for whom, Fr Lev Gillet said at his funeral, prayer was "as natural as breathing," Paul Evdokimov was also quintessentially a man of the world. He was married, father of two children, widowed and remarried. He supported himself in his student days by washing railways cars and working at the Citröen plant in Paris, while also doing university studies in literature and philosophy at the Sorbonne and theology with the likes of Bulgakov, Kartashev, Berdiaev and others of the "renaissance" at St Sergius Theological Institute. While his wife Natasha supported the family by teaching, he wrote a doctoral dissertation on Dostoevsky's theology, also caring for his very young son and daughter and the rest of the household chores—and this in the early 1930s! During World War II, he worked first with the Resistance, primarily in hiding those targeted for arrest by the occupying Nazis and then and for a decade thereafter, directing an ecumenically sponsored hostel for displaced persons, and later political refugees, Third World immigrants, students, and the socially marginal folk.

Few theologians had the privilege, as his son, Fr Michel Evdokimov, puts it, of such a life of worldly *diakonia*, of service to others. Finally, in the late 1950s, his second wife, Tomoko Sakai-Evdokimov, assumed the leadership of the hostel and enabled him to teach full-time on the faculty of St Sergius and as a visiting professor at L'Institut Catholique, the Roman Catholic graduate theological school at the Ecumenical Center at Bossey and at many other ecumenical and Orthodox schools and religious houses. His writings filled an equally diverse range of scholarly journals, as the selections collected and here presented in translation attest. He knew personally many of the contemporary figures he mentions and quotes, and not just from churchly circles, the community of believers, but very much from beyond, in the world: Sartre, Simone de Beauvoir, Jung. At the third session of Vatican Council II he was appointed and attended as an official ecumenical observer and though not explicitly cited by name, his influence on the constitution on the Church in the world, *Lumen gentium* is not hard to detect.

Not only did Paul Evdokimov have a different foundation of experience for his theological work, I also believe he had a distinctive

understanding of the place and mission of theology in both the Church
and world of our time. He was part of the rediscovery or rebirth of litur-
gics, patristics, and scriptural exegesis among the Russians both just
before and after the Revolution. Though a layperson all of his life, he
had an unusually insightful understanding of monastic life and spirituality. Trained in both philosophy and theology, from the start he began to
search for theological insight beyond the borders of these disciplines, in
literature, social theory, psychology and art. It is therefore no surprise
that his essays and books are filled with references to and discussions of
Freud and Jung, Marx and Heidegger, Gogol and Dostoevsky, Sartre
and de Beauvoir, Camus and Simone Weil, along with a long train of
fathers and mothers of the desert, patristic writers and saints. His major
work, *L'orthodoxie,* still not translated into English, is a kind of *summa* of
Orthodox theology but of a very different sort than the usual efforts of
academic theologians to create their own dogmatic synthesis. Entwined
with the major doctrinal work of the ecumenical councils, Evdokimov
weaves the beauty of the icons, the heavenly transcendence of the Divine
Liturgy, the wonderful sayings of the desert fathers and the lived experience of the Christian, a "liturgical existentialism," without the angst of
the philosophers who go by this label.

Evdokimov was to produce as one of his principal volumes a still
fresh, lyrical study of the distinctive theology and power of the icons of
the Eastern Church, *The Art of the Icon, A Theology of Beauty.* Among
others, Olivier Clément considers the understanding of the Kingdom
of God as the pinnacle of all beauty to be Evdokimov's principal contribution to theology in our time. But, in fact, I think it is very difficult to
so characterize the central insight or perception of Evdokimov's work.
One could just as easily argue that for him the core of Christian faith,
of the liturgy and the icon, of the Eucharist and the Church, is God's
emptying out of himself, his *kenosis* in absurd, foolish love for us. Or it
would be equally possible to point to the Mother of God as a the
person whose *fiat,* whose "yes" to God as the ultimate "liturgical
being," is the quintessential icon of the Church, of the liturgy, of the
life of every Christian.

Likewise, it is not hard to notice Evdokimov's consistent interest in
the mystery and the gifts of woman, the depths of the feminine in a

time of feminism. Here even some of his closest friends, including Elisabeth Behr-Sigel, question his thinking. Yet his concern with the feminine opens us up to another seemingly incongruous fascination and connection throughout his writings, namely the callings of the monastic life and that of married life for the Christian. *The Sacrament of Love*, his analysis and contemplation of marriage as sacrament and vocation, remains one of his best known books. In it, surprisingly, the connections between married life and monasticism are followed. This, however, is not so unusual as it appears, for in working through Evdokimov's writings, one finds that monasticism's gifts to the rest of the Church, the teaching of monastic spirituality for all Christians, is yet another major theme. Borrowing from and adapting a phrase from the nineteenth-century Russian bishop and theologian, St Tikhon of Zadonsk, Evdokimov argues that all Christians by their baptism and chrismation are called to the royal priesthood of the Church and tonsured in these initiation sacraments (the newly baptized still are tonsured in the Eastern Church) to an eschatological way of life not essentially different from the "maximal" vocation of monastics. For him, St Tikhon's "untonsured monasticism" becomes an "interiorized" monasticism that can be lived by all Christians. It is both hard to precisely capture his language and intent here and easy to misunderstand this concept. It is not at all the case that monasticism is the "superior" vocation, all others inferior to it. Neither does Evdokimov envision any simple imitation of monastic life, its dress or details. The vows of poverty, chastity and obedience taken by monks and nuns are, after all he notes, none other than Christ's reply to the three temptations of the Evil One after the Lord's forty-day time of prayer and fasting in the desert. The roots of monastic life in the Eucharist, daily liturgical prayer and reading of the scriptures and in doing the works of love for the neighbor—these are the same roots for those who are married, raising children, studying or working in every profession or job.

Contrary to much superficial and uninformed dabbling in "spirituality" so widespread in our culture in these last years of the twentieth century, Evdokimov, in what Clément calls his real masterpiece, *The Ages of the Spiritual Life*, presents the classical and substantial tradition of the life of faith from the time of the early Church to our own era. It is not possible to recreate the ancient Church's exact existence nor is it right to do so. Neither is it living Tradition to adhere slavishly, obsessively to the details of the spiritual life of the third or for that matter of any other century. It is the Holy Spirit's promise to us that he will constantly come down, that there will always be an *epiclesis* or descent of his life and light. But it is also the Spirit's challenge to us to find the ways of living the Christian life, of worshipping and being the Church appropriate to our time. Here we encounter one of the principal conflicts of Christianity in our time, that is, the clash between "traditionalists" and "liberals," as one set of labels would characterize them, between those opposed to any change or adaptation whatever (in the extreme) and those convinced (also in the extreme) that virtually all of the Christian tradition is expendable. Evdokimov's position here is that of his colleagues of the "Russian religious renaissance," simply that the Holy Spirit remains, and where he is, there the Church is also. His nuanced, moderate, yet profound sense of Tradition assures us that there has always been diversity in unity and the constant work of the Spirit to breathe new life and new ways into the life of the people of God. The lives of holy men and women throughout the history of the Church are held out to us, in the Church's daily calendar, readings and other liturgical feasts and their texts as "living icons" of holiness, of the divine life incarnated into human lives.

The Christian life, for Evdokimov, does not have only a vertical dimension, that is an axis of communion with God, the Mother of God, angels and saints of the heavenly Kingdom through the liturgy, prayer, Bible and icons. The cruciform or Cross pattern stretches out horizontally, as Christ's arms did on the Cross, and in these are the open heart of the Father and healing wings of the Holy Spirit. There is no Christian life with loving care and service toward the neighbor. The "liturgy after the liturgy," in the well known words of St John Chrysostom, is celebrated on the altar that is the face and the heart of every sister and brother around us. Paul Evdokimov did not simply write or teach this, he lived it. The tributes to him at the time of his death in 1970, from family, friends and academic colleagues, from clergy of all the churches—Orthodox, Protestant and Roman Catholic—and from monastics of all these communions, from some of those who lived in the hostels he directed, these testified to a man full of God and full of tender, simple care for them. It is revealing to read, in the essay included in this collection, Evdokimov's own very restrained and modest remembrances of all these faces and lives and his life with them as friend, sometimes listener, sometimes counselor, always as servant, in the common priesthood of all the faithful. Today, even one of his beloved commitments, that of ecumenical prayer, study and conversation, is attacked and condemned by some of his fellow Orthodox in the name of truth and the purity of the tradition. The canons are invoked to reject shared prayer or any "contaminating" contact with heretics. One can carefully read pages after pages, thousands of them, in Paul Evdokimov's writings and never encounter this epithet for a fellow Christian, "heretic." He wrote, spoke and acted, a colleague said, as if there had never been a schism, either in the eleventh or in the sixteenth centuries. In his own words he lived not only face to face with the mystery of the division or separation of the churches but in awe of the yet greater mystery of God's desire for their unity and granting of this despite schism and disagreement. Likewise, Evdokimov followed the lead of his teacher Fr Sergius Bulgakov in rejecting the "penitentiary theology" of previous centuries, the use of fear, threat and force by the Church to bring souls around from sin back to holy living. Like Pope Jon Paul II more recently, Evdokimov could freely and easily point to the abuses of the clergy and faithful in times past as well as present, acknowledge these evils, ask God's forgiveness, and move on to the work of the Gospel. Thus, as several of the essays express it, the Church is more interested in healing than punishing. The Fathers could even wonder about the limitless love of God in the resurrection and salvation of all (*apokatastasis*) at the end, or better, the fullness of time and revealing of the Kingdom, the universal redemption so threatening to our human sense of "justice," that union upon which Fr Bulgakov meditated at length in his larger trilogy, as did Origen and Gregory of Nyssa, among others.

The first of the selections in this collection, "Eschatology," is precisely about the end or fullness of time, death, life after the grave, judgment, hell and damnation and the resurrection of all. Like the rest of the essays selected and translated here, it originally appeared in a now difficult-to-access location, a collection long out-of-print or a back number of a scholarly journal. In choosing these essays, we have tried to include a variety of the issues about which Paul Evdokimov spoke and wrote. "Eschatology" contains much of what he learned from his own study of the Fathers as well as from a contemporary "Father" and teacher of the Church, the much (and illegitimately) maligned theologian of the Russian emigration, Fr Sergius Bulgakov, one of Evdokimov's teachers at St Sergius in Paris. "Some Landmarks on the Journey of Life" is the closest one comes to autobiographical writing in Paul Evdokimov's publications. Though reserved and spare in personal detail, his autobiographical "souvenirs" speak eloquently of what he treasured most in life, in the world, and in the Church. We included his 1950 open letter "To the Churches of Christ," an impassioned plea in the wake of WWII and in the intense hopefulness of ecumenical interaction in France at that time. Paul Evdokimov's incisive social criticism (and ability to apply the Fathers) is revealed in the essay, "The Church and Society: The Social Dimensions of Orthodox Ecclesiology." The longest piece in this collection, a primer about the spiritual life itself, is "Holiness in the Orthodox Tradition." The very last paper Evdokimov presented, just days before his death is his most challenging work about the Mother of God, "Panagion et Panagia," "The All-Holy One (Spirit) and the All-Holy (Virgin)." Another essay focuses on perhaps the best known theological expression Paul Evdokimov used, "l'amour four de Dieu," the "foolish" or "absurd" love of God, actually a phrase from the fourteenth-century Byzantine lay theologian, Nicholas Cabasilas. Here Evdokimov dwells upon the apparent "silence" or absence of God in our time and experience. A pair of essays, "Culture and Faith" and "Freedom and Authority" display Evdokimov's deft interplay of Christian tradition and the contemporary controversy and conflict. Though not lacking criticism even from his life-long friend, the lay theologian Elisabeth Behr-Sigel, Evdokimov did write extensively on women and their gifts and place in culture and society and the Church. His thinking is amply represented by the essay "The Charisms of Women." The collection concludes with what might at first appear to be a rather formal, almost textbook presentation, "The Eucharist, Mystery of the Church." However as in virtually all of Paul Evdokimov's writing, no matter how difficult the material, how rigorous the analysis, how serious the intent, another voice is nevertheless heard. It is not the sentimentally pious one of devotional tracts. Neither is it that of radical criticism, so characteristic of 20th century theological expression. (Evdokimov, as other selections here well attest, could very well write as an impassioned prophetic critic.) What is heard in this final piece bears echoes of Fr Sergius Bulgakov, and of Frs Nicholas Afanasiev and Alexander Schmemann, also of the Paris Russian community, who would awaken the Church to her true heart, the Sacrament of Sacraments. In the end, one hears in Paul Evdokimov the voice of the Mother of God, that of prayer, of a "liturgical being," and encounters not just theological issues and problems but a Person, the crucified and Risen Christ who is, in the words of the prayer of the Cherubic Hymn, "the Offerer and the Offered, the Receiver and the Received," the Eucharistic Lord who in his Body and Blood in the Bread and Cup, opens to us the Kingdom, the life of the Triune God, and in the same, communion with each other.

Michael Plekon

I

ESCHATOLOGY

On Death, the Afterlife, and the Kingdom; the "Last Things"[1]

The mystery of salvation

"If true wisdom means knowing reality, we would call a person wise only if he embraced in his knowledge the things to come." This is what St Gregory of Nyssa asserts.[2] The last things are covered by a veil of mystery. While the patristic tradition most often leaves the explanation of these to scriptural texts, scripture is not always sufficiently explicit. Except the articles of the Nicene Creed which mention the *Parousia* (the second coming of Christ), the last judgment and the resurrection, Orthodoxy possesses no exhaustive dogmatic synthesis of the eschatological realities, the "last things." One sees here the Church's great pedagogical wisdom, for, according to St Paul, it is only the "foolishness of the Cross," and not established doctrine, which is able to bring together the unforseeable ways of God.

Thus it seems that in the central mystery of the divine economy, in the love of God, his mercy and his justice appear to be mutually contradictory. The scholastic manuals of theology customarily conclude with a final chapter on the last things, but their format is highly misleading, for it is so thoroughly rationalistic and anthropomorphic. Fr Sergius Bulgakov calls this simplistic solution "penitential theology," one which, in moving away from the mystery of God, ends up by constructing a juridical code. The significance of this approach is quite dubious, in the light of St Paul's

---

1   "L' eschatologie," in *Le buisson ardent*, Collection Bible et Vie Chrétienne, Nouvelle Série, direction P.P. Fransen et Poswick, Abbaye bénédictine de Maredsous (Paris: Editions P. Lethielleux, 1981), pp. 135-167.
2   PG 45, 580c.

words: "O the depth of the riches and wisdom and knowledge of God! How unsearchable are his judgments, how inscrutable his ways."[3]

The biblical and patristic understanding of salvation as healing

On the Cross, Jesus said: "Father, forgive them, for they do not know what they are doing."[4] The Church can only emulate this word. Not to know what one has done is exactly the situation of one who is disabled, one who is insensible because of deafness or blindness and who is, therefore, not entirely responsible.

For the Eastern Church, salvation is not at all juridical. It is not the sentence of a court of law. The verb *yacha* in Hebrew means "to have some elbow-room," to be at ease. In the most general sense it means to deliver, to save from danger, from an illness, ultimately, to save from death. It describes that which delivers. Precisely and most particularly, it means to reestablish a living balance, *to heal.* The substantive *yécha*, salvation, refers to complete deliverance with peace-*shalom* at the end. In the New Testament *sôteria* in Greek, coming from the verb *sôzô*, the adjective *sôs* corresponds to *sanus* in Latin and means to return health to one who had lost it, to save from death, which is the natural terminus of every illness. That is why the expression "your faith has saved you," is tantamount to "your faith has healed you," the two expressions being synonyms of the same act of divine pardon, an act which touches the soul and the body in their very unity.

Corresponding to this fundamental vision, the sacrament of confession is *metanoia* or transformation more than *penitentia*. Confession is understood as a "clinic," that is, a place of healing. Believing psychiatrists know the sacramental action of absolution and send their patients to receive appropriate treatment in the "ecclesial clinic." For Clement of Alexandria, the confessor is like an angel of God, capable of opening up the soul of a sinner. He is, above all, a physician for the healing of the sick, "God's therapist." The prayer before confession says: "You have come to the physician, may you not return without being healed."

3 Rom 2:33.
4 Lk 23:24.

The Council *in Trullo* (692) defined this charism: "Those who have received from God the power to bind and to loosen should act as physicians, attentive to finding the particular remedy which each penitent requires yet lacks."[5] The *epitimia* or penance corrects, it is not a punishment. Once again, it is not so much the juridical principal of "satisfaction" as it is the fact of healing. The spiritual father searches for the organic connection between the sick person and the therapeutic means, and then prescribes the conditions under which the person is no longer troubled by sin. St John Chrysostom describes this quite precisely: "Time is of no matter. We do not ask if the wound has been treated often but if the treatment has been successful. The state of the wounded one indicates when the disease has been removed."[6]

St Ignatius of Antioch called the Eucharist *pharmakon athanasias*, the "medicine of immortality." Jesus the Savior appeared thus as the Divine Healer, saying: "It is not the healthy who need a physician but the sick...I did not come to call the righteous but sinners."[7] According to the canon cited from the Council *in Trullo*, "sin is the sickness of the spirit," and an atheist is a sick person who ignores the malignant nature of his condition. Spiritual death is more terrifying than anything which menaces the body. The healing of such a one would be the elimination of the demonic germ, the removal of the veil which blocks out the light of Christ, the calming of the spiritual revolt.

According to the *Shepherd of Hermas*, a very early Christian text, "the name of God sustains the world," keeps it in equilibrium. The name of God creates the cosmos out of chaos. This is why the Church sings the *Trisagion* or Thrice-Holy prayer at the moment of catastrophes: "Holy God, Holy Mighty, Holy Immortal, have mercy on us." The invocation of the Trinity calms, it brings order into chaos. This is the same reason for singing the *Trisagion* in the burial service, when the body is interred. Such a prayer expresses faith in the resurrection, the re-establishment of what is normal, ontological healing.

5   Canon 102; Mansi tr.XI, col. 987.
6   The sick nature is healed by the medicine of salvation, St John of Damascus teaches, PG 94, 1332; Origen, is the first who places salvation in connection with the parable of the Good Samaritan-healer, PG 13, 1886-88; 14, 856 A.
7   Mt 9:12-13.

Evil's malignancy encounters the power of the cure. The sick one undergoes treatment by God, who is the surgeon. In the place of the patient, it is the Physician who dies, is raised and inaugurates his universal and radical therapy: "Unless a grain of wheat falls into the earth and dies, it remains just a single grain; but if it dies, it bears much fruit."[8] The Cross is planted on the threshold of new life, the water of Baptism receives the sacramental value of the blood of Christ.

Forgiveness places us at the heart of the relationship between God, the Holy One, and the person, a sinner, and it is necessary to grasp the profundity of this act. It is not God's almighty, obliterating or annihilating power which figures here. Rather it is "the Lamb immolated from the foundation of the world" who acts. Forgiveness comes from Christ, who, according to St Paul, "forgave us all our trespasses, erasing the record that stood against us with its legal demands. He set this aside, nailing it to the cross."[9] The creation of the world is rooted in this sacrifice. The power of forgiveness comes from the price of the blood shed by the crucified Lamb. Christ takes upon himself the sins of the world, responding to the love of the Father by his indescribable love in our place, which manifests the "moral" power of removing our sin, of forgiving and restoring us as children of the Father.

But the human *fiat*, "let it be so," the expression of the total act of faith proclaimed by the Virgin Mary, demands the same freedom as the creating *fiat* of God. And this is why God accepts his being refused, ignored and rejected by the revolt of his own creature. On the Cross, it is God against God. He has taken the side of humankind, and has begun our healing.

There is a well-known saying of the Fathers: "What Christ has not assumed, is not saved, is not healed."[10] Christ assumes the place of every person in the midst of sin, in the midst of atheism and the atheistic revolt. At this stage in history, atheism is the "murder of the Father." It has severed the umbilical cord linking man to the beyond, to the Transcendent. It has rejected the link with the abyss of the Father's love

8   Jn 12:24.
9   Col 2:13-14.
10 PG 31, 181 C.

and has settled not in the nonexistence of God but in his absence. Christ's "bloody sweat," his indescribable anguish in his piercing cry: "*Eli, Eli, lama sabachthani*"—"My God, my God, why have you forsaken me?"—is the horrifying, consummate experience of the Father's silence and absence, of his abandonment of the Son. This one Man abandoned, as is every person's terrible experience, is the only begotten Son. He passes through the door of the great silence, charged with the sin of all.

Predestination

Eschatology sheds light on the destiny of man, on our participation in being saved or lost. Grace makes us feel the "breath of the Spirit." Grace "provokes attention" and thus, according to the Fathers, protects free will not only in action but also in choice (Acts 16:14). "If anyone listens and opens the door, I enter" (Rev 3:20). Rendered attentive by the Spirit, man is able therefore to decisively formulate his yes or no.

We can define the relations between God and his creature in the categories of causality. In this case, God is the first cause who puts all things in motion, shows the way and returns all to this path. Human freedom is only the secondary instrumental cause drawing its origin from the primary, and determined by it. If the secondary cause sins, it is only because the primary tolerates it. Causal determinism is fatally situated in time, the primary movement finds itself inevitably there. That which establishes the primary cause is the universal pre-cause of all, and the prefix "pre" introduces time into the eternity of God. Humankind does not appear except inevitably, as the object of divine action. In such a causal scheme, the dubious Augustinian idea is led, through the iron logic of Calvin, to its conclusion: predestination to glory, condemnation to hell. The circle is buckled in upon itself without any possible exit: "Therefore according to the end for which humankind is created, we say that it is predestined to death or to life."[11]

For the Eastern Church, God is never the primary cause, but the Creator. It is creation "in the image" of the Creator which places the

---

11 *Instututions*, VIII, p. 62.

"second freedom" outside any causal determinism, and the patristic conception of humankind as *autexousia*, self authoritative, rightly defines its mysterious capacity to transcend every necessity and the very condition of the creature over against divine freedom: to see oneself as *microtheos*, as God-in-miniature. One can even say that God, the Lover of humankind, is much more determined himself by his creation and his covenants than the creature by his Creator: "The Lord has sworn and he will not change his mind" (Ps 110:4). The Incarnation appears as God's reply to his own promise: the divinizing of his creature. The fall of man reveals the titanic fullness of our freedom, which in turn, determines our own destiny. Satan did not lie in saying: "You will be as gods." Man has created something which never existed before. We created evil and introduced it into our innocent nature. What is more, our salvation determines the shape of the Incarnation as Love crucified. Divine blood has been shed to safeguard our freedom in grace, for, according to the Fathers' saying, "God is not able to force anyone to love him."

But all autonomy pushed to the breaking point is against nature, for it encloses man in his lower nature, hardens our "selfhood," destroys our ontology, our very being in the form of God. On the contrary, when man ceases to see himself in his pure subjectivity and rather in relationship to the divine Other, there we discover our "identity by grace," our being "eternally accepted."[12] Then hell's isolation is destroyed and man is lifted toward the joy of the friend of the Bridegroom, St John the Baptist, and the Servant of the Lord, the Blessed Virgin Mary, the Mother of God.

"I knock at the door," says the Lord, and he knocks at the door of his own image in man, at the image of divine freedom in us. God empties himself. He "waits," determining nothing. God's decrees and even the predictions of the Apocalypse reveal a conditional character (Jer 18:7-10; 26:2-3,13). Human freedom has the power to change even these.

The miracles of faith, the absolute newness of holiness, the charism of prophecy, all lead to the marriage-like relation between God and man, where love reigns, love which transforms all submission and

---

12 These are frequent expressions in the writing of St Maximus the Confessor.

subordination into the "complete otherness" of the Kingdom. The mystery of the *Deisis* or "Supplication" icon of Christ the King, seated between John the Baptist and the Virgin, discloses this. This icon is placed at the very heart of the icon screen which stretches across the front of the sanctuary, before the altar. Its aim is to present the image of judgment and at the same time its own transcendence through the image of the marriage feast of the Lamb.

God persuades, "not by power, nor by might, but by his Spirit."[13] Now, "where the Spirit is, there is freedom." The error of *pre*destination and of *pre*science is to introduce into God the Creator the temporal "before." The primary cause placed in time foresees and predestines, determines all. The *pre-* deforms the "eternal" character of God and the capacity of faith to surpass the framework of time. Freedom bears the only interior necessity: to express oneself in choosing. Its fullness contains the most fearful choice; that of a revolt and a determination of oneself against God. Its archetype, the first choice of Lucifer before any concrete existence of evil, reveals that even in the initial state of innocence, freedom is safeguarded intact, and it is God who protects against his own omnipotence.

In non-Orthodox commentaries on Romans 8:29, predestination is conditioned by God's prescience or foreknowledge and the "we" of Ephesians 1:8-12 is taken in the limited and arbitrary sense of only "the elect." Now, according to St Paul, those thus called "elect" are the Christians, the two being synonymous. Despite terminology often confusing and inadequate to his vision, his theology is strongly voluntaristic. The principal theme of the letter to the Romans is salvation by faith *and* by the grace-filled life conformed to faith. The Pauline opposition is not at all between faith and works but between the works of faith and the works of the law. Deeper than any doctrinal prejudice, predestination is for St Paul nothing but a conventional form for designating the mystery of God's love, *and this love determines or predestines God and not humanity,* if one wants to use the concept. It is rather symptomatic that in Romans 5:19 "For just as by the one man's disobedience the many were made sinners, so by the one man's obedience the

13 Zech 4:6.

many will be made righteous," the Greek terms *parakoé* (disobedience) and *hypakoé*, (obedience) are extremely rare even in classical Greek. Their rarity points to a meaning of something most unusual. To the abyss of disobedience corresponds the abyss of obedience. The transgression of limits here is not juridical but ontological. Christ's obedience is that of the Son to his Father, of the life within God. His indescribable fullness and "the image of the Son" leads us towards "another humanity," the mysterious humanity of the age to come according to the phrase of St Gregory of Nyssa.[14]

In Romans 1 and 9, St Paul speaks of the "historiosophic" mystery of Israel, that is, the action of divine Wisdom in human history and, as in the case of Jacob and Esau, this has mostly to do with the paradoxes of Providence, the historical theme, of the metahistorical meaning of the history of salvation. Even here, the image of the potter only reveals but one of the multiple aspects of divine Wisdom, but does not describe exhaustively the totality of the infinite, the completely inexhaustible range of the relationships between God and humankind. St Paul has a sufficient enough sense of true mystery not to slip toward such a simplification. Certainly *it is God who brings to birth and will and action*, but there is also the reverse of this: *Work out your salvation in fear and trembling.*

God has imprisoned all in disobedience so that he may be merciful to all (Rom 11:32). To every limiting rationalization Paul responds by the confession of the true mystery: *how inscrutable are his ways*. It is fitting for us to honor these in silence. The *docta ignorantia* ("learned ignorance") is opposed to every "asylum of ignorance." The Savior's plan, *that all be saved* (1 Tim 2:4; Rom 8:32) is infinitely more mysterious and *impenetrable* than predestination which is so human and so impoverished in its rectilinear logic. The "complex of the elect" is a morbid state, symptomatic of an unhappy conscience, and anxiety about hell.

The descent into hell

In the office of Holy Saturday the Church sings: "You have descended to earth to save Adam and not finding him there, O Master, you have

14 PG 44, 1225.

gone to search for him even into hell." Humanity since Adam has been destined for hell, for the realm of death, and it there that Christ goes to find us.

Primitive catechesis draws attention to an aspect of the sacrament of baptism much forgotten in history. Baptism by immersion reproduces the complete and figurative course of salvation, and every baptized person follows the same itinerary of the Savior. The triple immersion replicates the three great holy days of the Lord's passion, death, burial and resurrection, the *Triduum*. The descent into hell—the coming out of the baptismal font—is the return to the day without end. The sacrament of baptism is thus the very real descent with Christ in his death. It is the descent into hell. St John Chrysostom expresses this tradition most clearly: "The action of descending into the water and ascending from it symbolizes the descent into hell and the leaving of that abode."[15]

The "light upon the Jordan" is seen in the baptismal light—*photismos*. This means the "illumination" of hell's darkness. Illumined, the newly baptized joins the souls ascending with Christ from hell to eternal life. Thus baptism is not only dying and rising with Christ, it is also the descent into Sheol or hell and the leaving of it, following him. Hell is more fearful than death. One thinks of the words of a father of the Church: "and the annihilation which they seek will not even be given to them." It is here that the definitive victory takes place.

Christ descends there, a place full of sin, and he transports all those stigmatized, that is, all who are marked by the cross, by Love crucified. The ultimate consequences for us of this action must be emphasized here. Every baptized person, risen with Christ, bears also the stigmata, the marks of the wounds of the pastoral care of Christ the High Priest, of his apostolic anguish for the destiny of those held captive in hell. According to the early Church document, *The Shepherd of Hermas*,[16] and Clement of Alexandria,[17] the apostles and teachers descend to hell after their death to proclaim salvation and to baptize those who desire it. Quite differently from Dante, whom Péguy reproaches for having

---

15 *Hom.* 40 on 1 Cor 15:29; see also Cyril of Jerusalem, PG 33, 1079 and Gregory the Theologian, PG 46, 585.
16 IX, 16, 5-17.
17 *Strom.* II, 9, 43.

descended to hell "as a tourist," these saints have already encountered Christ and themselves shine with the brilliance of his light.

God created man as "another freedom" and the risk God has taken is already to be seen in the suffering of Christ, the "Man of sorrows," in the shadow of the cross, for according to the Fathers, "God does everything except to constrain us to love him." In expectation of this love God renounces all his power, empties himself in the figure of the Lamb sacrificed. God's destiny with us depends on our "yes," our *fiat*. To assure the complete freedom of such love, Christ even renounces his omniscience, leaves the abyss of silence and gives his life. The impassible, that is nonsuffering, quality of a hidden God is only apparent, for according to Gregory of Nazianzus, the God who seems unable to suffer nevertheless does suffer. God sees the sadness ahead, and his love is no less vigilant, because man is able to refuse him and build a whole life upon this rejection, upon an atheistic revolt against him. Which then is more important, love or freedom? The two are infinite and hell bears this question in its fire.

Death

The silence of death weighs heavily upon the living. However, since Christ, death has become part of the Christian reality, no longer an intrusion but a beginning. Upon this mystery, the name of the Virgin Mary, the Theotokos—the new Eve, Life—is set as a seal, and thus it is death's own annihilation that is sealed. Since Christ's resurrection, then, it is not life that is a phenomenon of death, rather death that is an event in life. Death has submitted to life. It has no existence of its own but is a perverse form of life, a provisory and transient state. As every regulation is subordinate to, comes after affirmation, death has become a secondary phenomenon, essentially a parasite.

Death is neither a reversal by God nor a contradiction, for it cannot destroy the living. The equilibrium is broken. Death becomes the "natural" destiny of "mortals." This being completely against nature, thus we have the anguish of the dying. Death, the "king of terrors" according to Job, halts our habitual profanation and forgetfulness and places the dying immediately in a place that is deep and striking in the grandeur of its mystery.

The wound is so deep, the evil so virulent, that divine healing is required. The depth of the tragic abyss is to be found in the necessity of *God's own dying* and following on this, our own passage through the *catharsis* of death. The *anastasis* or resurrection of which the Gospel speaks is not just the soul's survival, for the Bible does not teach any natural immortality.

Before Christ's coming, *sheol, hades,* hell was a kind of survival of the soul which without being a return to nothingness was a state of exile at the frontiers of existence and nonexistence. It was a diminished mode of being, its shadow without joy or light, for it was situated outside God under the captivity of fearful *Thanatos,* the spirit of nothingness.

The Incarnation of the Word, "Emmanuel, God *with* us" already is the Resurrection. For in this, the Word unites himself to "dead nature" to vivify and heal this ultimate misery. "He took on a body capable of dying so that, himself suffering for all in this body he had entered, he could annihilate the master of death."[18] "He came to death in order to become a corpse and to give to this nature resurrection."[19] "He has destroyed the power of mortality and transformed the body into incorruptibility."[20] "Christ has transformed the sleeper into light."[21] Patristic thought is most explicit. Immortality comes from the Resurrection, from the penetration of the human in its totality by the energies of the divine Spirit. The Apostles Creed confesses this: "I believe in the resurrection of the body," and the Nicene Creed says, "I look for the resurrection of the dead."

The saints greet death with the joy of being born into the true world. St Seraphim of Sarov taught the art of "joyful dying." This is why he addressed everyone he met with the Paschal greeting: "My joy, Christ is risen." Death no longer exists, life reigns. For St Gregory of Nyssa, death is something good, *agathon an eiê ho thanatos.*[22] In the first letter to the Corinthians, St Paul presents an astonishing vision: "All things are for you, whether in life or in death" (3:22). Both are gifts of God, charisms

---

18 St Athanasius, *On the Incarnation* 20.
19 St Gregory of Nyssa, *Cathechesis* 32, 3.
20 St Cyril of Alexandria, *On Luke* 5:19.
21 Clement of Alexandria, *Protreptikos* c. 114.
22 *Or. de Pulcheria,* PG 46, 877 A.

put at our disposition. In assuming it totally, man is the priest of his death, he is the one who creates his own death. The anointing of the dying is when we exercise this final priestly action, giving us the "oil of gladness," sustaining the exaltation of our hearts beyond the agony of the body. Diadokos[23] says that our final sickness takes the place of martyrdom. To each of us then is given the charism of being a martyr. Face to face with the robber whom death seems to be, we can call her "our sister" and confess the Creed, which asserts our having already passed from death to life.[24] The great spiritual teachers even slept in their coffins as in a marriage bed and showed an intimacy with death, regarding it as nothing more than the ultimate passage—Pascha.

If philosophy cultivates the knowledge of death and according to Plato teaches the art of dying well, only Christian faith knows *how* it is necessary to die in the resurrection. In actuality then, death is completely within time now, since it is behind us. Before us we find that which we experienced in baptism, the "little resurrection" and in the Eucharist, eternal life.

In the case of a martyr, death is passionately desired: "There is in me living water which speaks and tells me, 'Come to the Father.' "[25] There is the wonderful account of the death of Macrina by her brother, St Gregory of Nyssa: "She reached out toward her Beloved with a most urgent intensity. Her bed was turned toward the East."[26] When "the heart is wounded by the splendor of God,"[27] "love overcomes all fear."[28] "Your tomb, O Christ, is more beautiful than paradise," the Church sings in the Divine Liturgy.

Death is liturgically called "dormition"—a part of the human being sleeps (the psychic faculties attached to the body) and a part rests in consciousness (as it is the organ of consciousness, the soul remains in the spirit).

23 *Chap.* 94.
24 Jn 5:24; Col 2:12.
25 St Ignatius of Antioch, *Rom* 7, 3.
26 PG 46, 984 B.
27 St Macarius, *Homil.*, v. 6.
28 St Anthony, *Philokalia* v. I, p. 131.

Purgatory

If the existence between death and the last judgment is called purgatory, this is not a place but an intermediary state of purification. The Greek Fathers spoke of purifying sufferings. They never spoke of penal satisfaction nor of "purifying expiation." If they spoke of pain, they were repulsed by the very notion of any "satisfaction," and they rejected any fiery suffering before the judgment, any *ignis purgatorius* the juridical character of the Western doctrine of purgatory. But in rejecting penal satisfaction, the Eastern Church did teach that there was purification after death, not as pain which purifies but as the destiny one assumed in death and experienced toward the end of healing.

Between death and judgment the attention of the dead is creative because of their heightened receptivity. Prayer, especially at the Eucharist by the living, and their good works for the poor on behalf of the dead, constitute a form of communion. The Church's liturgical services and the intercessory ministry of the angels intervene and continue the Savior's work. The collegial aspect of the waiting of all is strongly emphasized, and all are saved together by communion in the same eschatological destiny of the Body of Christ, *totus Christus*. The mystery of the Church is to be at the same time "the Church of the penitents, of those who perish" (St Ephrem) and the *communio sanctorum*, the "communion of sinners" in the "holy things," their participation deifying them into "the only Holy One." It is not our faults which are repaired but our nature, recovering the true "health" of the Kingdom, its fullness. Here is explained the frequent image of the passage of the dead through the toll or customs houses (*telonies*), where those who belong to them are left to the demons and those who belong to the Lord are freed. All this has nothing to do with torture or flames but with a maturation for the stripping away of every stain which weighs upon the spirit. Perhaps down through the ages one becomes conscious of its reality and is purified.

The word "eternity" in Hebrew is taken from the verb *alam*, which means to hide. God has enveloped in obscurity the destiny beyond the tomb and it does no good to try to violate the divine secret. Thus, the

Fathers affirm that the time "between the two," death and judgment, is not empty and as St Irenaeus says, the souls "ripen."[29]

The heavenly waiting of the saints

About the in-between time of the ages, the Fathers keep a profound, contemplative silence. St Ambrose speaks of the *locus caelestis* where souls dwell. According to the Tradition, it is the "third heaven" of which St Paul speaks, the heaven of *arcana verba*, of hidden words. It is useless to try to force the door open, with Bishop J. A. T. Robinson and Rudolf Bultmann. It is perfectly clear that heaven has nothing to do with an astronomy or places in outer space. The Bible says nothing about this. Here we have symbolic language which allows us to think, to contemplate by legitimately overstepping what we know. These are eschatological symbols, essentially mysterious. These approaches to the Kingdom indicate more than a historical state or a place. According to St Gregory of Nyssa, souls are part of an intelligible world, the city of the celestial hierarchies "beyond the astronomical heavens." "Beyond" here means an entirely new dimension, beyond the known dimensions of existence. It is Eden become the temple of the Kingdom. It also called the "bosom of Abraham, a place of light, of refreshment, of repose" (Orthodox service for the departed).

This ascension directed by the fiery swords of the Cherubim, strips away the weight of evil. The purified souls go up to another dwelling place (the *mansiones* of St Ambrose), being gradually initiated into the mystery of heavenly life they approach the Temple, the Lamb. The angels and souls enter a preliminary intercommunion, and singing the *Sanctus*, together ascend to the courts of the "House of the Eternal." This is the sanctuary which Our Lord himself entered (Heb 9:24) and where the "wounded friends of the Bridegroom," the martyrs and the saints, are reunited in the *communio sanctorum*, the communion of saints in the loving heart of the God-Man.

Once more, this is the life of disincarnate spirits, wrapped as in a cloak in the presence of Christ whose glorified body and shining light covers the nakedness of their souls. The interiorized meaning of the spirit captures

29 *Adv. haer.* PG 7, 806.

heaven. The communion of prayer with the Church on earth presupposes the active memory at the very heart of this preliminary "Sabbath rest." The saints now rest, and their works follow them (Rev 14:13).

This is the active waiting during which the Church dresses herself in proper clothes: the work of the saints (Rev 19:8). The words: "I sleep, but my heart watches," (Song of Songs 5:2) points to this vigilant sleep of the "little resurrection." Moving forward gradually, the souls await the day of the Lord. It is the mystery of the complete Body, of the "sheaf of grain gathered for the harvest," in the words of St Cyril of Alexandria, "for there is only one body which awaits...the perfect blessedness,"[30] and this is exactly the fullness which the abyss of the Father opens. The gaze of all is directed toward this final moment of the constitution of the *totus Christus*. Earthly history rejoins the heavenly and culminates in the eschatological Coming which prepares the unique destiny of man completely reconstituted in Christ.

The end of the world

The figure of this world is passing (1 Cor 7:31) but *the one who does the will of God abides forever* (1 Jn 2:17). Something disappears, something remains. It is not a simple separation of the things of this world, but a metamorphosis of chosen elements and their passage to the "*new earth*" and the "*new heaven*." The apocalyptic image of fire is the one used most often, for fire reshapes and purifies material, but the passage is within limits. There is a hiatus. Thus the "last day" was not yesterday and will not be tomorrow. It will not be numbered with other days. Being is raised again to its ancient measure. The hand of God seizes the closed circle of empirical time and lifts it to a higher horizon, a different dimension.[31] This "day" closes historical time but does not itself belong to time. It cannot be found on our calendars and for this reason we cannot predict it. It is like the death of every person which is not dated except by those surrounding him. But at the end of the world, the entourage will not be remaining in time which will no longer exist. When we read that "with the Lord, one day is as a thousand years," this

30 Origen, *On Levit.*, Hom 7, n. 2.
31 PG 44, 504 D.

is a symbolic expression, an image of the measure of ages which *cannot be counted*. The transcendent character of the end becomes an object of faith and of revelation. The end of the world is announced by the *Parousia* following upon the resurrection and the judgment.

The Parousia and the resurrection

Christ's ascension already proclaimed the *Parousia*. It is Christ, stripped in his *kenosis*, his self-emptying, yet coming in his brilliant glory, revealed to all. We cannot know more about it than this. The events of the last days are spoken of as signs in the Gospel and are already within history. The *Parousia* however, coincides with the transformation of nature and it will be visible not within history but beyond it, as we hear about the age to come: *we will all be changed* (1 Cor 15:51) *then we who are alive, who are left, shall be caught up together with those who have died in the clouds to meet the Lord in the air* (1 Thess 4:17).

All who are in the tombs will hear the voice of the Son of God and will come forth at the sound of his voice (Jn 5:25-29). According to St Paul, it is with the energy of a seed germinating that God will accomplish the resurrection: *it is sown a physical body, it is raised a spiritual body... clothed in immortality...and in the image of the man of heaven* (1 Cor 15:44). The eschatological texts present a symbolic compactness which excludes every simplification and literalism. Images replace definitions which are powerless to explain the transcendent dimension at that moment. The precise meaning eludes us and we are invited to "honor in silence" of which it has been said: *what eye has not seen, nor ear heard, nor the heart of man conceived, what God has prepared for those who love him* (Is 64:4; 1 Cor 2:9).

The resurrection is an ultimate super-elevation—*hyperhypsôsis*—which tears being from its own state. The hand of God grasps his creature and raises this being into a new and unknown dimension.[32] At most one can say that the spirit again finds the fullness of human being, soul and body kept in their perfect unity. St Gregory of Nyssa[33] speaks of the "seal" and the "stamp" which are given to the form of the

---

32 St Gregory of Nyssa, PG 45, 697 C.
33 *De Pif. Hom.* cap. 25, 27.

risen Christ, namely no more heaviness and impenetrability. The
energy of repulsion which renders everything opaque and impenetrable,
yields to the energy of attraction and interpenetration of each by all.[34]

Judgment

St Paul speaks of the faculty of seeing the face uncovered, this is already
the pre-judgment and the last judgment consists in the total vision of
all mankind. The great spiritual masters insist on this aspect of judgment more as a revelation of the light of God's love, not at all the
menace of punishment. God is eternally identical to himself. He is not
the fearful Judge but he is Love and the very love which subjectively
"becomes suffering among the outcasts and joy among the blessed."
"Sinners in hell are not deprived of divine love,"[35] but estrangement
from the source, poverty and emptiness of heart, make them incapable
of responding to the love of God, which in turn produces suffering;
but this cannot continue, for after the *Parousia*-revelation of God, one
cannot but love Christ. How can this happen without suffering when
the heart's substance is impoverished to the point of making it mute?
The Gospel employs the image of the separation of the sheep from the
goats (Mt 25:32).

No perfect saints exist. In every sinner there are fragments of good.
In the profound thought of Fr Sergius Bulgakov, that which justifies is
an interiorization, a personal appropriation of the sense of judgment.
There is no separation not between good and evil people, but such a
dividing line, rather, runs through the heart of every one of us. From
this point of view, the words about destruction, annihilation and the
"second death" do not have to do with human beings but with the
demonic elements they bear within themselves. It is the image of "fire,"
not as torture and punishment, but as purification and healing. Even
the "cutting off" of a member of the body, of which the Gospel speaks,
indicates a spiritual surgery, an ascetic therapy accomplished by negative means in order to surpass these in a positive accomplishment, a

34 Nicholas Lossky, "Resurrection of the Body," *Anglican Theological Review* 31 (1949)
pp. 71-82.
35 St Isaac of Syria, Wensinck ed., XXVII, p. 136.

shining, blossoming, a blooming. Certainly, in terms of justice, all deserve hell, but in each of us are fragments of paradise and of hell and the "grace of paradise," which, according to Clement of Alexandria, are never lost and which call out to God's mercy.

The divine sword penetrates the depths of the human heart and accomplishes the separation. It reveals that what is given by God as gift has been received and borne fruit. The sword therefore reveals the emptiness hollowed out by the refusal of God's love and the tragic loss of correspondence between the divine offer and the human response. The complex mixture of good and evil in this earthly life, described in the parable of the wheat and the tares, displaces every juridical notion of God and places us instead, before the great mystery of divine Wisdom.

The eternity of hell

Eternity has a different nature than that of time and it is not at all "bad infinity," the absence of finitude. Eternity is a qualitative determination and one can say that the eternities of paradise and of hell are different, for it is impossible to conceive of eternity in such a form devoid of its content (Mt 25:34-41). For the Hebrew mind, no autonomous nature existed. Nature exists for human use, is an element of human history. There exists no purely cosmic evolution separated from man, but there is an existential involution centered upon humanity and open to humanization. Biblical time is not objective, formal, independent of humanity, for its temporality is one of the structurings of human destiny, its principle of orientation. Mankind does not subjugate time, but rather has the power to govern it by determinative and qualifying intentionality. Time has a cosmic, cyclical form. There is historical time and its duration and there is existential time which opens itself to the eschatological dimension. Here we find the *kairoi,* the "favorable times," the eruptions of the beyond of which the Bible speaks.

The Incarnation has "redeemed time," ordering and orienting it within the axis of history. Since then, everything culminates in the messianic presence of Christ where time is opened and vertically united to eternity and is transformed in its own quality.

The current understanding of eternal suffering is nothing but a scholarly opinion, a simplistic theology of a "penitential" nature which neglects the depth of such texts as John 3:17 (*For God sent the Son into the world, not to condemn the world, but that the world might be saved through him*) and 12:47 (*If anyone hears my sayings and does not keep them, I do not judge him; for I did not come to judge the world but to save the world*). It is simply unacceptable to imagine that from all eternity God prepares hell as a destination for his creatures. This would be a contradiction of his divine plan and thus a victory for evil! The tragic tension described in the Gospel of St John—"The light shone in the darkness and the darkness did not receive it," (Vulgate) or "the darkness was not able to overcome it," (Origen's version)—speaks of the invincible Light and the resisting darkness. Metaphysically, the darkness is but the passive absence of light. In the infinity of the light an active reaction of opposition arises. The light reveals this, and its flight is wrapped in an opacity, a complicitous obscurity which hides the heart in darkness. But in his resurrection, "Christ has trampled down death by death," and in his transfiguration he has revealed the light of the age to come. The radiance of the moment of the Parousia shines with the fullness of Tabor made universal and illumines every darkness, rendering it nonexistent. This is not so much destruction as the clarification of the very essence of this opacity: "All is filled with light: heaven, the earth, hell" (Paschal Liturgy). "Death is swallowed up in victory. O death where is your victory? O death, where is your sting?" (1 Cor 15:55).

If even St Augustine rejected the *misericordes* (mercies), it was to avoid promiscuity and sentimentalism. Today the pedagogical argument for fear is totally ineffective, risking the transformation of Christianity into Islam on this point. On the contrary, holy trembling before holy things saves the world from its meaninglessness, and perfect love drives out fear (1 Jn 4:18).

The Fifth Ecumenical Council did not examine the question of the duration of suffering in hell. The emperor Justinian (who, in this instance much resembled the "just ones" in the story of Jonah, angry that punishment did not fall upon the guilty) presented to the Patriarch Minas in A.D. 543 his own personal doctrine. The patriarch then elaborated several theses against neo-Origenism and Pope Vigilius confirmed them. They have been attributed erroneously to the Fifth Council. Now this was only a personal opinion, and even St Gregory of Nyssa, who was opposed to it, never condemned it. The question thus remains open, suspended perhaps on account of human charity. One could give numerous supportive citations here, of which a few follow: St Gregory of Nyssa speaks of redemption of even the devil;[36] St Gregory the Theologian mentions the *apocatastasis*, the "complete restoration."[37] St Maximus the Confessor invites us to "honor in silence" the question of punishment, for the spirit of the crowd cannot grasp the depth of words.[38] Further, he says, it is not wise to open to the imprudent the insights into the abyss of mercy.[39] According to St Anthony, the *apocatastasis* is not just a doctrine nor the subject of academic inquiry but prayer for the salvation of all.

In the end, Satan finds himself deprived of the world, which is the object of his desire and limited to his own being which unlike that of God is not limitless. Pure Satanism disappears when the subject is without an object. On the other hand, the heart of the Church, her maternal intercession is without limit. St Isaac of Syria speaks of a heart burning with love for all creatures, for reptiles, even for the demons. Such compassion is universal and extends to every creature made by God: *"He who descended into the lower parts of the earth, also ascended far above all the heavens, that he might fill all things,"* says St Paul (Eph 4:9-10). The balance-sheet lies in the hands of God. In Hebrew, Jesus means "Savior," Liberator, and as Clement of Alexandria says so magnificently, "even the will of God is an action, and this is called the world, thus his intention is salvation and this is called the Church."[40]

The Eastern Church remains a stranger to every penitential principle. Sin is a sickness to be healed even if the cure is the blood of God. Without any "prejudice," the Church abandons herself to the Father's love for all mankind and redoubles her prayer for both the living and

36 PG 46, 609 C; 610 A.
37 PG 36, 412 A B.
38 PG 90, 412 A.
39 PG 90, 1172D.
40 *Pedagogos*, 1:6.

the dead. Some, the greatest of the saints, find the audacity and receive the charism even to pray for the demons. Perhaps the most deadly weapon against the Evil One is precisely the prayer of a saint. The destiny of hell does not depend only upon the transcendent will of God, but also on the love of the saints. We prepare our own hells for ourselves, closing ourselves in from the love of God who continues to dwell in us without change: "It is not right to say that sinners in hell are deprived of the love of God...But love works in two different ways, becoming suffering in the outcasts and joy in the blessed."[41]

Every one of the faithful in the Orthodox Church, when approaching the holy table for Communion prays "of sinners, I am the first," the greatest of sinners, without comparison, "the only sinner." St Ambrose stated it most concisely: "The same person is at once both condemned and saved."[42] St Isaac, an ascetic himself, said it another way: "The one who sees his own sin is greater than one who can raise the dead."[43] A parallel vision of naked reality teaches the true right of speaking about hell, that is, only when it concerns me, personally. My attitude is to struggle against my hell which menaces me if I do not love in order to save others. A very simple man said to St Anthony: "In watching those who pass by me, I say to myself, all will be saved, only I will be condemned," and St Anthony concluded, "Hell truly exists, but only for me."

In echoing St Anthony's words, one could also say that the world in its totality is also "at the same time condemned and saved." Even more perhaps than hell, it is in its condemnation that it will find its transcendence. It appears this is the meaning of the saying of Christ to a contemporary elder, St Silouan of Mt Athos: "Keep your spirit in hell and do not despair."[44]

The Eastern Church does not put limits on the mercy of God or on the freedom of man to eternally refuse this mercy. But above all it does not impose limits on being a witness, on love which is open and creative

---

41 St Isaac the Syrian, PG 34, 5440.

42 PL, 15, 1502.

43 *Sentences.*

44 See Archimandrite Sophrony, *Wisdom from Mount Athos: The Writings of Staretz Silouan 1866-1938,* (Crestwood NY: St Vladimir's Seminary Press, 1974), pp. 117-ff and *The Monk of Mount Athos,* (Crestwood NY: St Vladimir's Seminary Press, 1975), p. 115-ff.

in the face of this world's hell. Every baptized Christian is an invisibly "stigmatized" being—"Jesus is a wound which cannot be healed."[45]

It is the destiny of man, especially of those in rebellion to keep open this wound, to add to the sufferings of Christ[46] in agony until the end of the world. To "imitate" Christ is to descend like him into the very depths of our world. "Imitation" is complete conformity to Christ and according to Origen, martyrdom for "the love of God and the love of humankind are but two sides of the same, single love."[47]

Hell is nothing else but separation of man from God, his autonomy excluding him from the place where God is present.

The ability to refuse God is the pinnacle of human freedom. Yet it is precisely God, who is limitless Love, who desires that it be this way. God cannot force an atheist to love him. We dare to say that to do this would be the hell of his divine love. If Judas escaped into the night of solitude (Jn 13:26-30), it was because Satan had entered into him. But Judas carried in his hand an awesome mystery, the morsel of bread from the Lord's Supper.[48] Thus hell holds in its very heart a fragment of light, thus comes true the saying: "The light shone in the darkness." Jesus' action of giving even Judas the bread of life reveals the final mystery of the Church. She is the hand of Jesus offering his body and blood. The appeal is addressed to all, since all are within the power of the Prince of this world. The light does not dissipate the darkness but the darkness has no hold over the invincible light. We are all ensnared in the ultimate tension of divine love. God is not "impassible," that is, without passion, suffering. The Book of Daniel[49] tells of the three young men cast into the fiery furnace. The king perceived the mysterious presence of a fourth: "I see four men who walk in the fire without being burned and the fourth has the likeness of the Son of God."

Thus we find the necessity of hell, which comes from human freedom. With respect to God, who will not force anyone to love him, hell

---

45 *Saying of Ibn Arabi concerning Al Hallaj*, cited by Louis Massignon.
46 Col 1:24.
47 St Maximus, PG 91, 409 B.
48 This is the opinion of St Ephrem, St John Chrysostom, St Ambrose, St Augustine and St Jerome.
49 Dan 3:25.

witnesses to our freedom from loving him. This brings hell into being, for our freedom can always say, "May your will not be done" and even God does not have control over this statement. Emotionally, we would be shaken in our understanding of God if he did not love his creature with such abandon that he would not punish his child for such a cruel separation. It also would be most disturbing if God did not save his beloved without touching or destroying his freedom. The Father who sends his Son knows that even hell is his domain and that "the gate of death" is transformed into the "gate of life." Even the despair of hell is wounded by the hope it already contains, and the Church teaches the Christian not to despair.

During Matins on Pascha night, in the silence of the conclusion of Holy Saturday, the priest and people leave the church. The procession stops outside before the closed church doors. For a brief instant, this closed door symbolizes the Savior's tomb, death, hell. The priest makes the sign of the cross over the doors and under the irresistible force the doors, just as the doors of hell, open wide and all enter into a church inundated with light singing, "Christ is risen from the dead, trampling down death by death, and upon those in the tombs, bestowing life." *The doors of hell have again become the doors of the Church.* One cannot go further in the symbolism of the feast. In truth, the world in its totality is at once condemned and saved. It is at the same time hell and the Kingdom of God.

"Here, my brother, is a commandment I give to you," said St Isaac in his *Sentences*, "that mercy always keeps you in balance, till the moment when you feel in yourself the very same mercy that God has for the world."

The Vespers which follow the Liturgy of the feast of Pentecost contain three long prayers attributed to St Basil the Great. The first places the Church before the face of the Father. The second asks the Son to protect all the living. The third prays for *all* those who have died since the creation of the world: "You who are willing to listen to our prayers for those who are held captive in hell, and who give us the great hope that you will deliver them...we offer you our prayer for their souls..." Once a year, on the day of Pentecost, the Church prays even for those who have committed suicide.[50] Did not Origen and St Augustine say as much? "Many are outside who should be within, many are within who should be outside."

The love of the Church knows no limits. She carries the destiny even of those who turn from God and places them into the hands of the Father, and his hands, according to St Irenaeus, are Christ and the Holy Spirit.

The Father yields all judgment to the Son of Man and this is the "judgment of Judgment,"[51] the crucified judgment. "The Father is crucifying Love, the Son is Love crucified, the Holy Spirit is the invincible power of the cross."[52] This power bursts forth in the breath and outpouring of the Spirit.

The mystery of the cross

St John Chrysostom prays: "You, Lord, who are alone among the lonely and who are all in all! The One who cannot be divided is divided so that all may be saved, and even the lowest place is not deprived of the hand of God...We pray ...extend your arms over your holy Church and over your holy people always yours."[53] In extending his arms on the wood of the cross, Christ unfurled two wings, the right and the left, calling to himself all believers and covering them as a mother protects her little ones," says St Hippolytus.[54]

The divine philanthropy, God's love of mankind wills it thus. "God is patient," and grants a mysterious delay, for it is man who will return and "hasten the day of the Lord," already found within the *Parousia*, as the angels of salvation of whom the *Cherubic Hymn* in the Liturgy speaks. It has to do with the "intensity of our love," with our "bringing to birth" by faith which brings the world toward the coming of the Lord. Hidden germination prepares for the "springtime of the Spirit,"[55]

---

50 Julien Green, in his *Journal*, says that one who commits suicide is someone born into the Kingdom of God before his time.

51 St Maximus, PG 408 D.

52 St Filaret, Metropolitan of Moscow, *Homilies* (French translation), Paris, 1849, p. 154.

53 PG 59, 743-746.

54 *On the Anti-Christ*, c. 61.

55 St Gregory of Nazianzus, PG 36, 620 D.

the sprouting forth of the saints. Paschal joy overflows in "new harmonies,"[56] and despite destructive pessimism rises on the winged words of Origen: "The Church is full of the Trinity."[57] St Simeon the New Theologian[58] confesses: "Brothers, I know a man weeping and groaning to the point of taking upon himself the sin of another person, imputing to himself the faults the other committed...I know a man who desired with such ardor the salvation of his brothers, who prayed to God for them with burning tears and with all of his heart, and in the excess of his zeal, worthy of Moses, who prayed that his brothers might be saved with him, and that he might be condemned with them For he was bound to them in the Holy Spirit in such a bond of love that he would not enter the Kingdom of Heaven if he were to be thus separated from them." This is the miracle of authentic hope of salvation for others. In our faith in Christ, we cast ourselves into his faith in his Father, the *pros ton théon* of the prologue of St John's Gospel which shows us the Word *"towards God,"* turned toward him, toward the face of God saying to him: "Here I am, with the children you have given me."[59] And since that time everything is new, for our faith has become his faith and this why I say to you: *everything you ask in prayer, believe that you have already received it, and thus it will be given to you* (Mk 11:24).

Such faith transcends history. The hands of God, the Son and the Spirit carry the destiny of all even to the threshold of the abyss of the Father. St Peter speaks of this: *The Lord is not being slow in carrying out his promises, as some people think he is; rather is he being patient with you, wanting nobody to be lost and everybody to be brought to repentance. The Day of the Lord will come like a thief, and then with a roar the sky will vanish, the elements will catch fire and melt away, the earth and all that it contains will be burned up. Since everything is coming to an end like this, what holy and saintly lives you should be living, while you wait for the Day of God to come, and try to hasten its coming....* (2 Pet 3:9-11). This Day is not just the goal, not just the end of history, this Day is the fullness (*plerôma*) of the mystery of God.

56 Clement of Alexandria, *Protreptikos* c. 1.
57 PG 12, 1265.
58 PG 120, 423-425.
59 St Cyril of Jerusalem, 1, *Cat.* n.6.

2

SOME LANDMARKS
ON LIFE'S JOURNEY[1]

A young émigré finds himself in the West, a turning point in his life, a
rupture in the conditions of existence without breaking the spiritual
continuity.

As an adolescent, he passionately nourished himself on the genius
of Dostoevsky. While treading the stones of the Paris streets in the sun-
shine of France, pausing in the shadows of the ancient churches, he
would recall the words of this writer with veneration.

For the Russian, Europe is also as precious as Russia; each stone is
sweet and dear to my heart...Russians cherish these ancient foreign
stones, these marvels of the ancient world, this debris of sacred miracles; and it is all as precious to us as it is to them....

Exile offered the possibility of pilgrimage to many sanctuaries. I
wanted very much to know about Western Christianity, its treasures,
miracles and saints. The Spirit revealed all of this naturally, with a naive
freshness, to an ecumenical atmosphere that was still quite new and
tentative. Before confronting anything in the West, I was very much
aware that, stripped of everything from my homeland, I was still an
inheritor of my Orthodox faith. There were always occasions in which
to witness to Orthodoxy, but it was necessary, before all else, to understand, to penetrate the mystery of these strange forms which surrounded me and which already were questioning me.

The Russian Christian Student Movement (l'ACER) in France, of

1   "Quelques jalons sur un chemin de vie," in *Le buisson ardent*, (Paris: Editions P.
    Lethielleux, 1981), pp. 13-26.

which I was the first secretary, gave me the unique opportunities for so many powerful encounters. Everything I experienced told me that the Russian emigration was a providential event which required profound spiritual discernment. Through the active presence of a brilliant elite of Russian religious thinkers, Orthodoxy was suddenly led out of its secular isolation and made known in every country of the world. The encounter between Christians of the East and the West became an irrevocable fact of history. Very soon an appeal made itself understood, a passionate vocation was clearly outlined.

The great ecumenical meetings were marked by something infinitely simple and grand as well. These encounters communicated an astonishing, unspeakable reality. Can one "recount" love, a face, the color or the light, can one prove or analyze such evidence? There are happening impossible to describe: you see them, are bowled over by them, they burn themselves into you, but they elude any description. I have seen many bishops, quite rigid in their canonical and dogmatic limits, suddenly become "impatient with limits," realizing the limitlessness of the presence of God, of a heart radiant with the living Christ.

"God, sensible to the heart." This saying of Pascal often crossed my mind. Yes, the most profound, the most gripping ecumenical experience is located in this perspective of Pascal: "the ecumenical fact sensible to the heart." It was not at all sentimentality of the emotional or psychological kind, but nevertheless, it was experience "sensible to the heart" in the biblical understanding. A very rational, almost elegant geometric frame of mind would formulate the impasses. Then another perspective would be open to evidence and certainties, and in Pascal's sense of "memory" would reveal the possibilities of transcending and overcoming these boundaries. On the one hand there was fidelity to the Orthodox truth in which I had been raised and on the other, attentiveness to the high priestly prayer of the Lord. Thus, both attentiveness to history and to the world's destiny impelled one to understand their meaning in the light of all of Christianity, to see what one could possibly do, what we could become together. Kierkegaard's affirmation took on a striking resonance: it is not the way which is impossible, it is the impossible which is the way, and it is necessary to embark upon it.

Nicholas Berdiaev and Fr Sergius Bulgakov: the one a free-thinking philosopher, the other a priest and professor of dogmatic theology, each in his own way spoke of the freedom of Orthodoxy and of the prophetic mission of Orthodoxy in different terms, each deepening the "institution" by the "event," each placing great emphasis on the Holy Spirit.

In Fr Sergius' teaching, it was necessary to cultivate the "instinct of Orthodoxy" which placed you in the path of Tradition, a return to the source, where you rediscovered the immediacy of the Bible. But it was also necessary to plunge oneself into the thinking of the Fathers, to live in the Liturgy, to "consume the eucharistic fire," to discover the icon, eschatology, all of the faith that way beyond history, the meta- historical.

The more one found oneself in the ecumenical arena, the more one became conscious of one's own roots. Ecumenism, paradoxically, increased one's sense of and love for Orthodoxy. The initial need, to deepen the elements of one's faith in order to be at the level of ecumenical dialogue, was rapidly surpassed by intuitive evidence. The more one is Orthodox, the more one is ecumenical, precisely because one is Orthodox.

With Fr Sergius, Tradition revealed itself as essentially a very creative path. The thinking of the Fathers served as a guide, allowing one to overcome every provincial or sectarian tendency. At the ecumenical crossroads breathed the spirit of the capital, Paris. There beat the heart of Christianity, and Orthodox catholicity emerged.

The scope of this essay limits me to choosing two or three souvenirs from my ecumenical dossier.

At the end of the Second World War I found myself working in a hostel. It sheltered a highly diverse community, victims of recent events caught up in the clutch of many difficult problems. There were teenage mothers, a Prussian officer, a Communist clown, and so many others, social "debris," some might say, suicidal people, shriveled souls, over forty persons of all nationalities, forming a highly unusual ensemble. I proposed meetings to bring together in a Christian way at least some elements of these souls ravaged through suffering had created. These were overwhelming encounters, unforgettable and unique exchanges.

How should I define my task when it concerned pastoral care? I felt that this work did indeed constitute a ministry which I could exercise within the universal priesthood of baptism. It was great challenge to me. These souls and their suffering confronted me, made me a witness, a confidant, an intercessor. And in my prayer I was consciously able, in this lay priesthood, in its charism, to respond in a way beyond the purely humanitarian. The moment had come to experiment with formulas which I had not formerly realized, to put into practice such expressions as: "After God, see God in every person," to recognize in each face the human, living icon of Christ, to greet in each one the image of God and there venerate His presence. This radiant recognition was affirmed in an astonishing supernatural truth. The apocalyptic shock of the camps and of the war brought to life again something of the atmosphere of the Acts of the Apostles.

After a series of discussions and Bible studies, a group of German refugees told me of their need for prayer and desire to have a service of worship. And they requested that I lead this. I made it clear that I was Orthodox but would gather them for prayer. It was important that the elements of worship be familiar to them, part of the habit of their souls. I chose lessons from the Scriptures and prayers taken from a Protestant service book. I was deeply aware of thus exercising the universal baptismal priesthood in my own small way, personally, in the Fathers' definition of "priest, king and prophet." In these singular circumstances where the ecumenical voice made itself heard, I had been called upon to bring these souls into the presence of the Lord, in prayer, by the grace of God.

I had an entirely different kind of experience in Protestant churches where the service was led by a pastor. Every negative reaction, so easily aroused was squelched at such a moment by the reality of prayer. Being present as an Orthodox Christian meant not so much being there as an individual but as a witness, very much aware of what I carried within me the deposit of the entire history of the Church, unbroken since the time of the apostolic community. An equal attitude of openness, of active, prayerful presence was accompanied by an astonishing insight. I sensed that my presence transcended the personal and contingent and contributed something to this Protestant service. My being there linked it, in a way, through my Orthodoxy, to the sacred history of the Church, beyond all division and separation. An integration such as this must remain something of mystery, not capable of easy theological formulation, even less of canonical definition. But it is no less real, mystically, for those who live it. In a sense it greatly facilitated ecumenical understanding, even if it was the Protestants who first made the appeal to unity. "Protestation" gave way to "testation," that is, protest became witness to the irrevocable desire of transcending every division, an explosive element of universal importance was beginning to see the light of day and was embracing all Christianity, even Rome....

For several years, during the summer months, I was able to be present each Sunday at Mass celebrated by a very close friend, a Catholic Benedictine monk and priest who was a biblical exegete and who also was most familiar with Orthodox liturgy and iconography, (Dom Celestine Charlier). He celebrated the liturgy in a very old chapel he had himself restored, and this liturgy radiated and brought to life the atmosphere of the great centuries of the high middle ages. The Mass he celebrated very naturally took on the rhythm of the liturgy of the Eastern Church, with the very active participation of the whole assembly. He himself prepared a very large host, which he broke during the eucharistic canon. His words, distinctly pronounced, were intelligible to all, his liturgical gestures full, again approaching the liturgical richness of the East. The power of witness through the liturgy had attracted a congregation of previously dechristianized people. Here was the miracle of Western Christianity. One could touch the reality, bare, pure, transmitted across the centuries, stripped of the weight of mediocre Catholicism. But does not average, mediocre Orthodoxy also have its own poverty?

I felt myself completely at ease, transported into the place of an Eastern Church pilgrim visiting the Western Church before the schism. Within the eucharistic action of Christ, nothing hindered me from being one with this priest, his parish, his Mass. This anticipation of possible unity, one of the most noteworthy of my life, remains alive for me. True, it was not possible for me to receive Communion, but this suffering in a heart filled with joy seemed a most fertile promise, an ardent hope, an *epiclesis* (coming down) of the Spirit.

The last souvenir I have chosen is connected with the second wave of political émigrés, following the Second World War. These student-refugees were gathered in one residence. If the world seemed deaf to their souls' lament, they tried all the more to bring together in an action or

gesture their recent experiences. As in the time of the Old Testament, a
stone was set up as a memorial, a theophanic event revealing God. Here
the students, Catholic, Protestant and Orthodox together laid the cor-
nerstone of a chapel, an ecumenical place of prayer which they soon
completed. Later one of the students confided to us the almost ineffable
feeling experienced by all in the form of a parable: After the war we were
like people parachuting into an unknown land which remained closed to
us. We were placed together to be like the bricks of the chapel and we
saw ourselves in reality as the "living stones" of that holy place. A strange
thing: in entering by the door comprised of ourselves we understood that
only then did we enter France.

This door, a symbol of Christ who called himself the Door, was
their passage to universal Christianity. The chapel walls suddenly drew
back to embrace the ends of the earth and the fire of prayer uniting
these Christians.

The path I am describing runs a much wider course beyond what
was personal for me. Reflection on the universal aspect of this experience cannot be ignored. The dislocation stemming from the breakup
of Christian unity occurred rapidly. The path toward reunion however
is long. But in the action which shattered unity, God revealed a coun-
ter-action. The evidence lies before us. Before the mystery of union
exists also *the mystery of disunion.* The division which has impinged so
seriously even upon the Church's very nature is found corrected by the
shining presence of God amid the separated parts of Christianity. God
transcends what we humans have broken and divided.

We know where the Church is to be found. Who is able to say
where the Church is not found? The reciprocal acceptance of the sacrament of Baptism tacitly confirms the action of the Holy Spirit beyond
the sacramental jurisdiction of the Church.

In order to again attain "being for the other," *esse ad alterum*—in
order to restore a living dialogue maintained in the Christian past, it is
first necessary to be silent together, to unite in the silence of mutual
repentance. It is in this prayerful silence that the Spirit is received, the
One who is the revitalizing source of *essential words.*

The paradoxical coexistence of the churches, in the plural, is explained by the "conflict of fidelities." Fidelity to the faith of the Fathers

inspires the most profound respect, except when it is exclusive or virulent, in a sectarian manner. Quite rightly, the mystery of disunion, the recognition of the still saving, real presence of Christ in each other, conditions every ecumenical encounter and demonstrates that relationships with those outside of Orthodoxy are not at all to do with "saving" them. This is why every attitude of proselytizing, of seeking the conversion of the other, is out of place, dissonant in ecumenical dialogue. It makes impossible the recognition of what is of value in the other, in a kind of ecclesial positivism. Relationships between the Orthodox and the non-Orthodox are on the level of the fullness of the Incarnation, of the growth of the stature of Christ, of the fulfillment of the truths of the faith, as the prayer in the liturgy says: so that all may attain full knowledge of the truth.

This is the internal dialectic of the faith, a problem interior to Christianity. Its solution is not to be found at the end of a struggle but at the heart of a charismatic witness, full and free of the mutual works of love. According to St Paul, the usefulness of heresies is to stimulate each to show holiness before all, for it is the saints who transcend every limit, the saints who reveal the presence of God.

"That they may be one...in order that the world may believe" is an example of an "essential" word. It judges the entire Church "gathered at the Table," rejoicing in the mystical supper and forgetting that, biblically, this feast cannot but be messianic. The being "one in Christ" by an explosion of love is subordinated to the apostolic goal of the salvation of the world, the mission of the Church in the world. It is from the world's fragmentation, from its weeping, from its hellish dimension that the most urgent cry comes for unity. It is to be noted that it is the saints who bore the blame for the hardness of heart of a world closed in upon itself. In a crucified manner they heard this other essential word of St Silouan of Mt Athos: "Keep your soul in hell and do not despair."

An excessive Christocentrism has narrowed the dimensions of dialogue. Only "the Spirit who blows where he wills" expands the limits, reveals in an ecumenical assembly not one Church but the ecclesial nature of this assembly where each bears the presence of his or her own church. No one can deny his own charism. Rather he should be attentive to that most particular communion of charisms. Here we return to the source, the very abyss of "tri-solar unity," that of the Holy Trinity, which transcends theological systems impoverished by their centrism or unilateral stance.

A right theology of the Holy Spirit rescues us from shipwreck, leading us to the safe haven of the Father's "philanthropy," His love is for all mankind. But to pray with the Holy Spirit is to infuse the very familiar words of the Lord's Prayer with the Spirit's eschatological breath. In "approaching from behind," one comes "before." It is the martyrs and confessors who utter the "hallowed be Thy Name." This is the active waiting for the kingdom of the Holy Spirit, the eschatological *epiclesis* which makes this world already "the new earth." It is the final agreement of the will and the freedom of the Father with that of mankind, on earth as it is in heaven. It is the request for the truly substantial bread of the Eucharist, the only sustenance in the aridity of these last times. It is the sense of the ultimate and fearful temptation even for the saints, and last of all the praise, the doxology in which the fullness fills the heavens and already anticipates the Kingdom.

It is in this messianic and eschatological sense that the ecumenical *epiclesis* or calling down of the Holy Spirit is the essence of the prayer for unity, defining more than anything else what ought to be the attitude of one who so prays.

We are all united before the closed Bible. As soon as we open it, our readings begin to diverge. United by the fact that "God has spoken," we are divided by the fact that "we have spoken." The extreme poverty of our witness does not even approach the brilliant evidence of the truth which overcomes every controversy about faith. This weakness intrudes into prayers for unity, depriving them by an all too narrow human vision. A Catholic prays for universal agreement on the infallibility of the Pope and his universal jurisdiction. An Orthodox prays for the conciliar structure of one Church. A Protestant prays for the critical examination of every confession of faith by the Bible alone. These parallel prayers, although historically legitimated, however perpetuate existential conditions thereby canonizing the status quo, precisely where the ecclesiological actualities are incapable of resolution.

But we might look for guidance at a period in history immediately preceding the Council of Chalcedon. Alexandria proposed a dogmatic thesis on Christ, Antioch another, the antithesis of the first. The conflict seemed deadlocked yet it produced exactly the confessional situation we have today. The invocation of the Holy Spirit, the *epiclesis*, by the Fathers of the Council led to a brilliant response, a transcendent solution whose origin was divine. Each part found its truth, purified of its particularity and integrated into a synthesis completely new, and truly "catholic."

This lesson invites us to abandon ourselves to the Holy Spirit who will " lead from behind" in dogmatic truth without taking anything from it. But there must be at the same time "a foreboding" of the Paraclete who offers this royal gift of a unity unattainable in the actual state of things.

If God himself " is patient, not wishing that any perish but that all come to the fullness," the ecumenical *epiclesis* demands most especially openness and purity of heart. Such an ascetic catharsis is demanded of those who engage in ecumenical effort, which then ceases to be either an enterprise of conversion or an occasion of sentimental gentility.

In the Orthodox liturgy, before the confession of the Creed by all, each person is invited to take on the only proper liturgical attitude: "Let us love one another that with one mind we may confess—Father, Son, and Holy Spirit, the Trinity, one in essence and undivided!" It is this open heart of love which sets the stage for the *epiclesis* to occur. St Peter formulated this imperious demand and the precise nature of the attitude required to invoke the "holiness" of God. Should not our sanctity and prayer hasten the Day of the Lord?

A kind of parenthesis exists between spiritual actions and the sacraments, the latter serving as "guiding images." In this sense one can speak of "ecumenical baptism." It means dying to every spirit of imperialism, to every temptation to impose at any cost our own manner of thinking, believing or living. It bears in advance the expectation of an ecumenical Pentecost. The narrative of the Acts of the Apostles explains why this is a Pentecost. The first manifestation of the very essence of the Church took place in the apostolic breaking of bread, in the one and the same Supper of the Lord, and then the Lord added a great number of believers to the Church.

The *Parousia* of Christ, his second coming, carries within itself at one and the same time judgment and salvation. Thus the saying of the Lord will be accomplished: "I did not come to condemn the world but to save the world." The *Parousia* presupposes as preliminary the pentecostal unity of all Christians. For this to happen the Lord must then add the greatest number of brothers and sisters, those who return from the descent into hell, from despair, toward the light without end of the unique supper of the Lord.

It is possible to paraphrase the Gospel and say: seek the salvation of the world and unity will be given to you in abundance, freely, as the ultimate grace of the ministry of salvation, in full accord with the universal praise of God.

An image is perhaps clearer than words. Orthodox churches have an iconostasis, a wall separating the sanctuary from the nave, an image of the separation of the Kingdom from the world. At the beginning, this was a low barrier separating the faithful from the altar space in order to keep order during worship. In time, liturgical sense has adorned this line of separation with icons, which finally have come to cover the entire surface of the iconostasis. The Christ of the *Deisis* icon, the icon of "Supplication," of prayer is enthroned in the center and all around him are the saints who sing to him and reflect his light. What was a wall of separation has now become a bridge. In his saints, Christ has become the passage of all into the Kingdom.

The ultimate deepening of the presence of Christ is his manifestation in the saints and even more particularly the eschatological group of saints known as the "fools in Christ," whose charism or gift is to transcend their very own character. His presence is an ongoing miracle and transforms separation into connection, into a unity. The Orthodox, the Catholics and the Protestants walk the path of holiness to its goal—towards an ecumenical Pentecost if they surrender themselves, without an afterthought and tirelessly to the power of the Holy Spirit. The Paraclete would then make them to be living icons, reunited in the iconostasis of the unique Temple, whose royal doors open upon the expectant Father.

"I have come to bring fire upon the earth and I want it to be ignited." At this critical moment, when the ecumenical movement suffers entombment in institutionalism, when prophecy drowns in theological discourse, now more than ever we need the freedom of true monastics and the magnificent faith of the martyrs, capable of moving mountains and raising the dead.

"Let the one who has ears hear" no longer the governing by human pretensions or meticulous reason, but the essential word of *epiclesis* raised from the liturgical, praying heart of the Church, and the response coming from the Father, his *fiat* to the *totus Christus,* the whole Christ.

3

TO THE CHURCHES OF CHRIST
(A Message)[1]

We are faced with a brutal historical reality. For various reasons, the Church now appears to be thrown back to the pre-Constantinian era. The Church is a remnant, a tiny minority in a world quite hostile to her message and without a grasp of history. More precisely, it is a post-Constantinian era, for the world is no longer pagan, but profoundly atheistic. It listens to other gospels and to other prophets. Dynamic forces are at play, seeking to establish a new integration of the world with realities incompatible with the Christian ethic.

To every affirmation of the transcendent, the skeptical human spirit says: "What is truth?" Pilate despised the Old Testament Hebrew mentality. How much more is the world justified in finding historical Christianity repulsive. This is a treacherous and offensive era. In the throbbing daily scene of life, God cannot find a voice sufficiently pure and detached to be his herald. All is horribly compromised to the point where roles have become reversed: now the Church is being judged by the world.

Christians have done just about everything to sterilize the Gospel. One could say that it has been plunged into a neutralizing solution. Everything that is striking in it, all that transcends and turns things upside down, has been moderated, sterilized to death. Religion, having become inoffensive, is now flat, shrewd and above all, reasonable, and remains simply to be vomited out. "God does not demand much of us"—such a conviction makes the salt of the Gospel insipid and tasteless, that salt which is God's terrible jealousy, his insistence on the

---

1   Published originally as "Message aux Églises," in *Dieu vivant* 15 (1950), pp. 31-42 and reprinted in the posthumously published collection, *L'amour fou de Dieu* (Paris: Éditions du Seuil, 1973) pp. 159-174.

impossible. One cannot even say that the Gospel has encountered a wall, for a wall is hard and resistant, offering some opposition. Today the Gospel meets total indifference. It resounds in a vacuum, passes through and is received by no one.

The Church is no longer, as in the first centuries, the triumphal march of Life through the graveyards of the world. In all the recent theological definitions of her nature, the Church is conceived in an astonishingly static manner, as essentially a self-serving, self-preserving institution. She has settled on maintaining the subsistance of her own membership. In losing the apostolic sense of the Body, the living organism of the real presence of Christ, of Christ who came neither just for the apostles nor for a handful of parishes, the Church no longer exists for the world. Christian faith has thus strangely lost its character of ferment, of disrupting everything. She is no longer the leaven which raises the dough. Christians no longer have any sense of mission. They do not know how to be ambassadors, *envoys sent out*. Their life has become a closed circle! After two millennia of Christian history, the worst judgment that the world can pass upon the Church is that she has become a faithful reflection of the world itself. She recognizes the world as her own, a Christian heresy, flesh of her flesh.

Christianity and the world now face the breakdown of the Incarnation, of humanity-made-divine. According to the formula of the fourth ecumenical council of Chalcedon, the divine and the human are united in Christ *without confusion* and *without separation*. Now if divine monophysitism in theology has devalued all that is human (the tragic though eloquent absence of any Christian understanding of what is human) human monophysitism in the many, diverse forms of humanism separates the divine from the human and suppresses it. [Trans. note: Monophysitism is the heresy that claimed there was only one divine nature in Christ, not the two, divine and human.] But what is infinitely more serious is the reality that every heresy of thought is the result of the heresy of one's life. Arius was a judaizing monotheist in his life, in his piety and from this came his heretical theology. Actual Christians are heretics in their day-to-day existence and the theology they produce is that of eunuchs. St Athanasius said, "Can eunuchs give birth?" Even if their theology is absolutely correct, it is barren, devoid of any life.

One sees even in heroic efforts at actual evangelization the consequences of this breakdown we are describing. The two dominant approaches do not converge. On the one hand there is the conversion of individuals who are carried off by a kind of religious, almost sectarian sniper-action, in a purely vertical orientation. On the other hand there is a movement of incarnating Christianity into the world, in a horizontal sense, thus undergoing secularization. There is no meeting of the two. The power of the Christian message however, lies precisely at such a juncture. Salvation is not possible except in the Church, but the Church, well rooted in the world, lives only in that cry of the last times, "Come, Lord Jesus" (Rev 22:20). The fulfillment of history is beyond the limits of the Church *in situ*, which, living in the light of the second coming of Christ, is actually in history, realizing and accomplishing it.

No movement of renewal will be effective or lasting unless it makes a person an organic member of the Body of Christ and parishes living crossroads where the fullness of the coming Christ surpasses the Christ of history. Mainstream Christianity professes a somber religion of darkness so serious and ponderous as to make one atheistic. Or else it gives simplistic and optimistic bribes, the easy smile and denial of death, in any case a ridiculous vision of reality.

A psychoanalytic examination of our contemporary Christian vision would reveal one of the most profound causes of the lack of realism in its message. Christianity is not a doctrine but a life, an incarnation of its action. The average person today primarily reacts to what Christians do. In Communism, it is not Marxist speculation which is of interest but Communist action, the Communist "new being." One grasps the Christian message today either in the light or the darkness of Christian action. The average Christian today testifies to a striking phenomenon. Christianity is not at all a "new people," but just one typical sociological group among many, and it is here that we come to the heart of Christianity's failure.

Faith is no longer the source but has become an imposition, something merely added to the structures of the world in which the faithful engage—a striking example of sociological alienation. The clergy employ a distinctive religious vocabulary, but their manner of thinking, perceiving and acting, all of this is sociologically determined. The "unique" reality which is the Church defends either owning property or collectivization. For one group the demonic element is "socialism," for another "capitalism." The Kingdom of God is just an ethical category or "instrument" of propaganda which crowns the edifice. A stoic, one who follows Spinoza, an atheist—each of these is engaged according to his own moral belief. But all Christian virtues break apart before the saying: "The pagans themselves, do they not do as much—to love those who love them" (Mt 5:47). Holiness is not virtue at all but the radiance of the transcendent. Every ethical preoccupation is centered upon Christ, the Logos or Word, every moral perspective turned upside down, for the transcendence of Christianity is not that of the existentialists inside their own closed world, but the transcending of the world itself, in its totality.

Since Constantine the Great, the Church's hold on history regrettably has neither come from above nor from within, but by identification with the historical structures of the world. Christianity, whether feudal, bourgeois or proletarian has therefore lost any power of a new, a second birth, of the bringing forth of that which is *from above*. Monasticism arose from the revolt against the alienation of the Church by the Empire. Only the heroism of the desert seemed powerful enough to respond to the absolute demands of the Gospel. The Church, mystery on the march, the Bride awaiting her King, has become a "religious association," dependent on the laws of natural evolution. And the consequences are disastrous.

In appearance, "the Christians are no better than the others," yet by the strength which comes from above, they should be capable of raising the dead. But since they nourish themselves solely with earthly food, they can only be the ones to bury the dead instead.

The Incarnation has been accommodated to this age. The Temple of God has become a huge "insurance company" for eternal life with minimal risk (for Pascal, "the wager"), with techniques of consolation and "strategies" for every imaginable situation. The Christian faith is preached as the healthiest, happiest, most effective arrangement for human life. Holy Communion is offered as a promise of eternity. A person disturbed by the instability of changing, contemporary values is attracted to what appears to be the "stability" of spiritual values. But this is exactly contrary to authentic spiritual reality. In losing Kierkegaard's idea of faith as finding oneself above thousands of fathoms of water, in searching for guarantees of salvation, such a person actually compromises his salvation. The respectable Christian middle-class has made of the Gospel a prolongation of the best aspirations of humanity for the best of all possible worlds, the Kingdom of God. It has lost historic Christianity in the optimism of sanctimonious piety, empty of all tragic existence. The Gospel however is not adaptable functionally. It is explosive. The Gospel is the demand of metamorphosis, transformation, of *metanoia* which shatters not only historical structures but makes even history itself radiate with light.

It is due to such an interiorizing, a making one's own of Christian truth that a specifically "Christian" science, philosophy, or politics can no longer exist, neither can they have legitimate practitioners. There can only be Christian people who work at their professions in a manner authentic or false, in all fields—art, medicine, business, or other areas. You cannot have a Christian mathematics but you can be a Christian mathematician. Each expression depends uniquely on the source not on the outcome. In your home you can install a holy water font or paste up biblical passages on the walls but these will only be appendices, mere additions to being an *ecclesia domestica*, that is, living the Christian life in your home, as a little church.

An authentic Christian is one who, to all he knows and does attaches the claim of God's existence. The difference between believers and non-believers today is the fact that the former are metaphysicians a bit more than the latter. Some believe in allopathy, others in homeopathy, and the third group in prayer. (Dr Carrel's clinical observations reveal that the mystical element makes these more resistant to illness. Healers show that faith brings about good health. The miraculous is sociologically channeled.) In the behavior and thinking of the average Christian, however, there is no place for the *further, other Reality* which transcends, which by its existence even announces *the wholly Other.* Faith here appears as one of the elements of a functional sort, a sociological category and thus the Christian message is emptied of all its transforming power.

We thus can understand why Christianity, as a sociological form, is no longer attractive. We meet impassioned people searching for truth in other places, searching for the beyond, for the purity of existence, and theirs is more than a desperate effort.

In our parishes, one is struck by an impoverished humanity, by the number of mediocre people looking for compensation. One could say they are there because they dream of being first of the least in the Kingdom of God. "God has chosen the weak things, the lowly, the despised of the world," not because he does not know how to choose but because he chooses "the foolish things to confound the wise" (1 Cor 1:27-28). Now for the mass of Christianity, the greatest wisdom is to flee like the plague everything that is "foolish," all that transcends, is mystical, even the very heart of the Gospel. Rather than confounding the world, such Christianity is itself confused with the world. It has become refuse, without radiance or value.

In the Middle Ages, the Church had a powerful weapon, namely the fear of hell. In time, though, the mystical understanding of life disappeared and the devil with his hellish paraphernalia has become nothing more than a fairy tale for children. Paradise, just like hell, is no longer part of our spiritual experience. Having become radically transcendent, both heaven and hell have turned into pure abstractions. Both the fear of hell and the joy of the Kingdom are now exterior to us, outside of our experience. We remain the only truth and the sole meaning of our existence. This is where we are the most vulnerable and accessible.

Evil dominates us and our thinking, makes us suffer without release, and in turn allows us to make others suffer. The world is fallen because we cannot imagine the depth to which it is fallen. There is no sense of being culpable. The very idea of *sin* is meaningless and thus tragically, there is no reason for *forgiveness.* No one asks for forgiveness because there are only the unfortunate victims of chance, cast into existence. They can only make themselves less sensitive to their pain, forgetting it. They can attempt courageously to exist without any meaning. Or again they can try to refashion humanity by suppressing all metaphysical anguish.

So we live without continuity, carried along in jerks and starts, plunged into life, out of time. Life thus no longer has any mysteries. There is only initiation into techniques. Who dares to speak of love when surrounded by techniques for lovemaking, sexual acrobatics?

Who can speak of the *mysterium tremendum*, the terrifying mystery, of "the place which is holy," of any sensation of the sacred at all? In biological terms what could one say today of the Virgin Mary?

The faces of those who make history do not allow us to imagine them on their knees, in contemplation of the holy. There is no solution to the mystery of evil, aside from the Fall. History with its infinite defects appears as a fault on the smooth surface of nothingness where nothing occurs. The disintegration of our human substance is so deep that the idea most innate, most natural, of the first Adam and of the second Adam-Christ, is now impenetrable, even for Christians. A complete indifference enshrouds the Christian message. "About all this let us speak again, at another time" (Acts 17:32). All words are rendered ineffective in principle, in advance, by prejudice.

Modern man is terribly practical when it comes to money. If nothing else, he is calculating. If it should even dawn on him to ask what this Christian adventure "tells" him, he eyeballs Christianity and sees nothing singular there. As in the world he sees hypocrites there. He also sees the repressed who try to conceal their weakness and the shrewd ones who make religion the opium to help them accomplish their goals. And if the world is more bored of religion's discourse and if the words do not move anyone, then we have a situation worse than that of the tower of Babel. It is not so much a confusion of languages but utter chaos at the very heart of language itself. We no longer understand each other. Communion is completely shattered and we exist only in isolation from each other.

Having been tossed on the sociological trash heap, is it at all possible for Christianity to become once more the place where the presence of the God-Man shines forth? Can the face of Christ again "radiate in the faces of those who belong to him," as an ancient liturgical text puts it? Here lies the entire matter. The only message which is powerful any longer is not the one which simply repeats the words of Christ, the Word, but the one which makes him present. Only his presence will make the message, as the Gospel says, *light* and *salt* for the world.

The Gospel is an explosive seed. It is revolutionary. It overturns not the structures of the world but those of the human spirit. What is important here is the manifestation of God in us, the coming of Christ in humanity. In the words of St Seraphim of Sarov, "Acquire peace within and a multitude of people around you will find their salvation with you."

The man and woman of our modern era has already been transformed by the magic spell of the conviction that "all is permitted." Yet we are unhappy in the very depths of our souls. Our misery is echoed in our hunger for freedom. It is possible for us, once more, if just for a moment, to put all else aside and to see Christ, to enter into conversation with him. But in order for this to happen it necessary that the Christian message no longer be the repetition of a catechism lesson. It is necessary rather that we become persons who speak of God and to allow ourselves to be ones in whom God himself speaks. If we find Christ again in the Gospel, it will be because each word read there already contains his presence. The one who then becomes the messenger must identify with Christ who is speaking, so that his presence may shine. And the messenger must always still his own voice.

There is no salvation except in the Church. The ministry of the Word comes through the ministry of the sacraments and is fulfilled in the ministry of *incorporation—into us*. But the Body of Christ overflows the limits of history, and it is precisely this transcendence which frees us from all sociological alienation. This is clearly described in the account of the calling of the apostles: "Let the dead bury their dead" (Mt 8:22). Our vocation, our call, transcends the sociological cemeteries.

During the ages of the ecumenical councils, monasticism raised a powerful appeal, announcing the end and many generations of Christians were moved, yes, transformed by the striking image of the heroism of these holy women and men. Today monasticism is above the world but not within it. Christianity is called now, more than ever, to find itself at the same time both above and within the world, and this is essential. It is not so much a problem of new language but of avoiding the real danger of reducing the message, lowering its demands. We must again raise this message to its proper level. "The one who is near me is near fire." It is neither paradox nor dialectic which consume, but fire. We need to return to the simple and striking language of the parables. "Never has anyone spoken with such power" (Jn 7:46). With all of his being Christ proclaimed the "wholly Other," and thus overturned the established perspectives, leaving not "a stone upon a stone."

The message ought to rip us out of every sociological straight-jacket, to strip and clothe us again in Christ. In Russia, the rejection of the State at the time of the revolution was such that one feared that with the fall of the monarchy would also come the fall of the Church. Nothing like this happened. With the monasteries closed, monks and nuns entered life as free men and women. They radiated the light of Christ by their silence. This is the freedom we need to recover most of all. The oppressors and the prison camps put Christians outside the law. With what speed and ease these conditions liberated them from every sociological category and captivity.

"Seek the Kingdom of God." This call contains the greatest of para-doxes. One must find that which cannot be found in this world, the eternal in time, the absolute in the relative. How can we do this? From all *"having"* we must pass into *"being."* "Blessed are the poor in spirit." This does not mean, blessed are those who do not own, do not possess the spirit, but rather blessed are those who have become spirit, who are spirit. Only such as these become the true scandal or stumbling block for the world, yes, and for the Church. Only they reveal the power of the Christian message. To become spirit is already to live in the Other, to become the Other—it is the eschatological experience. The King-dom of God has come among us.

Every human activity—culture, art, thought, social action—has its religious meaning but this meaning always overflows the borders of history. At their peak all these forms of human accomplishment express not their own values, but in transcending these they become symbols, signs, sparks of the fire that heralds the coming of that which is greatest, the reign of the Father. The fulfillment of history lies outside of itself. It is this which makes history the pathway, and not by its own strength. The historical task is "the fulfillment" of cul-ture and of history but as a figure of the Kingdom of God, as its icon. This ultimate challenge is evident in the response of a priest in Soviet Russia to the question, "What is the real goal of Russian Orthodox spirituality?" His answer: "The *Parousia,* the second coming of Christ." The Church does not accomplish its historical fullness except in preparing for the return of Christ. Evangelization must be seen only in this perspective.

Here we arrive at the solution of the problem of the *Christian style* or *way of life*. Formerly this expressed, in its details, the spirituality of the age in which it found itself. But we now live in a very different time. Now is not the time for Christian spirituality to reflect the age. Rather in every aspect our spiritual life must point to the Other, by its adaptability, its suppleness, by detachment, and by the freedom of possessing all things as if we did not possess them. This is the apocalyptic style which places its invisible but nonetheless perceptible seal on everything. King Midas turned everything he touched into gold. By one's interior attitude, each Christian can make everything around him beautiful and light, can turn them into icons, images of their true nature. Such an authentically spiritual life would accomplish much, much more than many sermons. And it is uniquely in such freedom that the missionary vocation of the faithful, of the laity can be seen.

Here is the significance of the "worker priests" who entered the factories and shops without giving up their priesthood, who in their freedom dispelled all the categories, myths and complexes surrounding the faith. In their struggles, these clergy were both above and within the world. The faith became the source for every task and transformed all of their work into prophetic ministry. This is prophetic speaking by one's life, the most powerful form of proclamation: "I place before you life and death" (Deut 30:15). The demonic impulse in the world has made its choice in advance. How often do we reject the message because we fear the change it may bring to our lives, because we fear the demands of the transcendent, and in our isolation we find nothing to sustain us.

A Christian community, if it truly is this, buries itself as a splinter in the body of the world. It imposes itself as a sign. It deals with the world as the place where God is encountered. The community is where the world comes into contact with Christian reality, where we come and see, and live. Such a place is where the Christian presence exists to serve the world. Do not the people of the Church possess the social awareness and understanding of actual situations, the intelligence to humanely tell others the meaning of existence, of work, of their place in the world?

One need not improvise as a messenger. To approach another person in our modern era is truly an art. The essential ingredient is the marvelous power of putting yourself into the place of the other, to look at the world with his eyes, to appreciate things with his tastes and to allow to surface what is slumbering there—communion. And we must be able to remove ourselves from the picture, permitting Christ to speak.

So often our theology, formulated in so many abstract terms, falls to pieces in the face of crime, death or loneliness. I have seen miserable, squalid, downright ugly persons—like old precious stones encrusted with grime and dirt. Yet if for a moment some living warmth is placed in the hollow of their hands, suddenly, light beams from their faces. Behind the facade of intellectual objections, of cynicism and indifference we all hide our loneliness, our need for the presence of another.

To receive Christ is to "eat" and "drink" him and afterwards make our way into the world as living sacraments, as the Eucharist on the way, moving along through life. It is only through us, even if we are silent, that Christ speaks once again to the world, that he again gives himself as food, for the life of the world.

The Fathers of the Church knew how to reconcile the ways and wisdom of the world with the life in Christ so that for them, *everything was Christ*. This is the breath of authentic catholicity. They knew how to put theology together with the experience of the Church. They knew how to live in a completely eucharistic manner, consuming all as if it were the Body and Blood of Christ.

If it is indeed a good thing to make atheists less certain of the nonexistence of God, it is also good to make theologians less sure of their own speculation. It would be most interesting and beneficial to see in our seminaries a chair or professorship of atheism established, to make our theologians less free in their affirmations, more sensitive to the ordinary person's situation and suffering, and so, to make Christ more accessible. Christ is so often kept from us by theological and religious mumbo-jumbo. You don't worry about adjusting the furnace when the house is on fire, nor do you wallow in secondary, unimportant things while the world is going to pieces. All of our creativity ought to focus on lifting the generation before us into the immense joy of freedom, the joy of serving others, into the joy (as St John the Baptist) of being the friend of Christ, the Bridegroom.

And if the moment comes when we find ourselves marginalized from social life, then this generation would have to mature. They would have to become "confessors" of the faith, a generation capable of "conversing with Christ," as the letter of the martyrs of Lyon in the ancient Church put it so magnificently.

The historical task, however, is not the search for the forms of primitive Christianity but for her cry: *Marana tha*—"Come, Lord," for union with the Church in the final hour. This hour makes all the other hours real. This last hour make the Christian message real again, for us.

4

THE CHURCH AND SOCIETY
The Social Dimension of Orthodox Ecclesiology[1]

A fter the great Geneva Conference on "The Church and Society,"
Pope Paul VI's encyclical *Populorum progressio* expressed the Roman
Church's caution. In that church's view, such great organizations as
UNESCO, the World Health Organization, the International Labor
Bureau, the Organization for Economic Cooperation and Development
have proposed both solutions to world problems and pilot projects aimed
at them. After their consultations and work, the problems of underdevel-
opment do not appear to be unsolvable either in theory or technically. We
know the very tangible solutions. All that is lacking is the will and agreement to employ them. We can fathom the depth of the problem only if we
consider that the solution to social and economic problems, though
urgent, depends before all else, on a spiritual principle.

Certain commentators at the Geneva Conference stressed that the
actual positions taken there had no connection either with theology or
with classical humanism and its secularized ethics. Their critique was
in part aimed at the abstract character of theological systems no longer
effective. The salt has lost its taste, as the Gospel tells us. On the other
hand, the critique also rejected a social ethics reduced to itself, as lacking the transcendent power which could say to the afflicted: "Rise and
walk." Long ago Dostoevsky, addressing the socialists of his era, said:
"Without Christ you will never be able to share bread...."

Are such hopes utopian? They put into play the very foundations of
our faith and how we enact them. Are the "good words" of an honest
person any more utopian than God himself or his vision of humanity?

1 Published in *Contacts* 59-60 (1967), pp. 190-231.

The "Legend of the Grand Inquisitor" of Dostoevsky emphasizes this most singularly. If we are to be honest, Christian hope is not the problem. According to St Gregory of Nyssa, "One hope's in that which already exists." Such hope is not a simple supposition, not the mere "perhaps" of alternatives without any foundation. According to the Letter to the Hebrews, faith is the *guarantee* or assurance of things hoped for, the *proof* or conviction of things unseen. Thus in the Gospel, the Kingdom of God is not the revelation of a static truth but on the contrary, the dynamic revolution of what is "absolutely new." Because it is *near*, this newness is already overturning the foundations of the world. The newness has to do with the ultimate destiny of humanity because it is rooted in the *humanism of God* and not just in that of humankind. The 'death of God,' which is so much spoken of today, really means the death of the God of a cerebral theology which is abstract, static and horribly pessimistic. The living God is the God of the dynamic reality of a human being deified, who has become a participant in God's own life, a concelebrant who shares with God in his limitless work: "The one who believes in me will also do the works that I do, and he will do even greater things" (Jn 14:12). Here we are not speaking of miracles but of something even greater than a miracle. Here we mean the righteousness or justice of God, the presence of his radiant truth in the struggle against the dehumanization of the world, against suffering, hunger and death.

The Church has something to say about this justice of God, a message to proclaim. Without becoming entangled with technical matters which are the competence of sociologists and economists, the task of theology, as the Orthodox understand it, is to employ the tradition of the Bible and the Fathers of the Church in order to more precisely define the social ministry of the Church, to sketch out the fundamentals of a *social ecclesiology*, the Church's authentic relationship to society. In examining the teaching of the Fathers, one is struck by the realization that *the social teaching of the Church contains the very essence of Christianity*. As early as the fourth century, St John Chrysostom emerges as the most radical and severe judge of the amorphous and passive state of Christianity: "I see the body of the Church prostrate in the sun like a corpse. I see the members lifeless. I do not see anyone accomplishing its functions....We call each other brothers and sisters since we are all members of each other, but in reality we are at each other as savage beasts...nothing would make us more imitators of Christ than to take an active concern for the neighbor...miracles and martyrdom will not be able to save us unless we have a perfect solidarity of love among ourselves."[2]

The "communion of saints" is inseparable from the "communion of sinners." A "fool for Christ," prayed, with tearful intensity: "That all may be saved, that the entire world be saved." It was in this sense that the 1925 Stockholm Conference, seeking to reawaken the social conscience of the churches, asked what was the biblical message concerning society. This question addresses the prophetic ministry of the Church and requires her response without equivocation. According to the Gospel of St John (16:13-15), without modifying any Christological truth, the Holy Spirit "goes after" Christ in order to "announce beforehand." Faith reveals the concealed meaning here. The "inspired" manner of "thinking in advance" tells us that a "responsible" society can never be effective if it does not find its leading images, its guidance in the "responsible" Church. As the world's moral conscience, the Church engages the hearts of all. Only the Church can do this, for she leads humankind toward its ultimate destiny, and the Church herself is illumined by an eschatological light. With reference to the Apocalypse and the absolutes of divine justice, only the Church can give a soul to social development which is itself just a means in the service of the Spirit. Berdiaev said it profoundly: "Bread for me is a material question, but bread for my neighbor is a spiritual one." In our completely new and urgent social situation all ecclesial provincialism must be transcended in favor of the universal. The task for the Orthodox is to make the voice of the Fathers heard again, and where the problems are "contextual" to our era, to formulate the leading principles with fidelity to their teaching.

The Church, the moral conscience of humanity

"Be perfect as your heavenly Father is perfect" (Mt 5:48). The patristic commentary on this saying is forceful and explicit. In every effort

2   *Hom.* 27, 2 Cor, PG 61, 588; *Hom.* 25, 1 Cor, PG 61, 208, 210.

towards perfection, personal holiness is inseparable from the social dimension. St John Chrysostom energetically condemned every "transcendent egoism" of individual salvation: "Seeking only one's own salvation is the surest way of being lost...our life is a hard struggle; our King orders us to stand in the ranks without following our own interests."[3] Vladimir Soloviev could not help but echo this: "The one who will be saved is the one who saves others."

In this common struggle, no social arrangement can be "dogmatized" or "canonized." Always relative, no particular political, economic or social system incarnates the ideal of divine justice or the good. The Church, which is the presence of the "Word that judges," transcends all political regimes and economic orders. The Church can exist under capitalism, indifferent to religion, or follow the path of martyrdom under an atheistic Marxist regime. Despite the many errors of the historical past, no dependency of the Church upon a political system is justified, except in the case of violent constraint. It is this freedom which gives the Church the power of standing as the moral conscience of humanity and shapes her ministry in society. Such a charismatic ministry seeks approaches to the absolute through the changing and relative forms of history.

The New Testament

The New Testament canonizes no particular social system. Christ announces the coming of the Kingdom, but he never presents himself either as a reformer or the lawgiver of a specific social order. In his preaching, he neither concerns himself with nor criticizes any of the political, social or economic institutions of his time. The difficult saying, "Give to Caesar the things that are Caesar's and to God the things that are God's" (Mt 22:21), in its most immediate sense poses a clear distinction between the Kingdom of heaven and the kingdom of this world and avoids the danger of confusing them. "Seek first the Kingdom (of heaven) and everything else (the earthly) will be given to you in abundance" (Mt 6:33). A hierarchy of values thus establishes the project of following the Gospel and affirms that it is the invisible Absolute

3   *Hom.* 59 on Mt 5.

that determines the true relationships and gives them their own visible and relative value. Therefore, everything relative is actually not relative but is always related to that which is not relative, the Absolute. Caesar is not Caesar except in relation to God and this is the meaning of St Paul's affirmation: "There is no authority except that which comes from God" (Rom 13:1). If God does not exist, there is no Caesar, he is only a manifestation of nothingness and the absurd. In Dostoevsky's *The Possessed*, an officer told of the nonexistence of God cries out: "But if God does not exist, am I then a captain?"

It is always because of this hierarchy of values, because of God, that the human person receives his inestimable dignity of being a place of *theophany*, of the presence of God: "The one who does not love the brother whom he can see does not love the God he cannot see" (1 Jn 4:19-20). St Irenaeus says "The criteria of our love of the Holy Spirit is the measure of our love for all of the faithful."[4] Love of the human is well founded, for man is the object of the divine love which Nicholas Cabasilas called *manikon eros,* the "foolish" or "absurd" love of God for man. This is why the great spiritual masters say, "After God, esteem all others as God himself." They teach that there must be infinite respect for this "presence of God" which is the human person. Even more the Lord has said, "Whatever you do to one of these, the least of my brethren, that you do to me" (Mt 25:40).

In the words of St Macarius of Egypt, a "kinship" of likeness between God and ourselves as his children surpasses mere human solidarity. In becoming incarnate, in becoming flesh, God has identified himself with the human and thus revealed the ontological norm. Created in his image, human nature is conformed to the Trinitarian mystery of unity in the many, for God is one and three at the same time. The revelation of the Godlike image excludes any isolation or solitude which is the exclusive lot and tragic destiny of the demonic world. This is why *unus Christianus, nullus Christianus*—"one Christian is no Christian," and "where two or three are gathered in my name, there am I in the midst of them" (Mt 18:20). This is the unshakable evangelical foundation of the social. Origen emphasizes this: "It is only in the

---

4 *Adv. Haer.* III, 24, I.

community of the faithful that the Son of God can be found, and there because he only dwells among those with whom he is united."[5] Christ does not show his presence except where there is mutual love. From the beginning, the time of the apostles, to be a Christian meant to be in communion with the Twelve, to be found *epi to auto*, "in one and the same place and for the same thing," that is, to participate together in the breaking of the eucharistic bread.

From the start, the People of God became in Christ "neither Greek nor Jew," but a *tertium genus*, a third race, the *totus Christus*, or whole Christ, which includes all of humanity. The Church then formulates the social dogma of the fraternal communion of all people for it is this communion that Christ makes the place of his presence. The Church preaches this and this is the sign of the Kingdom, without any distinction between herself and society. The gospel does not know of society as sociologists do, that is, as a complex collection of different institutions. The gospel rather, recognizes only "the world," the totality of humanity, the creation of God and the object of apostolic mission.

"God so loved the world...." He has loved it in its sinful state and "he came to search for those who are lost" (Lk 19:10). In the person of the apostles, Christ sent the Church out saying, "Go then and make disciples of all nations...You will be my witnesses, even to the ends of the earth" (Mt 28:18-19). The *Letter to Diognetus* (from the end of the second century) describes the original vision of Christianity as placed in the world, without any separation between the two, for the world is the great field of missionary action. "Lift your eyes and see, the fields are white for the harvest" (Jn 4:35). Just as the love of God cannot be separated from love of the brethren so the Church cannot be separated from society. The whole of humanity is governed by the same dogmatic principle, its leading image: unity amid diversity. This is how God is present and shows himself in the human community.

Without specifying the forms of social structures, the gospel is nevertheless precise about the basic attitude in relationships among human beings, something St John Chrysostom later would qualify as sacramental: "The love of the neighbor is a sacrament," he would say, a

5 *Comm.* on Mt XIV, I.

sacrament because beneath the visible form of the neighbor is given the grace of the invisible presence of Christ. It is this presence which makes me the neighbor of all. The last judgment is centered upon this "sacramental attitude" towards the sick, the hungry, the poor and prisoners.

We can understand, then, that wealth might be considered as one of the most serious obstacles on the path of the Kingdom. The rich risk losing their souls and the poor risk losing their bodies. In the parable of the rich man and Lazarus, Abraham notes the reversal of social inequality: "Now, here, Lazarus is consoled and you, the rich man, you are in torment" (Lk 16:25). If the Beatitudes speak of a future age where the poor and those who weep will be consoled, the messianic ministry implies the revelation of the righteousness of God here and now. The song of Mary, the *Magnificat*, sings of the coming of God's justice to the earth, the fulfillment of the prophets' preaching. "He has cast the mighty from their thrones and sent the rich away empty" (Lk 1:53). Beyond any appeal to revolution, the Word judges the social disequilibrium and sketches out for us the normal, primordial time in which human relationships followed divine righteousness.

The apostolic age

The apostolic community of Jerusalem realized, according to Troeltsch, a "communism of love." The story of Ananias and Sapphira witnesses that this communism was not imposed at all. In actuality it was not the desire to keep a portion of their property for which they were punished but for lying to the Holy Spirit. This apostolic community only had a brief life. It disappeared in 70 C.E. without leaving a trace or imitators. Its unique image was radiant with the gifts of the apostolic era. Utopian in its context, this community remains a driving force and image, a source of inspiration for renewal, for returns to the ecclesial Ideal. Later on, this inspiration was evident in the monastic communities. The Orthodox Church's liturgy guards this principle in its integrity, underscoring the intimate relationship between eucharistic communion and the "sacrament of the brother." Eusebius, in speaking of the Christian communities of Asia Minor noted that "the Christians share not only in the bread and wine at the altar but also what they possess, distributing to the needy clothing and other necessities, because in them they recognize their brothers."[6] St Cyprian said the same: "At the table of the Lord...we learn to see in our neighbor another me, another self."[7]

In the first century, the waiting for the *Parousia*, the coming of the Lord, took the Church's concerns beyond immediate material interests. Yet from the beginning, there was one thing of great importance. Alongside the ministerial priesthood of the liturgy and the preaching of the Word, the apostles proposed to select persons charged with a function both religious and social at the same time. This was the ministry of "serving at table," the service of bread and its distribution to the poor. The deacons elected were the social ministers of the community. They incarnated the *diakonia* of the Church, distinct from the priestly ministry. This was a ministry for exemplary Christians "of good reputation, full of the Holy Spirit and of wisdom," hence this was a charismatic ministry, bearing within itself the seed of the future ministry of the laity. When later on, the deacons formed the first degree of the order of the priesthood, their social task passed naturally to the lay members of the parishes.

The apostles did not criticize the economic structures of the ancient world. For the moment, love was superabundant and changed human relationships, moving them to a spiritual level. Thus St Paul does not condemn slavery but teaches us to recognize "beyond the slave, the beloved brother." St Paul does not become involved with the institution of slavery as such. St James recovers the prophets' radicalism and condemns the wealthy without criticizing the social and political regime. Social evils receive a corrective in the works of love, in the *diakonia* of the Christian communities. But already the *Didaché,* probably from the beginning of the second century, goes even further, for it touches upon the very principal of personal ownership of property and prepares the way for the Fathers' teaching. "Have all things in common with your brother and do not say that you own things yourself for if you want to share in the things eternal how then ought you to treat the things that are perishable?" One sees here the right of giving charitably

6   PG 21, 42.
7   PG 79, 1198.

has become the obligation to love and to share because no one has absolute proprietary rights.

History

In the fourth century Christianity became the official religion of the Empire. The Church proclaimed and preached the principles of the new Christian way of life but had no real power to modify the economic structures of the Greco-Roman world. The easy justification of social evils as the inevitable consequences of sin and thus their passive acceptance provoked the violent opposition of the church fathers. Further we will see their authoritative teaching expressing the Church's doctrine.

In the course of centuries, the Church sought to transform the cruelties of culture and the injustice of society. The Church established hospitals and built schools and hostels for the suffering and needy. St Basil inaugurated a immense hospital center, financed by the Church of Caesarea, for the sick, the handicapped, and the poor. St Gregory of Nazianzus called it a "new city," and in time it became known as the *Basiliade*. In monastic communities there was a flourishing of common life and work, always attentive to the social disorders of the world to the degree that they became veritable institutions of social protection for the oppressed. The Church condemned usury, preached a commercial ethic, defended just pricing, judging mercilessly all speculation especially during times of war and famine, and these very perspectives eventually became part of civil law. The corporations of the Middle Ages formed the conscience of social responsibility and assured mutual assistance among their members. The bishops authored programs of reform for the princes, for better control of the judiciary, suppression of alcoholism, and the removal of excessive and unjust taxes. Even those who left the world and fled to the desert defended the poor and the weak before the rulers. The theology of the medieval period explicitly formulated the idea of society as *corpus Christianum,* the Christian body.

Monasticism, with its origins eschatologically outside of history, quite rightly had a role to play, providing both a necessary retreat and freedom, and in time monasticism became a shaper both of history and of Christian spirituality. In the East, St Basil in his *Monastic Rules* founded the life of such communities on love of the neighbor and service to all. In the West the *Rule of St Benedict* proposed an evangelical balance: "All that had been done out of fear of hell now should be done for the love of Christ." The rigorous ascetic and bishop St Paphnutius was granted a vision which revealed to him what the ideal of perfection according to the Gospel looked like in action. He saw the following as models of love: a robber who saved a woman abandoned in the desert, also a just and generous head of a village, and finally a merchant who shared his possessions with the poor. More and more the great spiritual masters accented the social aspect of the spiritual life and affirmed it. No asceticism which lacked love of the neighbor could draw near to God. The true disciple of Christ bears in his soul the whole world and all beings, for, according to St Gregory the Theologian, such a soul is "the treasure chest of divine love for all."

The Fathers' sacramental and ascetic therapeutic approach rehabilitated the understanding both of the cosmos and of the human being. For St Gregory Palamas, the fact of being an incarnate spirit is the unique privilege of the human person and the reason for superiority even over the angels. Here is the seed of an immense theology of culture, the beautiful grounding of God's creation, namely deification. Furthering this theology of creation, incarnation and deification, Nicholas Cabasilas saw in marriage the fullness of the human person. The Fathers recognized and promoted the integrity and fullness of humanity. In our time, a monk of the Eastern Church (Fr Lev Gillet) in his book, *In Thy Presence,* writes: "Do not allow your word to be in my life as a sanctuary, separated from the world by some kind of cloister or wall." Truly, the only accusation at the last judgment will be of being insensitive to the suffering of others, inattentive to the presence of Christ in their suffering. The "neptic" or "vigilant" Fathers insisted, "When you see you brother, you see God." Such an attitude though certainly not a rule but a style, is the fruit of the ascetic culture and the heritage of the Fathers and one can only call it an *ecclesial evangelism.* Here we find the very best perspective of the Church on the world and society, but this tradition is enclosed within the shadows of monasteries and in the teachings of the great masters of the spiritual life. It would seem that the monastic solution by reason of its very "eschatological maximalism," is marginal to the world. Those who remain in the world perceived another way and tried to build a Christian city, a Christian society, culture, even empire. Theocracies, so-called Christian empires and states put an end to this hope and show conclusively that it is not possible to impose the Gospel from on high as a law.

The Renaissance and the modern period have broken with the social tradition of Christianity. There is no longer any *corpus Christianum*. Religious individualism (*devotio moderna*) goes hand in hand with modern economic individualism. Spirituality without any concern for the problems of work, the body, the cosmos and the modern world has closed itself off to the real problems of the spirit. The capitalist system in which alienation means the objectivation or reification of the human person, his transformation into an object or a slavery of objects, encounters no moral resistance. Now we realize that it is not capitalism which is guilty of inhumanity, but rather the once Christian but now decadent which tolerates and eventually allows economic and political and social exploitation.

With the French revolution, the social ideal decisively became hostile to all religious elements. Socialism has inherited this attitude but in its origins, socialism is Christian. Socialism goes back to the medieval movements of evangelical poverty, to the spirit of the *anawim*, the poor ones of Israel. Utopians of the sort of Saint-Simon, Fourier, Pierre Leroux were romantic Christians, not to mention Lacordaire and Lammenais. It is in this unconsciously religious climate that socialism developed and it is here that Marx would take and transpose these idealistic initial aspirations into an economic plan of dialectical and historical materialism, into which he would further project a secularized messianic vision. The most powerful and well known movements of the nineteenth century forced the social problem into the consciousness of the Church and awakened her. Pope Leo XIII spoke of economic immorality. Pope Pius XI condemned certain aspects of capitalism. The encyclical *Populorum progressio* of Pope Paul VI followed the path of his predecessors but this pope's incontestably new contribution was to even more forcibly stress the opposition of human community to all economic individualism. In the English speaking world, again today, socialism is not separated from Christianity and Christian perspectives. Exiled Russian thinkers such as Fr Sergius Bulgakov, Simon Frank and Nicolas Berdiaev underscored the opposition between Marxism and the social truth of Christianity, speaking of the "dignity of Christianity and the indignity of Christians."

A moralist such as Rousseau, metaphysicians such as Kant and Hegel, even positivists such as Comte, the agnostic Herbert Spencer and the materialist dialectician, Karl Marx all nevertheless converge in their belief in the utopia of an earthly paradise. But since the end of the nineteenth century and especially in the Soviet experience, such a purely mystical faith in nature has become an exhausted deception. The brutal reality of history has shattered the utopias and their dreams. It is now clear that a perfect society is not possible. Each evolution of society is finite and the sterile immobility of each cannot be escaped. In actuality, our realizations are always partial and relative and in need of a view of the Absolute. Here is the significance of the Kingdom of which the Gospel speaks, of Christian eschatology. Because the King has come his Kingdom will also come. Only a Christian personalism has any chance to bring a solution, for it offers the fundamental value of the human person as the subject and does not envision the full growth or blossoming of the person except in the universal community of "the unique," the Orthodox "sobornost." Both capitalist individualism and Marxist collectivism are anti-personalist and anti-communitarian for they deal not with unique persons but with a world in which anonymity rules—*das Man*, "they," "one...." In the conflict of empirically dominant ideologies the average Christian finds himself marginalized, without any direct influence upon history. The Church herself always seems to be at least a century behind, accepting all reform and revolutions *post factum*. Now the fact that the Church is able to exist under all sorts of political regimes does not signify her indifference to them. The actual exegesis of Romans 13, "All power comes from God," reveals that these words do not apply only to the infant Church in the political condition of St Paul's time.

The Orthodox Church, living in a free political situation today, lags behind the encyclicals of the popes and the social activism of English-speaking countries. On the other hand, her experience in Marxist societies is advanced and on this basis she has found that freedom itself is not sufficient for formulating and expressing judgment. This experience is of great importance, namely that one should speak with prudence and caution. It would seem that in such Communist contexts the Church has again found what it means to be "poor and servant," with the privilege of being persecuted and having many martyrs. The "sacrament of the brother" flows from the God of the *kenosis,* the suffering God, stripped and purified of every "triumphalist and terrorist" religion. Would this not be the most disarming and effective response to the atheism of today?

The identification of the Church then is not with the powerful of this world but with the suffering of the oppressed. This touches the essence of God and recovers an expression adequate to his mystery: to put one's feet into the footsteps of Christ *elcomenos*, the suffering and sorrowful servant of Yahweh. St John Chrysostom's comparison of charity, our sharing with others, to the Eucharist is not lyrical romanticism. It is because Orthodox ecclesiology is eucharistic that giving to the poor, real sharing, is the most dramatic and authentic expression of both Church and Eucharist. The social teachings of the Fathers is of the very essence of Christianity. This is why the problems of transcending capitalism, of technocracy, of the situation of the Third World —the developing nations, of war and of hunger, burning issues on the international scene are the most pressing for the churches and for Christian conscience.

The only true revolution will come from the Gospel, for here it is God himself who will overtake us in order to bring about the Kingdom and establish its justice. In the Book of Revelation, Christ is "the One who is, who was and who is to come." That he is "the One who is to come," testifies that we have already entered an entirely new historical age. In its light, we can see the alternative of the final struggle between an eschatological Pentecost, the time of an outpouring of gifts and charisms, and on the other hand, the darkness of a new barbarism, the dissolution of the human person and the possible destruction of the world. But eschatology is a two-edged sword. It is never enough to speak of the end of the world if this means a kind of passivity, or a theological obscurantism and indifference to our world. The eschatology of the Bible and the Fathers is explosive, demanding solutions in this earthly life in connection with the Apocalypse and the deepest meaning of our present crisis is that it is the visible judgment of God upon the world and the Church.

Every age has its own eschatology, its own crisis and judgment. We must pay attention to this and not to the precise time of the end of the world, which is hidden in the transcendent will of the Father. The Fathers' commentary on the parable of wise and foolish virgins discerns in the image of the empty lamps the drying up of love. The Fathers teach that the social question has its own proper eschatological dimension and is of concern to every Christian. Technology is autonomous today and is not focused on the end and meaning of existence. The real danger is that the secularized world of our time no longer hears the voice of Christ. The risk is that a passive Christianity will be reduced to a weak minority with no grip on history. The Swiss socialist Ragaz stressed the tragic rift between those who believe in God but are not interested in his Kingdom and the atheists who want to build the Kingdom, but who do not believe in God.

The extreme rationalization of our life has brought us to the moment where we even doubt reason and we are all threatened by irrational forces which can plunge us into the absurdity and anguish of which Heidegger, Sartre, and Kafka wrote. In philosophy, Foucault's structuralism thrusts reflection into "archeological" darkness. In modern drama and literature, in the work of Samuel Beckett and Robbe-Grillet, we find the same perspective, where the subject, the object, the very text, and even the reader disappear. It is possible to see similar dehumanization in abstract art. Modern music demands a completely new consideration of human destiny and the social dimension which at the same time it both expresses and determines. Ancient humanism is transcended and technocracy provokes visible breaks from it. In Berdiaev's profound thinking, if the individual is part of society, then reciprocally, society is a part of the human person, our social and communal dimension. According to the Fathers it is the same. The human person is a microcosm but the Church, the human community is a *macro-anthropos*, which means nothing less than that a new social form cannot come from the mind of sociologists but from the Spirit. The tragic experience of nations newly emancipated from European colonial rule demonstrates that natural instinct seizes upon new forms of slavery, worse than the old ones. The three responses of Christ to the three temptations in the desert reveal the only true *metanoia*, a total transformation, for this happens only in freedom and reveals the primacy of the Spirit over every cosmic, political, and economic power. Christianity, according to the Fathers is not a religion of personal or individual salvation. Rather it is the religion of the *metabolé*, the transfiguration of human conscience, which is a projection beyond. Christianity can intervene in the disruption of social order in order to introduce there this projection toward the transcendent, toward a qualitative change in human relations in the image of St Paul's understanding of the communion of new creatures.

The social ethic

Orthodox spirituality does not have to do with "domination" of the world, yet it is rooted in the "violence which takes the Kingdom by force" (Mt 11:12). This "violence" of which the Gospel speaks is opposed to any flight from the world. Rather it imposes "regulation" of it by ascetical mastery of nature, for nature is where the Resurrection occurs and is also the object of salvation. Only through history is meta-history attained. With its eschatological preoccupation, Orthodoxy has historically shaped nations, their political institutions, culture and society. In these Orthodoxy has bequeathed a union of the ethical and the esthetic in an iconographic contemplation best expressed by the Greek word, *kalokagathia*, a symbiosis of the Good and the Beautiful. If secularized humanism denies God, if extreme asceticism denies the world, if pietism places an exclusive accent upon God's transcendence, Orthodox ethics are rooted in a total vision balanced between transcendence and immanence, between the heavenly and the earthly. It is the Gospel ethic of the "friends of God," St Macarius' ethic of the heart, Berdiaev's ethic of creation. The Church canonizes her saints and fathers, also princes, physicians and iconographers, all of these active shapers of culture.

This kind of ethics, in its political and economic realism, meshes well with rather diverse social structures yet condemns morally unacceptable social institutions and processes. This ecclesial ethics distinguishes two

functions in the economy, production and consumption. For a biolo-
gist nutrition-consumption is a physiological function. For an econo-
mist, it expresses the struggle for existence, for a philosopher the form
of a cosmic communism, participation in the very flesh and blood of
the world in an incessant communion-exchange. For the theologian it
is eucharistic consumption, the anticipation of the banquet of the
Kingdom (Mt 26:29). The eucharistic bread and wine appear as a part
of the age to come.

Production results from the effort of human energy expended to
create material value. Such action humanizes nature, introduces into it
the human project, the light of our spirit. In this dynamic interaction
nature becomes the cosmic surface of the human body just as a tool
extends the human hand. Man advances in history as an "economic
being," charged with the task of production. Lord and master already
fallen beneath the power of cosmic forces, man regains his dignity in
the struggle and in the work of assuming anew his mission "of the
economy of nature," of becoming once more its economic *logos*, or
meaning. Further, it is in the human being as cosmic *logos* that nature
becomes conscious and waits groaning for her liberation by the man of
the Eighth Day. We assume the necessity of earning our living by the
sweat of our brow, but work itself, the creative and productive effort, is
by no means a curse. According to the Bible it is the condition of work,
"thorns and weeds," which are hard and painful. If those of genius are
rare, "genius" is nevertheless inherent in each human soul capable of
interiorizing and raising to the "priestly dignity" every effort and even
the most ordinary task. Monastic spirituality cultivated a "praying attitude" so that every action was done before God and in him.

It is not the empty terms "happiness" or "good fortune" which are
the goals of ethical action but the flourishing of the adult person in the
adult community. This is why one of the prophetic manifestations of
Christianity is its full response to the social question. It has nothing to
do with restoration of the past, for history clearly teaches the principle
of irreversibility, and the Gospel counsels us not to put new wine into
old wineskins. "History does not use the same plates again," as Celine
would say. In actuality, the conservatives conserve nothing, the liberals
liberate no one, the socialists do not really socialize anything, the

radicals show very little radicalism in their actions, the Communists do not achieve true communion. These are the ghosts haunting history who conceal, by their illusions and lies the real forces in history. Having passed through false uprisings and revolutions, it is now time to discern the prophetic voice of the people of the Eighth Day.

Fedorov located at the center of his vision the "common cause," a veritable cosmic "liturgy" which unites the dead and the living in one single community of Christ, ascending to the Kingdom. He scrutinizes the ontology of the economy and reveals the limitless possibilities of technology when it puts itself in the service of the Kingdom and the resurrection of the dead. For Dostoevsky it is the Church, her total spirituality, which best expressed Russian socialism. Bulgakov and Berdiaev opposed to Marxism the social truth of Christianity, because in Christ God had made all things new and the search for justice was the search for precisely the "new society." In place of the theocracy that had been thrown off, they proposed an evangelical Christocracy. For it is only in Christ that man becomes the "measure of all things," also the measure of society and the economy, based not on profit but on need.

Technology imposes its rhythms and its speed but morally it is neutral. It is only an instrument in our hands. Technology's capacities of power grow faster than the mind of the technician, like the apprentice-sorcerer, the consequences going beyond our use and control. Science exerts an effective control on our biological constitution, modifying time and cosmic conditions, reaching outer space and making the universe intelligible. We must become conscious of the extent of this new power when it acts upon our political systems and leads to unintended consequences. In the face of the dynamic automation of technology God calls upon us to master it, for it too is a gift of God and we are responsible for it. We must be the masters of ethical options in our social context. As they say, an electric toothbrush in the North presupposes a daily bottle of milk for every child in the South. Technocracy is not balanced except with the active participation of all in the vital decisions for the life of every country. Ethics must find a means of conferring a theological dimension to modern technology in order to open it to the meaning of history, in light of its goal or end.

In place of a natural theology, Orthodoxy cultivates a theology of the new creature, called to be concelebrant with God to fulfill the creation. From the abyss of the Fall, the saints invoke the abyss of God's mercy. They tell us that sin is self-sufficiency and the mistrust of our neighbor. An angel revealed to St Pachomius that "the will of God is that we put ourselves in the service of others...for the love of God consists in this, in our caring for each other."[8] Perfection is the fear of "wounding love, as little as that may be."[9] The ancient Christian writing, the *Shepherd of Hermas* recounts that anyone who did not come to the assistance of another in distress would become responsible for their loss. St Maximus the Confessor believed that we would have to render an account "for the evil accomplished but even more so for the good that we neglected to do because we did not love our neighbor."[10] An unwritten saying of Christ goes even further than the warning not to say vain things: "Every good word which they did not say, of these they must give an account at the day of judgment."[11] "In the evening of life we will be judged by our love," sings St John of the Cross.

The human person is not decisively defined by differences from others but mostly by the ability to identify with them, to create an "intersubjectivity" in Christ which is communal and ecclesial. Society (or the world) is more desired by God than the Church for it is the ethical task of a social ecclesiology to transform the world into its proper reality. The Gospel of St John (13:20) gives us a saying of the Lord which is perhaps the most serious addressed to the Church: "Whoever receives the one I have sent receives me, and whoever receives me, receives the one who sent me." The world's destiny depends on the Church's creativity, her ability to welcome, her charism of being a servant and poor in the service of the poor and the little ones of this world.

Theology of revolution

Without discussing Sartre, who poses himself as the incarnation of revolutionary consciousness, we are struck today by efforts to construct a

8   *Coptic Life of St Pachomius.*
9   Cassian, *Conferences,* IX.
10 PG 90, 936 A 13.
11 Resch, *Agrapha,* 13.

"theology of revolution." From the ethical perspective, any religious justification for war-making seems ambiguous. In its original struggle for justice every revolution fatally unleashes destructive forces, complexes of vengeance, and thereby risks being stranded in new forms of injustice. Every idol is an abomination, the one which is opposed as well as that which is born already dying. There is a very real dynamic of good and evil in conflict. For constant scrutiny the "limping of two opinions" of which the prophet Elijah spoke (1 Kings 18:21), Christian judgment is a "crucified judgment." It discerns the dangers of passionate ideologies, from the idolatrous dialectic of violence to the dynamism of ruptures in the social order. It knows that no revolution provides a total solution or brings about the Kingdom of God. On the other hand, the Gospel speaks of violence seizing the Kingdom. It rejects stagnant immobility and conformity to lifeless social forms, hostile to the "absolute newness" of the explosive messianic Reign. In the tragic coexistence of the two Cities, of God and of this world, we ought to search ceaselessly for a more just order, impelled to do so by divine justice. The violent will carry away the Kingdom and bring the justice of God here on earth: "Seek the Kingdom of God *and its righteousness.*" Every social order is a *penultimate* value, which cannot be understood and evaluated except in the light of the ultimate, *last things.* Ultimate realities are not realized except through the penultimate. The clarity and transparency of the Gospel and the apostolic age are located at the dawn of pre-apocalyptic time where everything is in confusion. The situations of this time are more and more "situations of distress."

For centuries ecclesiastical authorities have compromised with the unjust violence of the powerful of this world and were protected because of these complacent compromises. Today the *metanoia* of Christian conscience is so radical that it imposes moral demands which appear unimaginable and utopian. Berdiaev tells us that utopias are the most realizable things in history. It is necessary to choose, for there are moments where silence on the part of "good" people is more tragic than the brutality of the violent. To call an evil is already an act of violence in language which then obliges us to action of the spirit. Every "ethics of conviction" demands our moving toward an "ethics of responsibility."

St Paul speaks of the "present distress" (1 Cor 7:26) and locates this in the time between the ascension of Christ and the *Parousia*, his second coming, and here we are at the heart of the *ethics of distress.* The world of violence and disorder creates many situations where each option is never tranquilizing but always ineluctably tragic. Most often, it is not a choice between good and evil neatly delineated from each other but inextricably confused, the choice of the "lesser evil." Between the violence of a revolution and the pacifist objection of conscience, between Camillo Torres in Columbia and Pastor Martin Luther King Jr. in Alabama, the violent Christian is the artisan of peace but there are moments when love immolated in violence is perhaps greater than peace. Ghandi said to Pierre Cérésole, "I am nothing but I have been delivered from desire and from fear such that I came to know the power of God." Dr. King, in his six principles, sought to "pray everyday and ask God to make me his instrument so that people could be free." In truth violent "non-violence" is a defiance of good sense. This is why Ghandi called it "enigmatic," for at the core, it is the mystery of the God who suffers. According to the Liturgy, it is not man who is the measure of everything, but rather the Cross which is called the *balance of justice.*

The tragedy of struggle and the spirit of discernment

The fourth verse of the prologue of the fourth Gospel expresses, in a very compressed way, the Johannine theme of the struggle between the light and the darkness. The double meaning of the Greek word *katalambànô* justifies both the Western, Vulgate version which is more pessimistic: "The light shone in the darkness and the darkness did not receive it," and the Eastern version as used by Origen, a more optimistic one: "The light shone in the darkness and the darkness did not conquer it." The rich dialectic of these two versions, when brought together, shows the coexistence of light and darkness. The ceaseless struggle reveals the tragedy of the light, of God himself, of his destiny in the world as crucified Love. Certainly God's first words in the Bible, "Let there be light," are fulfilled in his last: "There will no longer be night." But between the two, and in the shadow of the Cross, we find all of human history. One of the characteristics of Orthodox theology is its conditional understanding of the Apocalypse. The most somber predictions depend upon human freedom. It makes all the difference if human beings are attentive to the Word or if they ignore him. The last judgment will not take place if it were possible to avoid it. We could call this vision "tragic optimism," for it depends upon human freedom and thus makes the social conscience extremely sensitive. From fearful events it overtakes and surprises conservative souls. Vladimir Soloviev's prophecy in his legend of the Antichrist is being realized before our eyes. From the abyss emerge false prophets in the figure of social benefactors who bring bread and peace.

The Church cannot remain solely on the defensive. She is called to respond positively to the social question. In dialogue with the world she maintains a kind of evangelical pessimism which promises neither a paradise of triumph nor apparent success and puts distance between the Church and the State in order to distinguish the Kingdom of which the Gospel speaks from earthly utopias. Drawing upon her reserves, the Church reaches out to all and engages them in creative *diakonia* or service to society.

In reality, humanity keeps advancing without knowing where it is going. The conflict between the pure economics of Marxism and the pure vision of psychoanalysis is a symptomatic sign of the break between the visible and the invisible, between private life and social life where all are strangers. Gogol had observed this, noting that in history we have lost the "brother." Depth psychology explains the reason for this loss which is veritable fratricide. Jung suggested that the excessive development of the functions of the human soul is accompanied by atrophy of others. Thus the primacy of cognition leads to the atrophy of the ability to discern, to appreciate, to distinguish values. These come from the heart and this is why *hesychasm*, the practice of silent prayer, urges the descent of the intellect into the heart. In the Fathers' profound distinction, *reason is an energy produced by the force whose source and organ is the heart. Dianoia* is the intellect which thinks, *dianoesis* is discursive and demonstrative reason. On the contrary *noûs, noesis,* is total intelligence, the spirit which contemplates revelations and can grasp the evidence of divine Wisdom. The rupture of the unity of these two functions is at the root of the ontological disorder which has repercussion in the social realm. The Fathers knew this well.

Over against the capitalist and Communist blocs, the Third World expresses another opposition. This is the conflict between the rich and the poor nations. The criterion of material affluence and technology is not sufficient for determining the degree of development in a nation whose reality is complex and of many forms. The countries called "wealthy" are also underdeveloped with respect to other inherent qualities. It is necessary to say that every nation has its own Third World which is not so obvious yet within. Thus the problem of the Third World is that of the whole world and of each nation in particular. The Geneva Conference has stimulated reflection and it is here that the Fathers' teaching reveals its fullness and decisive importance, for it brings to our thinking the unshakable foundation of the great tradition of the Church and the doctrine of a social ecclesiology.

Patristic teaching

If at the beginning of Christian thought there was no urgency about social reform, later on the patristic perspective presupposes this. The Fathers' fundamental understanding of property was as gift or more often as a loan, something that God has given to the rich for use of all. Every owner is therefore a steward, someone charged with the social administration of goods for the benefit of one's poorer brethren. When they refuse to so share, the wealthy become evil and, paradoxically, thieves with respect to their own property, for they divert it from its proper destination and thus have deprived it of its being a loan for social use.

St John Chrysostom was the most radical, truly an apostle of social ethics. "The rich are stealing from the poor even if what they have is honestly acquired or legally inherited." "In refusing to give and to share we thus earn the punishment of thieves. We are as guilty as the tax collectors who use the money of all for their own needs." "The rich are a kind of robber." "Do not say, I enjoy what is mine. You are enjoying the property of others. All the things of this earth belong to all of us together, just as the sun, the air, the ground and everything else."[12] Even later, in the eleventh century, St Simeon the New Theologian

---

12 *Hom.* 11 on Lazarus; *Hom.* 10 on 1 Cor, 3:4.

would echo what St John Chrysostom said in his homilies: "Money and all other goods are the common property of all, just as the light and the air we breathe."[13] This principle entered into the conscience of the Russian people. The sole owner of the earth is the Lord and this is why the earth is holy and belongs to all. According to an unwritten law, it is spiritually forbidden to speculate on property and even to sell it. One can only share according to the needs of each.

In the homilies on the Epistle to Philemon, St John Chrysostom surpassed even the attitude of personal charity of St Paul, to consider a slave as a brother, encouraging the immediate liberation of all so held by their Christian masters.[14] Here we have a significant evolution in social consciousness. The radical contrast between wealth and poverty collides with a sense of social justice. He so insisted on the spiritual necessity of sharing, of giving alms that he is called "St John the Almsgiver." "The rich expend so much money on the decoration of their homes and even on the care of their animals that they thus crush their poor brethren in inhuman misery and need. The person or better the Christ in him is bound by hunger. Your pack-animals carry your wealth and Christ dies of hunger at your door. What fire will punish such criminal souls." "Women who embroider biblical scenes on their clothing would do better to live out these stories." St John invites us to pass from symbols to lived reality. It is more here than simple charity or even the ethical principle of doing good, it is the recognition of Christ who identifies himself with the suffering poor person. It is this Gospel identification (Mt 25) which constitutes *the dogmatic and sacramental element* of social relations for the Christian.

St Basil who, according to St Athanasius "was weak with the weak on their behalf," in his homily against the wealthy cited Isaiah 5:8: "Woe to those who join house to house and field to field until there is no more room and you are made to dwell alone in the midst of the land."[15] Then St Basil comments, "My possessions are mine, you say. But it is only because the rich have acquired their possessions first that they so strenuously insist on the right to own them." St Ambrose

13 *Catechetical Discourses,* 9.
14 *Hom.* 2 and 3.
15 *Letter to Palladius,* PG 26, 1168 D.

echoes the same truth: "Avarice has abolished the right to own property."[16] "You are a thief," St Basil says, "if you transform in your possessions what you have received only as a steward. The bread you have belongs to the hungry."[17] For St Basil, poverty which produces misery is a social evil, a flagrant evil, and he recalled that during a famine the poor sold their children for a mouthful of bread. Gold, he said is a "prolific monster which gives birth and devastates."[18] St Simeon is even more radical: "The rich person is the murderer of the one who has no food."[19]

Proudhon's well-known saying, "Property is robbery" is but a summary of the Fathers' sermons. Basil, the two Gregorys, and Chrysostom sketch the outlines of a Christian social order. Exile and martyrdom could not shut the "golden-mouth" of St John Chrysostom and only makes the voice of the Fathers resound more loudly across the centuries to us today. Their reflection surpasses by far individual acts of charity and demands profound, radical social reform. St John Chrysostom wrote of the city of Antioch from which he came. The Church of this city, where he also was bishop before coming to Constantinople, fed every day 3,000 poor people, cared for the sick, for prisoners, pilgrims, widows. And the budget of the Church of Antioch, sufficient to cover all these expenses, did not exceed the total wealth of any one rich person in the city. The social fabric of Antioch, it should be noted, was made up of a minority of wealthy families and a minority of the poor and between them the majority of citizens of the middle class. To be certain, St John's calculations were simplistic. He estimated that if there were equitable sharing of wealth, misery would immediately disappear if a hundred inhabitants of the city assumed charge of providing for just one person in need. What is of interest here is not the technical accuracy of his proposed solution but rather his conviction that a solution should be sought after because divine justice demanded it. Here is an urgency both imperious and precise but not at all naive. Social obligation towards the community imposes a social reform, a form of

16 PL 15, 1303.
17 *Hom.* 6 and 7.
18 *Hom.* 2 on Psalm 14.
19 *Catechetical Discourses*, 9.

sharing which radically suppresses insupportable injustice. Etymologically, does not justice have to do with rights, with law? It is that which attributes "to each his right." Its object is the common good which establishes the community's law about particular rights and the use of its goods. St John was not speaking just about the Church of Antioch but about the city and thus the society of Antioch in its totality.

The Fathers never suggest hatred or class conflict with its violence. But when they speak of charity, of alms, it is in a much more generous and greater sense than we now understand such giving. Sharing is fundamental and central and for them constitutes the most radical *spiritual revolution*. Over time, the giving of alms or charity has come to have a far too narrow meaning. In the thinking of the Fathers this had nothing at all to do with the gesture of throwing a coin into a beggar's hat or patronizing a "charity bazaar." Leon Bloy's anger and vehemence has stigmatized this manner of taking care of one's charitable debts. For the Fathers, authentic charity was an act of sharing which was forceful enough to be a sign of the Kingdom here on earth. It was part of the divine economy of salvation, so strong an action as it was. A disciple of St Sergius of Radonezh, St Cyril of White Lake, provides an excellent definition of charity's greatness. He wrote to Prince Andrei, affirming that for those who live in the world, the sharing of charity replaced the asceticism of monastic life and as such was a basic, constitutive and indispensable element of the Christian spiritual life. Likewise, for St Tikhon of Zadonsk and more recently for St John of Kronstadt, "charity is the most powerful form of prayer." Clement of Alexandria said that charitable giving mobilizes the poor to assault heaven. The rich person, he also said, is one in despair, being unable to give charitably.[20] St John Chrysostom put it thus: "The ascetic see his asceticism but saves no one else, while the one who gives out of charity is a blessing to all. Charity is greater than miracles and covers over all our sins, for to feed the hungry is to feed Christ and is greater than raising the dead to life. God himself becomes indebted to such a person. The wings of charity take us beyond the angels to the throne of God."[21] St John goes to the very limit in comparing charity to the Eucharist: "The Eucharist

20 *What rich man can be saved?*
21 *Hom.* 6 on Titus, 2.

only is celebrated on the altar in the church while charity is found everywhere in the streets, in every public place." In his epistle St James shows the true nature of charity in its hidden depth: "Visit the poor in their affliction." This is an act of being totally present, for Christ identifies himself with the suffering. For St Cyprian, "to share one's possessions is to feed Christ in the poor."[22] The *Didaché* had long before stressed this: "May your charity warm your hands." This is an astonishing saying reminiscent of the words of the disciples at Emmaus: "Did not our hearts burn within us as he taught us!" For St Gregory Nazianzus our attitude towards the poor is rooted in the human ascent to God and becomes our response to the essential mystery. It is by charity that we acquire our heavenly "solidity" and our truth, our participation in eternal, divine love.[23] For St Gregory of Nyssa, to spurn the poor is to destroy the hidden unity of the world. It is to refuse the one God.[24]

The community of Jerusalem did its charity through the hands of the deacons and bestowed on them the apostolic seal of sharing the community's possessions. Thus we can understand why St Jerome put charity before the construction and adornment of churches.[25] Chrysostom echoed this: "God has never condemned anyone for not having embellished the churches with superb ornaments but he threatens with hell those who will not give charitably."[26] Charity, in the Fathers' meaning, is radically opposed to "paternalism," the work of those "obliged." Because we are not the masters of our wealth, charity has nothing to do with what is superfluous, but real sharing. Monasticism provides a wealth of instruction here. At first monastic work was not only ascetical exercise. St Theodulus said: "Our work ought to feed the poor and the sick." Monasteries formerly were located in the cities or very close by, making their action on behalf of the indigent actual "social security." St Abraham of Smolensk had painted on the entrance to his monastery an immense fresco of the Last Judgment with the citation of Matthew 25:31, 46. This is

22 On almsgiving/charity, PL 4, 601.
23 *Hom.* 14 on giving to the poor.
24 *On the love of the poor*, sermon on usury.
25 *Hom.* on Mt 50:3.
26 *Letter* 130, 4.

the authentic "evangelical churchliness" which monasticism preached vigorously to all, speaking the Gospel with its mouth while expressing the moral conscience of society. Berdiaev stressed with reason that the Gospel is infinitely more severe toward wealth, exploitation and social disorder than toward any sexual failing. The real problem of social obligation has been repressed and replaced by a veritable obsession with matters sexual, even up to our time. According to the Gospel, it is the rich who will not enter the Kingdom, while repentant prostitutes enter ahead of the righteous and their affluence.[27]

For St Ambrose the things of this earth are destined in an inalienable manner for the good of all. This is why "The rich person returns to the poor what is his." Any idea of charity as what is superfluous or left over after our consumption is completely out of the question here. Charity is the result of a global judgment upon personal fortune and the indigence of another. Such judgment signifies that a rich person who neglects his own salvation is one who denies his neighbor. In his *Dirty Hands*, Sartre is ironical but says something true and fearful at the same time: "It is so convenient to give, it allows us to keep our distance." And so Lanza del Vasto replies: "Then don't give, share!"

St Simeon in his *Catechetical Discourses* explains the inequalities of Byzantine society by contrasting the earthly kingdom with that of heaven. Justice calls for social giving, for charitable sharing but this is the tendency of justice to surpass itself. St Augustine said, "You give your bread to one who is hungry but it would be better if no one were hungry and that you gave to no one." Between ideal charity and our well established social disorder, God places justice as a mediation.

Christian approaches to a solution

The Fathers do not reject personal property. "What society has ever existed on earth without people owning things?" Clement of Alexandria asks. But then he cites Luke 19:9 to show that the principle of possession is clearly conditioned and limited: "Today salvation has come to this house." Salvation visited the wealthy Zaccheus because he "gave half of all he owned to the poor." Even if honorably and legally

27 Jn 8:11.

acquired, property is never an absolute. It is always held according to
the conditions of the community established by God and founded on
law. Thus the "apostolic sect" which in the fourth century preached
communism by an enforced sharing was condemned by the Church.
For the Fathers a middle class is normative because this allows for charity. So community of goods and private property are both founded in
law but property is always a loan, never automatically given to the exclusive use of anyone except as its steward, its administrator. The responsibility of such a one in the administration of what actually
belongs to God subordinates personal rights to the superior value of
the needs of the community. The poor person does not as such have
the right to personally appropriate the wealth of the rich. The Fathers
teach above all our spiritual transformation, the Gospel's *metanoia,* but
they also recognize the need for constraint on public power in the case
of urgent necessity.

Here there is a direct analogy with evil. God does not suppress it
automatically by his omnipotence. Likewise he does not suppress social
inequality by force, but makes possible a spiritual victory over the passion of possession. In extreme cases, public authority ought to intervene. However, the state is not called upon to realize the Kingdom of
God on earth. Its task is to prevent the world from becoming a hell and
thus to place limits against the progression of evil among us.

The Stoics had a famous saying about all of this: *volentem ducunt
fata, nolentem trahunt,* meaning that destiny leads the one who desires
it and carries away the one who refuses it. In all these cases there is but a
single destiny which is accomplished by fate. The Bible and the earliest
Christian texts speak of the two well known ways—of life and of
death—and underscore that the Last Judgment will only reveal the
consequences of a free choice between these two destinies. The paradox
of freedom is that it needs to be realized. Man is free in his choice but
the act of choosing is imposed and even his refusal is already a choice.
So we find an antinomic and most enigmatic constraint at the very
heart of freedom itself. It suppresses every neutral state of indecision
and obliges us to choose freely, to give in full accord with divine justice
or to refuse this, also freely. In overstepping the limits of justice, freedom degenerates, becomes arbitrary. In leaving the life of grace one is

buried again in life under the law and punishment. If justice is not freely and consciously followed it restrains individual freedom and imposes on the mass of humanity measures decreed by public authorities and dictated by international law. But are public authorities able to enforce decisions which really belong to the freedom of our souls? This classic objection sounds hypocritical. One forgets flagrant violence committed in history by ecclesiastical authorities as accomplices of injustice. The true humility preached by the great spiritual teachers is not weakness but the greatest strength and power. It is to come to the end of all selfishness, self-love and arbitrariness. According to these great masters, humility is the art of finding oneself exactly in the place that the will of God desires. Rather than wanting to be the Master's Beloved and Spouse (the calling of the whole Church), the better path is that of being the friend or servant of the Lord (like John the Baptist or the Mother of God).

The Fathers of the Church responded to the problems of their times. In the Middle Ages, the Church's way of thinking and expressing herself began to conform to that of society. In reality the theology then produced, both in academic settings and in pastoral ones became unreal, detached from the world. The more recent distinction made between static religion and dynamic faith could apply. Now more than ever, the question of society and the problems of social life are the existential issues of our era and of every person. Once again, as Berdiaev has put it, bread is at one and the same time a question of economic life and death as well as a spiritual problem decisive for the future of society. The Last Judgment raises the very real economic problems of hunger, sickness, isolation, and suffering, but these are in fact problems of the soul, of the human spirit. Throughout history we can see that the Church has had a critical and suspicious attitude towards the power of the state, its laws and institutions. The Church has developed her own canon law and in monastic communities shaped her own economic system. But now all of this is no longer sufficient, for the social question now resides on the international or global scale and has changed in its very nature and is expressed in terms of international law, all of this challenging the Church to rediscover her universal dimension. In place of the *corpus Christianum*, no longer in existence, the Church proclaims a social *koinonia*, but this demands sacrifices and suffering for there can be no authentic communication without identification with the sufferings of others. This is the radiant meaning of the Cross in history and in each person's own existence. The "responsible society" envisages a finality with an ethical content. The "responsible Church" here adds theological substance. The consubstantial fraternity of all is rooted in the deified humanity of Christ and in the doctrine of the Trinitarian community of God. The Church as *macro-anthropos* includes the cosmos and society and sketches out an immense and forceful image "before the clear heaven and the free sea."

The Fathers insist that God is able to do everything except to constrain us to love him and our neighbor. Now the constraint of social obligation is a powerful reminder and an appeal coming from spiritual truth. We are called to realize necessary justice but in freedom. The Lord himself was submissive to the supreme call of his Father. He said to St John the Baptist, "Let it be so now, for it is proper for us in this way to fulfill all righteousness" (Mt 3:15). Christ "accomplished" the Law and the word "accomplish" means "to fulfill." The fullness of the Law is its metamorphosis in grace. The reminder of obligation can make us attentive and sensitive to the mystery of justice or righteousness. It can open us to the grace of love in freedom and to the gift of ourselves. With respect to the underdeveloped nations, international law can impose on all the obligations which give to all the social right of existing and acting as full, adult human beings. Such a right corresponds to the imperative of divine justice in order to free the poor person from his misery and the wealthy from their murderous passion and greed. Certainly, to share the totality of what we own is not possible except by a strictly personal action. Total giving is the sovereign right of a human being, and it can never be decreed by law. In the Old Testament there was legislation demanding taxation to support the Temple and worship there and tithes for the poor, a very basic type of social security. In actuality there is but one economic sphere where each by means of imposed taxes participates in the national economy. It is from such taxes, based on a percentages of one's wealth, that roads, schools and hospitals are constructed. Such imposed payments construct the system of social security. The word for tax in French, "impôt," comes from the Latin *impositum* literally "placed upon," and these taxes are "placed upon" the head of each person, imposed upon all are social obligations about which there are no discussions. It is for us to confer upon this *obligation* the spiritual meaning of *gift* and of *charity*, in the understanding of the Fathers of the Church. The encyclical of Pope Paul VI urged the establishment of a global fund to be constituted from deduction levied upon "conspicuous consumption, waste and the buildup of armaments."

A substantial and regular tax, accepted by all nations, could radically reshape the situation of the Third World. It would be an act of solidarity and of sharing beyond the kind of "do-goodism" which wounds human dignity. If unable to impose the pure action of charity, which must arise from a personal right and decision, nevertheless all could participate in a global system of social security. International law offers a solution organized and regulated by justice. The Church has never decreed the obligation of the rich to rid themselves of their wealth nor has she preached the right of the poor to seize it. But the Church today in our situation of urgency can invite us to confer upon such an act of international law the quality of a genuine act of giving, to accept freely and fully the solution imposed by life, to show an authentic probity in the disposition of the industrialized nations' economy and the new relationships. The Church provokes among countries, all this in order to resist the destruction and death of the human person. It is the quality of a disinterested gift, the giving of a simple glass of water, which can be our justification at the Last Judgment, so the Gospel tells us.

Law requires each citizen to help another in danger. To refuse to do so is a crime. In the absence of a spontaneous action, it is the imposed obligation which defines the attitude which should be taken. The desperate effort of those who beyond bearable limits resort to revolutionary force and violence takes the place of the Law and of obligation, but this extreme solution is fraught with danger. Just as with war, revolution in principle already belongs to the period that is ended. The Gospel proclaims: "Know the truth and the truth will make you free." The freedom of choosing the truth precedes the freedom of living in the truth chosen. Totalitarianism suppresses above all the freedom of choice and declares: "Submit to my truth and I will make you happy." The Church must say today: "Accomplish the justice of social law and on the way you will know the justice of God and it will set you free." When the most urgent social justice is accomplished, we become conscious of personal freedom of going further in the disposition of what one has and what one is.

It well may be that today there are too many experts and not enough persons of true wisdom. Lacking prophets, what passes for ecumenism of the average sort happily reinforces dialogue between specialists and theologians. The churches are about the business of setting up their own institutes, conferences and committees. An enormous vista has been opened by dialogue among cultures, by the encounter between the East and the West with the movement toward an open and intelligent fraternity between them. Given the profound opening of "intersubjectivities" among various nations and cultures, it is easy to see that all countries both give and receive at the same time. The modes of providing assistance must avoid crushing the will and effort of those who receive and the reform of our social structures must reflect authentic personal conversion. Here the idea of human community is fundamental. *It is necessary to transcend even the category of sharing and to imagine a global economy, to institute the management of resources in a universal plan with participation of all the nations in this international cooperation.*

The encounter of the "heads of state" bring together political professionals. The absence of the spiritual dimension in their deliberations reduces their vision to the all too human and thus renders their action ineffective and their agreement impossible. The "wisdom of the serpent" lacks "the simplicity of the dove." The saying which Christ left to the world judges society. It also judges the Church and obliges her to immediate action that no one else can accomplish. The Church no longer leads history. She no longer is the major shaper of events. Quite the contrary, this situation places the Church above the immediate as an *authentic moral conscience of humanity,* and it is this prophetic charism which gives her today a completely different power.

Such a conscience is not the same as moralism. Above all, it is the brilliance of a militant eschatology, a forceful witness to the Kingdom. The Church must avoid naive confidence in human values and autonomous technology, for pure humanity does not exist. For the Fathers nothing was neutral and nothing was profane. There were only sacred realities, deified, full of God or else the demonic, where God was absent. A moral conscience is a powerful reminder of the biblical message that each human being is potentially recapitulated in Christ just as the world is potentially under the sign of the Prince of this world.

Perhaps we are coming to the last opportunity for Christian witness on the global level now, in this explosive time of the twilight of the gods. The Church, under the eschatological pressure of the Holy Spirit, cannot rid herself of her direct and supreme responsibility for the world's destiny. The immediate and urgent situation in the world today (1967) demands rapid and effective solutions. Why should there not be a meeting, for example, of the Pope, the Orthodox patriarchs, the leaders of the Protestant churches and representatives of Islam and Judaism? Such a gathering, a veritable council of all the communities of faith issuing from the Bible, of the entire "family of Abraham," would have the spiritual authority to make the political heads listen to the voice of the moral conscience of humanity in its religious and eschatological fullness and through this voice to make present the judgment of God. Without becoming engrossed in technical details, such a gathering would expose to the nations the urgency of an immediate and unanimous accord on economic sharing for the countries of the Third World and of a definitive effort to assure peace and protect the freedom of every human being.

Atheistic humanism cannot but ratify such decisions which meet its own aspirations, especially when these are inspired by the one and only true preoccupation of humanity and its destiny. The multiplication of the loaves and fishes by the Lord is a great symbol of the dynamism of sharing, of the possibility of working a miracle when love is authentically expressed. "Very truly, I tell you, the one who believes in me will also do the works that I do, and in fact, will do even greater works than these, because I am going to the Father..And I will ask the Father, and he will give you another Advocate, to be with you forever" (Jn 14:12, 16). The ascension of the Lord, his going up to the Father, is the Trinitarian *epiclesis* of the Son who asks the Father to send down the Holy Spirit.

This is the unleashing of Pentecost. The diffusion of charisms, of the gifts of the Holy Spirit, gives us power over both cosmic and human nature, and then we will be able to do the things that Christ did and even greater things. This is a promise without limits. The world is free to listen to the voice of conscience, to hear the appeal of God himself. The world can, if it wants to, accomplish the miracles of "even greater things." Then we can transform the face of the earth. The beautiful words of the communist poet Paul Eluard are appropriate here: "Everything is not needed to make a world, just love, and nothing else."

It is in such a convergence that the signs of a universal accord would be able to accompany the transcendent signs of the Kingdom and its righteousness. If the effort of political people has along with it the deep unity of believers and if together all of these effect an *ecumenical epiclesis,* a common calling down of the Spirit of God, then God himself would place the world very clearly and visibly before the ultimate option: "Look, I place before you life and death. Choose life, so that you may live" (Deut 30:15-20). And since God has become human, he himself, perfect man, would bring all the weight of his crucified love to bear upon the decisive choice we make.

More than ever, we are at the threshold of the impossible which becomes possible, of the miraculous and its supernaturally natural prodigies. According to St Gregory of Nyssa: "The divine power is capable of inventing hope where hope no longer exists and of opening up a path amid the impossible." The signs of the times tell us this but the time is short and the Gospel incessantly calls to us: "The one who has ears, let him hear" (Mt 11:15).

5

HOLINESS IN THE TRADITION
OF THE ORTHODOX CHURCH[1]

The concept of holiness

If all words are shaped by realities of this world, then there is an exception in the case of "holiness," for it has no direct reference to the human dimension. Wisdom, power, even love have analogies in human life but holiness is par excellence of the "wholly Other," the most striking manifestation of the Transcendent One. Holiness belongs to God himself. "Holy is your name," said the prophet Isaiah (57:15) But if each divine Person is holy, according to St Cyril of Alexandria, the Holy Spirit is the very essence of divine holiness, and for St Basil the Great, "holiness is the essential element of his nature." The Holy Spirit is holiness hypostasized, personalized.

Contemporary language frequently employs such expressions as "sacred" obligation, will, or commandment, a "holy" person. In semantic evolution the terms "sacred" and "holy" were detached from their roots and have taken on a *moral* meaning quite different from their original *ontological* significance.

Above all, holiness is the opposite of the reality of this world and presents itself as the eruption of what is absolutely different, that which Rudolf Otto termed *das ganz Andere*. The Bible supplies the fundamental definition. Only God is holy, and a creature is such only in a derived sense. The sacred and the holy can never be of the creature's

1   First published in *Contacts*, nos. 73-74, 1971, pp. 119-190, republished in *La nouveauté de l'Esprit* (Abbaye de Bellefontaine, 1977), pp. 108-190, and earlier translated, in part, by Constance Babington Smith in *Man's Concern with Holiness*, Marina Chavcharadze, ed. (London: Hodder and Stoughton, 1970), pp. 147-184.

own nature but only and always by participation in the nature of God. The terms *kadosh, agios, sacer* and *sanctus* imply a relationship of totally belonging to God, and of being set apart. The divine act of sanctification or consecration takes a person or an object back from its empirical condition and places it in communion with the divine energies and grace which change its nature and immediately makes it experience, within its natural or original location the *mysterium tremendum*, the sacred trembling before the coming of the supernatural and its "awesome purity." This has nothing at all to do with fear of the unknown, but is rather a mystical awe which accompanies every manifestation of the Transcendent One. "I will send my fear before you and will destroy all the people to whom you will come" (Ex 23:27). Again: "Take off your shoes from your feet, for the place where you stand is holy ground" (Ex 3:5).

This is, in the world's false realities, the overwhelming experience of a reality which is "innocent" because it is sanctified, purified and returned to its original state, to its destiny of being the pure vessel of a presence. The holiness of God abides there and shines from it. Thus "this place is holy" because of the presence of God as that part of the Temple was holy because of the presence of the Ark of the Covenant, as the Holy Scriptures witness to the presence of Christ in their words, as every church building is holy because God dwells there, speaks to us and feeds us with himself. The "kiss of peace" is holy because it seals the communion of those who exchange it in Christ, who is present. The prophets, apostles and the "saints" of Jerusalem are holy because of the charism of their ministry. Bishops have the title "holy brother," a patriarch is addressed as "His Beatitude/Holiness," not because of any personal virtue but because of their participation in the unique, holy priesthood of Christ. Each baptized person is confirmed or chrismated, anointed, sealed with the gifts of the Holy Spirit in order to "share in the nature of God," (2 Pet 1:4) participate in "the holiness of God" (Heb 12:10), and it is in this sense of participation in divine holiness that St Paul calls the members of the community "saints."

The liturgy teaches this holiness most explicitly. Before offering the eucharistic gifts, the celebrant says: "Holy things for the holy" and the assembly responds, moved by this awesome invitation, confessing their unworthiness, "One is holy, one is Lord, Jesus Christ, in the glory of

God the Father. Amen." The One who is uniquely holy in his nature is Christ. Those who are his members are holy only through sharing in his unique holiness.

Isaiah (6:5-6) provides a most illuminating image of this. "Woe is me!...I am a man of unclean lips...Then one of the seraphim flew to me with a live coal in his hand which he had taken with tongs from the altar, and he laid it on my mouth and said, Lo, this has touched your lips and your iniquity is taken away." The energy of divine holiness is a fire which consumes every impurity. When it touches a person this fire cleanses and sanctifies, conforming him to the holiness of God. The priest, after receiving communion, recalls this vision of Isaiah, kissing the rim of the chalice, which is the image of the pierced side of Christ, saying, "Lo, this has touched my lips and taken away my iniquity and healed me of my sin." The spoon with which the priest distributes Holy Communion in the Orthodox liturgy is called in Greek *lavis*, "tongs," of which Isaiah spoke in his vision and of which the Fathers, with respect to the Eucharist say: "You have consumed fire...."

"Be holy, as I am holy." Every degree of consecration and sanctification is through participation in the one, unique divine source. Thus is every being in the world "deprofaned" and "devulgarized." This "permeating" of the world is the very action of the sacraments which teach that in every life there is a sacred power, that every Christian is destined for fulfillment liturgically by participation in the mystery of divine life. Thus as at the feast of the Transfiguration and at Pascha (Easter), the faithful bring to church fruit and other food to be blessed, for all our nourishment is like the Eucharist, an offering to be consecrated, a gift to be sanctified. The destiny of water is for sharing in the Epiphany mystery of the Jordan in which Christ was baptized. The destiny of wood is to be the tree of life and the Cross; of earth to receive the body of the Lord into the rest of Holy Saturday, the great Sabbath; of stone to seal the sepulcher and then be rolled back by the angel for the myrrh-bearing women. Oil and water are fulfilled in baptism, chrismation and the other anointings. Wheat and the vine culminate in the eucharistic bread and cup. One sees very clearly here that everything refers to the Incarnation, everything is presented to the Lord as a splendid liturgy, the cosmic synthesis of all created being. The most basic actions of life, eating, drinking, washing speaking, moving—all of these are integrated and directed to their ultimate end by the liturgy, namely participating in the holiness of God. "At last all things are the furnishing of our temple, instead of being our prison," Paul Claudel say quite rightly. Thus holiness by participation is the restoration of our nature in Christ, his healing, "the return from what is contrary to nature to that which truly belongs to it."[2]

Holiness: the healing of nature

St Isaac the Syrian asks, "What is a heart full of love? It is a heart which burns with love for all creation, for people and for demons, for all creatures...The one who possesses such a heart is moved by an immense compassion...He cannot endure that any sorrow, no matter how small, should be inflicted on any creature. He even prays for reptiles, impelled by the infinite pity aroused in the hearts of those assimilated into God." According to St Paul, all of nature is groaning and awaiting the salvation of man, the coming of the holiness which will save her by becoming her *logos*. The saint reassembles in his love the disjointed cosmos and this is the therapeutic action of grace.

In the Bible, salvation is not at all juridical, it has nothing to do with the sentence of a court. The verb in Hebrew *yacha*, to save, means "to set free," to unburden, in the most general sense, to deliver, save from danger, from sickness, from death and more precisely it means to reestablish the essential equilibrium, to heal. The substantive *yecha*, "salvation," indicates complete deliverance with *shalom*, that is, peace as its fulfillment. In the New Testament, the equivalent word in Greek *soteria* comes from the verb *sozein*, and the adjective *sos* corresponds to the Latin *sanus*, meaning to restore health to one who has lost it, to save from death, toward which all sickness leads. This is why in the Gospel the expression, "your faith has saved you" can also mean "your faith has healed you, the terms being synonymous, describing the one and the same divine act of forgiveness, the action which heals both the soul and the body in their unity. Corresponding to this, the understanding of the sacrament of confession in the Eastern Church is one of "medical

2   St John of Damascus, *On the Orthodox Faith* 1, 30.

treatment," and St Ignatius of Antioch calls the Eucharist the "medicine of immortality," the only true antidote to death.

As the Savior, Jesus thus appears as the divine healer, "the bringer of health," saying, "Those who are well have no need of a physician, but the sick." Sinners are the sick, people threatened by complete death, and the therapeutic meaning of salvation has to do precisely with this seed of corruption and mortality. Redemption is the corollary of Resurrection of the body. "By his death he has conquered death." This is not only spiritual victory but also the physical triumph over all the consequences of the Fall. This is the essential Pauline doctrine of the "new creature."

The new creature

Though man is certainly not the center of the universe studied by the astronomers, he is nevertheless its summit, for man is cosmic evolution become conscious of itself. Humanity was created as the crowning fulfillment of the six days of creation and now in history brings together all the plan of being (*microscosmos*) in order to become the fulfillment of historical existence (*macroanthropos*). This is why the time of the Old Testament was oriented toward the coming of the Messiah. But if the King has come, his Kingdom nevertheless is still yet to come. After Pentecost the time of the Church is oriented towards the *novissima*, the new things of the Kingdom, and humanity is borne towards its fulfillment as the new creature. This is possible only because God has become the new man, the absolute, and all will follow.

It is not so much a "repairing" or "reorganizing" of the old man, for this old creature is in ruins, while the new man is renewed day after day, as St Paul puts it. The metamorphosis of *metanoia*, the total redirection of which the synoptic Gospels speak and the "second birth" of the Gospel of St John, is most radical. It is not a re-creation but, for the Fathers, a return to the norm, to the normal, to the true, first nature. "Oh man, consider who you are and your royal dignity," cries St Gregory of Nyssa. "What is man?" St Paul asks, "You have made him a little lower than the angels, you have crowned him with honor, you have put all things under his feet" (Heb 2:7).

In the thinking of the Fathers, we are kings, prophets and priests, in the image of the three dignities of Christ. "King by mastery over passions, priest in sacrifice of his whole being and prophet in being initiated into the great mysteries." The great charter of the Gospel is joyously proclaimed by St Paul: "The old things have passed away, here all has become new; the one who is in Christ is a new creation" (Gal 6:15). And the Book of Revelation has God proclaiming: "See, I make all things new" (21:5). Christianity, in the radiant witness of its confessors, martyrs and saints is messianic, revolutionary, explosive. The Gospel calls for the violence which seizes the Kingdom, tears open the heavens and transforms the old image of the world into the new creation.

A new creature, the new man, these are synonyms of holiness. "All of you are called saints" (1 Cor 1:2), St Paul claims. The salt of the earth and the light of the world, the saints appear as the obvious and hidden leaders of humanity, those who will assume responsibility for history and accomplish it. At the beginning, the "wounded friends of the Bridegroom Christ," the martyrs, are "the sheaves of wheat harvested by the rulers of this age, and gathered by the Lord as the harvest into his barns." The saints take the torch from the martyrs and continue to illumine the world. But the Gospel's call is to every person. If since the Incarnation, the Church, according to Origen, is "full of the Trinity," then since Pentecost, the Church is filled with the saints. In the office for the feast of All Saints, on the Sunday after Pentecost in the Eastern Church, this truth overflows all boundaries: "I sing of all the friends of my Lord, and may every one who so desires join and become one of them." The invitation is addressed to each and every person. The "cloud of witnesses" comes to meet us and to proclaim itself *urbi et orbi*, to the city and to the world, says St John Chrysostom. The *communio sanctorum* and the Church reflects the holiness of God. She sings: "Your light, O Christ, shines in all the faces of your saints."

In the mystery of the Incarnation, God transcends his own transcendence, transcends his own burning holiness (according to some of the fathers, the very word "God" comes from the word "to burn") and makes his deified humanity consubstantial with every human being. This is the ultimate action of the love of God which Nicholas Cabasilas has called *manikos eros*, the "foolish" or "absurd" love of God for us: "I no longer call you servants but friends...."

In the time of the Old Covenant, theophanies marked those few privileged places where God manifested himself in radiant apparitions. These were "holy places," such as the burning bush. But since Pentecost, the world as a whole has been confided to the saints so that they would make of it a burning bush, for as God has said, "all of the earth is my domain," the place of his saints, in whom he is present.

Formerly one heard, "Take off your shoes from your feet for the place where you walk is holy ground" (Ex 3:5). A small piece of the world was sanctified because the holiness of God had touched it. An ancient iconographic composition of St John the Baptist reveals the passage into a new order. The icon shows St John walking the earth, soiled by sin, overgrown, but wherever the saint went wherever his feet touched the surface, the earth became paradise again. The icon seems to say, "Earth, be pure again, for the feet which have walked on you are holy."

When we say that someone has a strong personality, this means a particular blend of characteristics, certain of these being quite pronounced and despite which we get the impression of *déjà vu*, of a type known and easily categorized. The very face of a saint is striking, unique in the world, a personal luminescence of an absolute quality. Such a person has never been seen before. A saint is completely distinct from the ordinary and the newness is shocking, a kind of "foolishness." For the Marxist emphasis on *praxis*, a saint is a useless being. What good would be a "fool for Christ" or a stylite, one who perches on a high column? Yet it is this apparent uselessness, of being totally at the disposal of the Transcendent One, which challenges the world with the questions of life and death which it so easily forgets.

A saint, even the most concealed from view, is "clothed in space and nakedness," and bears on his or her weak shoulders all the world's burdens, the dark night of our sin, as well as protection from divine justice. While the world laughs, the saint weeps and draws toward us divine compassion. Before death a hermit saint such as this, a true "fool for Christ," made as his final prayer a definitive "Amen" on his entire work: "That all may be saved, that the whole world may be saved," he prayed. The saints enter a "communion with us in our sin" (for humility makes them understand themselves, as the Orthodox prayer before Holy Communion states: "...sinners, of whom I am the first"). By their love for sinners, the saints draw them towards "communion with the Holy One." What must surely scandalize nonbelievers does not at all disturb the saints, namely, the terrible reality that not all Christians are saints. Léon Bloy puts it well: "There is only one sorrow, that of not being a saint."

The holiness of the Church

"I believe in one, holy, catholic and apostolic Church." The Council of Constantinople in A.D. 381 thus designated the four "marks" or characteristics of the Church. Holiness thus is one of these and is a constitutive element of the Church's very being or *esse: unam sanctam.*

"Be holy as I am holy" (Lev 19:2). The fearful character of this demand corresponds to the sacramental superabundance of the Church which never ceases in imploring God for the life-creating grace which waters the arid desert soil of the human heart. "Send forth your most Holy Spirit who sanctifies our souls and illumines them." "By the Holy Spirit all creation is restored to its original state."[3] "Christ gave himself for the Church so that he might sanctify and cleanse it," (Eph 5:25-27) and to manifest the "One who is" and who is holy. The Church does not lack sinners but she is without sin. The dynamic tension between the "not yet" and the "already now" is inherent in the mystery of the Kingdom which both precedes and anticipates its fulfillment. The Church is at one and the same time holy and always being purified (*sancta et semper purificanda*).

What we see in the Book of Revelation/Apocalypse is an anticipation of our destiny—angels and human beings prostrate before the Lamb singing the *Trisagion*, the "Thrice-Holy" hymn: "Holy, holy, holy." Here is holiness chanted by all, the Church become the divine liturgy and the eternal communion of the saints.

"The splendor of the Trinity shines ever more brightly," St Gregory the Theologian says.[4] Each divine person participates in his own way in the same economy of salvation. So if Christ recapitulates and integrates humanity in the unity of his Body, what is personal to each should not

3   Prayers from the office of the feast of the Ascension and Sunday Matins, tone 1.
4   *Or.*, 31:26-27.

be dissolved in an impersonal incorporation. This is why the Holy Spirit works upon us as individuals and enables each of us to mature in the fullness of our gifts and charisms, each in his or her unique manner. The account of Pentecost precisely captures the grace descending upon each one personally: "Tongues of fire as if divided, came upon each of them" (Acts 2:3). At the very heart of our unity in Christ, the Spirit diversifies us: "We are as though merged in one body yet as persons still divided from each other as persons," St Cyril of Alexandria writes.[5]

As a result of the Fall, the Spirit's action is now *exterior* to nature and in the sacred baptism in the River Jordan the Spirit comes upon Christ and on the day of Pentecost becomes active *within* human nature, becoming an "interior reality" of human holiness. The Virgin Mary is "full of grace," (*gratia plena*), St Stephen, the first martyr, is filled with the Holy Spirit, and for St Ignatius of Antioch all the faithful and "bearers of the Spirit" (*pneumatophores*), are "filled with God."

The Church is holy with the holiness of Christ (Eph 5), and as the source of the sacraments and of sanctification she actualizes the communion of saints. Always in the struggle against the heresies of Montanism and Donatism, the Church presents the precise and clear understanding that she is not a society of perfected saints, of only the elect and the pure. Her mystery consists in being at one and the same time "the Church of the repentant, of those perishing" (St Ephrem) and the communion of sinners with the "holy things," of their deifying sharing in the "one and only holy One." The Church glories in the holiness of God. She venerates the "all holy" Virgin Mary (*Panagia*) and all of the saints known and unknown who are the Church's "golden band." The Church affirms that each and every sinner who lives her life will receive the entire measure of holiness given to that person.

In saying that "the Church is holy," we speak above all of the holiness that she confers upon her children, that which is realized in their lives, concealed in the mystery of silence, seen by God alone and by those to whom he reveals it in the Church, and in the case of these, canonization makes such saints known to all. From that point on, their ministry continues openly, known to all and in the service of the world.

5   In *Joan.*, XI; PG 59, 361.

The origins and development of the cult of the saints

In the Bible, it is the Book of Job which insists upon the intercession of the righteous: "Job, my servant, shall pray for you, for I will listen to him lest I deal with you in your foolishness (42:8). The same book also mentions recourse to the angels to receive illumination (5:1) and protection (33:23). In the Gospel, Moses and Elijah are on either side of Jesus during the Transfiguration and the Lord says of His friends, "If anyone serves me, my Father will honor him" (Jn 12:26).

Origen echoes St Paul's teaching on the unity of the saints with Christ: "If one is honored, all the members rejoice with him" (1 Cor 12:26).[6] "Jerusalem is our mother on high" (Gal 4:26). The Church extends from the heavens to earth. "Those who have fallen asleep in Christ dwell in the Lord" (2 Cor 5:6-8). Origen stresses that the entire letter to the Hebrews is inspired by the spirit of the communion of saints (1:14; 2:10-11; 13:7). In waiting for the day of the Lord when he will be "glorified in his saints," these continue their ministry of intercession for the living. The Book of Revelation speaks of martyrs in prayer before the throne of God and the Lamb. "Blessed are those who die in the Lord from now on, those called to the marriage feast of the Lamb" (14:13; 19:9).

Thus the tradition of the cult of the saints is formed from the scriptural understanding of the communion of saints. One of the most ancient documents in Christian literature is the *Martyrium Polycarpi*, (The Martyrdom of Polycarp), edited about 156 C.E., which mentions the cult honoring the saints by following their example. The cult of the martyrs is evident in the annual celebration of their death, the *dies natalis*, their "heavenly birthday," their birth into eternal life. "On the third day after his death, we returned to his tomb for the breaking of bread," the *Acta Joannis* (c. 72) tells us. Within a very short time the martyrs who had escaped death were honored as priests even though they were not ordained, this a recognition of the ministry of prayer inherent in their vocation. Those who have died for God continue to be in communion with the living, in Christ.

In the time of St Cyprian in Africa, the Church recognized the power

6   *De oratione*, II, 2.

of the martyrs' posthumous intercession with God.[7] The inscriptions on the tombs and the graffiti of the catacombs witness to the same intercession in the time of persecution. The martyrs were "advocates" of the faithful.[8] St Jerome writes of the mother of Blesilla: "She prayed to the Lord for you and obtained for me the pardon of my sins."[9]

According to Origen, a martyr is a source of grace for all of the faithful. In a time of peace, when Satan steals the martyrs, since there is no persecution, the Church, he says, is weakened. Speaking of the Liturgy, Origen echoes the fundamental truth that the prayer in heaven and on earth is one and identical, the martyrs and angels both participate in our liturgical assemblies.[10] Those in heaven continue the struggle of the faithful on earth because the economy of salvation is rooted in only one Body in which there is but one life. We are the companions of the saints, *sanctorum socios*, and by communion with them we are within the communion of the Holy Trinity.[11] "The Church of the saints sustains that on earth," Origen tells us, "impelled by their love, the saints are our physicians and benefactors."[12]

The ideal of the martyrs, that glorious company of the "wounded friends of the Bridegroom" in whom "Christ fights personally," made the spirituality of the earliest centuries of the Church unique. On the way to a glorious death as a martyr, St Ignatius of Antioch confessed: "It is now that I am to begin to be a true disciple...do not stop me from being born to life."[13] For St Polycarp, "the venerable chains of the martyrs are the diadems of the elect of God."[14]

A living image of the crucified Christ, the martyr preaches him in making of himself "a spectacle to the world," both to angels and men. "Your bodies are pierced by the sword, but your spirit was never able to be wrenched from divine love. Suffering with Christ, you are consumed

7   *De lapsis*, c. 17.
8   St Augustine, P.L. 38, 1209.
9   *Epist.* 25.
10 PG 11, 448:553.
11 PG 12, 437.
12 PG 12, 909; 11, 448.
13 *Rom* 5:3-6.
14 *Phil* 3.

by the burning coals of the Holy Spirit," the Church sings in the liturgy for martyrs. According to an ancient tradition, at the moment of death the martyr hears the same words Christ addressed to the good thief: "Today you will be with me in paradise," and enters immediately into the Kingdom where, as St John Chrysostom affirms, the martyr begins to intercede for us.

The peaceful existence of the Church, protected by law since the fourth century, however, did not soften the radical, violent character of her proclamation. Immediately, as it were, the Holy Spirit seems to have invented the "equivalent" of martyrdom. The "baptism by blood" of the martyrs gave way to the "baptism by asceticism" of the monastics. The well-known of *Life of St Antony*, written by St Athanasius the Great, described this holy man as one who had achieved holiness without tasting of martyrdom. Monastic sanctity formed a type which is called "very similar to God," a living icon of the Holy One. Thus the desert fathers, faced with the world's compromises, experienced the evangelical *metanoia*, the transformation of the whole economy of human life, its perfect metamorphosis. The awesome desert of the Thebaid, cradle of these giants of the Spirit, an arid, burning wasteland became completely illumined by their light. These astonishing masters teach us the art of living the Gospel. In the silence of their cells and caves, in the school of these teachers "taught by God himself," (*theodidacti*) the birth of the "new creature" gradually occurred, the restoration of a healed human nature, in the glorious appearance of these saints as "a spectacle" to the world. In the purity of their hearts these holy men and women saw God and through them, God let himself be seen.

Thus gradually did the tradition of the ministry of the saints unfold. In the third century already there was the strong conviction in their intercession before God on behalf of the Church. Certainly, Origen observed, only the Lamb of God takes away the sin of the world, the saints simply raise their prayer to him.[15] Even Tertullian emphasizes that the saints are not at all smaller "gods," but just intercessors.[16] St Cyprian speaks of the saints as those in whom death does

15 PG 12, 756.
16 PL 2, 99.

not interrupt their prayer for the living.[17] St Irenaeus of Lyons calls the Virgin Mary "advocate," the one who intercedes for Eve,[18] a role which St Gregory of Nyssa extends to all of the saints. St Gregory of Nazianzus refers to his deceased mother, Nonna, as one who responded to the prayers of her children, and he indicated his confidence in the intercession of his dead father as well.[19]

The teaching of the Fathers is firm and clear. The cult of the saints is a "cult of love and honor," without any placing of these on the same level as the divine power which alone gives salvation. The saints are but witnesses and servants of God, and after their death their ministry is like that of the angels. Liturgical practice very accurately and precisely expresses the Tradition and tells us of the prayer of the saints. Thus St Cyril of Jerusalem refers to the Liturgy which commemorates the patriarchs, prophets, apostles, martyrs and the saints "so that God by their prayers and intercessions would hear our supplications."[20] St Basil the Great mentions the prayers of St Mamas, St Gregory of Nazianzus invokes the martyr St Cyprian, St Gregory of Nyssa prays: "Remember, Lord, the tears I have shed before your holy martyrs."[21] It can be clearly seen that the prayer of the saints, ultimately addressed to God alone, reflects as the icon of a saint, the light of God reflected in the saint's own face. Of course, God has no need of the prayers of the saints. Yet, we should recall the Gospel parable of the judge and the widow, especially her insistence and faith. Also the prayer of the saints expresses their communion with us in mutual love, a manifestation of the unity of the Body of Christ, a point where grace touches, for as the letter of St James (5:16) has it, "the prayer of a righteous man, done in fervor is of great power." "All the members constitute the one Body of Christ in the unity of the Holy Spirit, and all should communicate to each other the goodness of the divine gifts," so St Basil the Great comments.[22] St John of Damascus synthesizes the tradition: "We venerate the saints

---

17 *Epist.* 60, 5.
18 PG 7, 1180.
19 PG 38, 52.
20 PG 33, 1116.
21 *Sermo asctia.*
22 *De Spiritu Sancto*, PG 32, 180.

because of God whose servants they are...the friends of Christ, the temples of the Holy Spirit. This honor goes back to God who is honored in his servants and we, as a result receive the blessing." So, "we honor the saints as the place where God is present."

Thus the cult of the saints is rooted in the *communio sanctorum* which transcends every limit of time and of space. The natural intercession of the living for each other finds in the risen Christ this absence of limits and therefore becomes the natural intercession of the saints, which is their way of heavenly participation in the destiny of the Church on earth. The saints surround us with their prayerful protection. This in no way separates us from Christ but unites us to him even more intimately. The saints are not "mediators" who diminish the unique mediation of Christ but our friends and companions on the same path of salvation.

A saint is one in whom "Christ lives" (Gal 2:20), one in whom "God has made his dwelling" (Jn 14:23), and this proximity or intimacy with the divine obviously does not cease at death. The Lord is attentive to the supplications of the members of his Body, to their manifestations of cosmic love made more dynamic and active by their liberation from earthly conditions. This has nothing to do with merits but the degree of the appropriation of the gifts and the charisms of the Holy Spirit, for "one star differs in brightness from another" (1 Cor 15:41).

Each of us stands before God personally, and we have a direct and immediate rapport with him, and this does not exclude but rather presupposes the fact that we stand together with all of the saints in saying "our Father." Any hesitation or doubt we have is stilled in the boldness of those with whom we join, those already in the light and radiance of the love of Christ. In praying to the saints we pray to Christ through the medium of the members of his Body. The Church, according to St Paul, is the "household of God," and thus a "family." So we recognize in the saints our brothers and sisters, our relatives in Christ, those who assist us in our search for the heavenly City.

From the start of the fifth century, the feasts of the saints began to have their liturgical place, so witness the *menologia*, the monthly lists and the *typica*, the directions for liturgical celebration. Special texts were developed such as antiphons, *troparia*, *kondakia*, for example, those composed by St Romanos the Melodist. St Ephrem, (†373) dedicated eleven texts to the Virgin in which she was venerated as an intercessor. To the feast of the martyrs was added that of all saints, instituted at Antioch in the fifth century and in Rome in A.D. 608. Iconography was particularly rich and expressive of the cult of the saints, for example the mosaic frescoes at Ravenna showing the glorious procession of the virgins and the martyrs.

Indications in the Scriptures, the experience of the Church in her prayer addressed to the saints, their iconography, the dedication of churches for whom each received a particular saint as patron and protector, the rapid diffusion of the "lives" of the saints, all of this constituted the very components of the tradition of the cult of the saints. The Church attentively cultivated this tradition and regularized it in the process of canonization.

The canonization of saints

Canonization is nothing else but the official act of the Church in response to God's judgment concerning his saints. This is expressed by various signs, the ecclesiastical declaration but establishes and records these. Most often one finds the origins of the process in the *vox populi*, the popular local veneration of a saint. This would attract the attention of ecclesiastical authorities and, if an inquest confirms it, the Church would canonize by this very act of investigation. This decision would not prejudge God's decree but simply identify the signs which manifest it and make it known to the Church on earth. Thus in place of the service of memorial and prayer for the dead usually sung: "Give rest O Lord to the soul of your servant who has fallen asleep," the Church sings a *Te Deum*, a service of thanksgiving honoring the saint and asking his or her intercession: "Holy father/mother, pray to God for us." This distinction is further marked by the liturgy of the Eucharist and other of the offices in which the new saint is named and thus placed in the ranks of those who surround the world with their prayerful protection.

Nectarios, patriarch of Jerusalem (†1680) formulated three conditions necessary for canonization: 1) indisputable orthodoxy in the faith, 2) a holy life and confession of faith which would go as far as martyrdom if necessary, 3) during life or after death evident manifestations of divine grace such as miracles, healings, spiritual assistance, and often, but not always, the incorruptibility of the saint's body.

The ancient Greek Church fixed the day of the saint's commemoration and inscribed the name in the liturgical diptych, or list, to be used in services as well as on the ecclesiastical calendar. Today, there is a solemn service confirming the act of canonization presided by the diocesan bishop, the metropolitan bishop, or the patriarch. In Russia, the synod of bishops issues an official declaration. In some cases canonization rests primarily upon a local tradition of venerating a saint, in others the tradition is received and acknowledged by all the Churches. It is always necessary to stress, however that there are no precise rules, formulae or statutes which determine the process of canonization, for it is beyond regimentation. St Vladimir, for example, was simply a Christian prince, the baptizer of the Russian people, and it was this, without any miracles, for which he was recognized as "equal-to-the-apostles" in the christianizing of Russia. The Council of 1546-47 canonized wonder-workers and martyrs, but it was the hard pastoral work of Leontius, bishop of Rostov (1077) which justified his canonization.

Miracles are signs, often striking and spectacular, but not necessarily so. In a miracle the power of God is clearly shown. God hears the intercessions of a saint, thus by this fact placing this holy one among the "friends" to whom he listens. There exists a category of saints to whom Tradition attributes no supernatural deeds or miracles in the strict sense of the word. Their lives however demonstrate great intimacy with God, a transcendence of their human condition, the hold of their spirit over nature. Thus the Virgin Mary and St John the Baptist are true "archetypes" of male and female sanctity, but they were not responsible for any miracles in their earthly lives.

Miracles are not always investigated. A saint resists all manifestations which risk pride, the sectarian dangers of the "pure" and the "elect." All ecstasies, visions, and other supernatural phenomena are considered as belonging to a kind of novitiate for the saint. This is why a saint's life is always hidden, mysterious, penetrated by humility and modesty. Many saints remain unknown to the world and known only by God. The recognition, the canonization of a saint, always occurs, as it were, against the will of the saint him/herself. Moreover every miracle, even resurrection from death is "supernaturally natural," for it is associated with the return of a person to his own true nature. In the life of a saint all is perpetual miracle and everything is "natural" as the amazing reality of his life in Christ, again hidden from all.

The contemporaries of a saint are always struck by his or her clairvoyant prophecy, the sense of the providence of God in the progress of history or in the destiny of a person. But even this charism, rather frequently found, is not exercised except in the situation when it is necessary to warn, to appeal to a free decision: "if you want," "if you will do this," as the Gospel constantly states it.

The natural state of the body after the death of a saint would be the natural result of the changing of his nature by the deifying energies, but here also there is nothing automatic or imposed, no violence to the human condition which would risk weakening this grace which is so majestically free in the "limits of reason" of which Kant speaks, in the experience of quasi-scientific proofs. The possible glorification extending to the body is a free gift of God. Absent or present, it is never a fact which determines whether the person will be canonized as a saint.

Participation of the saints in earthly life

The saints, even after their departure, continue in their own way to be effective members of the Church. They surround us by their prayers and represent a dynamic connection between heaven and earth. They are not mediators and do not diminish the unique mission of the one Mediator, Christ, but they assist us as friends and elder brethren in the experience of the mysteries of God. Confidants and vessels of grace, their intercession possesses a great power because of their intimacy and relationship with the holiness of God. They have realized the image of God in themselves and have thus become "most like" God (a title especially given to monastic saints), following their vocations and their personal gifts. The Church glorifies diverse categories of saints: patriarchs, prophets, apostles, martyrs, wonder-workers, theologians and fathers or teachers of the Church, monastics, ascetics, spiritual fathers and mothers, physicians and healers who did not charges for their services, princes and holy lay people. Holiness takes on numerous forms, as numerous as there are personalities and each person can find his or her individual form of sanctity.

According to the faith of the Church and her infallible experience, God gives to his saints the power of active protection of us on earth. They also help us to stand together before our Father. If we are aware of them we will thus never feel alone, having a great family around us, sustaining and conducting us to God. St Maximus the Confessor said that everyone had two wings which bore him to heaven and these are grace and freedom. Holiness is the triumph of this synergy which liberates the forces of active love. Saints are the "human hands" of God. All are equal with respect to both the Fall and the abyss of divine mercy. The difference is only in the mode of acquisition, of assimilation and personal appropriation of salvation. The distinction between the "sheep and the goats" at the Last Judgment indicates the qualitative differences among human beings and the judgment corresponds to one's creative liberty as a "new creature," to one's holiness.

In praying to the saints we pray to Christ present in them, addressing the power of Christ's love which makes all united as his Body. It is this indestructible communion of all, the simultaneous organic unity of the spiritual and the corporeal, which explains the *cult of relics*. The Church confesses and affirms that there is a special link between the spirit of a saint and his remains (whether these are intact or not is of no importance), a connection which death cannot break. The body of Our Lord was separated from his soul, his death being real, but the body maintained its connection with the divine spirit and because of this remained incorrupt. The same phenomenon occurs after the death of a saint. Through their sharing in the destiny of the living, the saints receive the grace of a union between the Holy Spirit and their bodies, as do their relics. It is a form of their presence analogous to that in the icon.

The liturgical calendar consecrates each day of the year to the memory and veneration of one or more saints. The *communio sanctorum* makes the glory of God shine in his creature: "God stands in the divine council, in the midst of the gods he will judge" (Ps 81:1). This is why the Liturgy of the Eastern Church, that of St John

Chrysostom and St Basil the Great, reserves a special place for the saints who have joined the angels in the heavenly choir of the Lamb.

During the "little entrance" at the beginning of the first part of the Eastern Church Liturgy, that of the catechumens, the doors of the sanctuary are opened just as the Kingdom of God was opened at the coming of Jesus. The procession of the celebrating priest, deacon and servers goes out of the north door of the iconostasis and eventually moves toward the central, royal doors with the Gospel book solemnly carried upraised, preceded by candles. This is a ritualized representation of Christ proclaiming his word, preceded by St John the Baptist, "a flame shining and brilliant" (Jn 5:35). Here the Liturgy prepares us for hearing the Word of God, especially the Gospel. The soul becomes pure adoration, like the good soil in the parable, open and receptive to the seed that the Lord will sow. Here the Liturgy attains one of its heights. With incomparable artistry, the service resounds with an astonishing fullness to worthily receive the coming of the Word. "I tell you, you will see the heavens open and the angels of God ascending and descending upon the Son of Man" (Jn 1:51). "A voice came from the throne which said: 'Praise God, all you his servants'" (Rev 19:5). This moment of adoration, the essential liturgical attitude, reunites heaven and earth. The angels who serve the "eternal liturgy" in heaven come to concelebrate with the priest and with all the faithful here. This is why the prayer of the entrance asks: "Grant that with our entrance there may be an entrance of holy angels, serving with us and glorifying your goodness." In the midst of the resounding irruption of heaven onto earth, the word "adoration" takes on the sense of "participation in the holiness of God" (Heb 12:1). "Blessed is the entrance of your saints," the priest proclaims, and there is the glorious praise of God by all the powers of the holiness of the Church, by her very being. The *troparia* or "proper" liturgical verses commemorate the saints of the day and the patron saint(s) of that particular church. These are part of the fullness of the "cloud of witnesses" (Heb 12:1) surrounding Christ, in the brilliance of the radiant glory of God in the whole assembly of the saints. All of the saints, the angels and the faithful form the cortège of the King.

"Come let us worship, and fall down before Christ, O Son of God, who is wonderful in Your saints, save us who sing to you. Alleluia!"

This is sung as the procession of the "little entrance" continues up through the royal doors of the iconostasis to the altar. All in the liturgical assembly bow during this chant. God, the Holy One hidden in the very mystery of his glory as in a cloud, approaches, adored by all the powers of his own holiness shining in the faces of the saints. Here, at the very heart of his transcendent holiness, God, the Lover of mankind, reveals his amazing immanence in his coming among his saints.

After the blessing of the entrance, the deacon (or priest) raises the Gospel-book being carried in procession and proclaims: "Wisdom, let us attend!" This is the call to the faithful to direct their adoration to Christ the Word, whose presence is witnessed by the Gospel-book raised for all to see. The Word will now resound among the *communio sanctorum*, hence the preliminary liturgical action of this entrance mobilizes all the force of holiness among those gathered. The Liturgy does not "teach" holiness, neither does it explain the holiness of God. It is indeed capable of doing so but it rather reveals holiness. The Liturgy opens the door to his coming and makes us powerfully aware of his presence. Here we have the very essence of liturgical worship, to carry over into direct and sensible experience the direct encounter with the wholly Other, the holiness of God. His glory truly fills his temple and the luminous fringe of his cloud comes upon the assembly. The angels are "amazed" and cover their faces with their wings and we bow down and worship. The deacon bows and addresses the celebrant: "Bless the time of the Trisagion, the Thrice-Holy hymn." The soul preparing to hear the Word of God finds the dignity appropriate to this mystery, its own place as a "person" of the Thrice-Holy Hymn, the *Sanctus* or *Trisagion*. This is a person of whom Psalm 104:33 says, "I will sing to my God as long as I live." Struck by this blinding vision the soul is raised up by such abundance of glory and gives itself entirely over to God as a pure offering, one who cannot but join with the song of the angels: "Holy God, Holy Mighty, Holy Immortal, have mercy on us." The celebrants bow deeply three times and lift their hands while saying the *Trisagion,* while the choir chants this overture to the Trinitarian Mystery from which Christ, the glory of the Holy God, approaches and appears before his reverent faithful. When the bishop is present at the Liturgy, he blesses the people with his special episcopal double and triple candlesticks, representing the Christological and Trinitarian realities. This is a very compact liturgical action, an iconographic gesture which reaches the juncture of the indescribable nature of divine holiness and the dogmatic icon of his love. From this depth comes the blessing: "Peace be to all!" Peace, *Shalom*, already introduces the world, by anticipation, into the Kingdom of the saints.

The cult of the angels

Pagan religions recognized the theophanic symbolism of nature. The authors of the biblical books communicate to us God's message but in order to do this use the figures and representations of their own cultural milieu. It is thus through folklore and symbolism that the essential kernel of the message is grasped. To the question of ancient philosophy—how does the Absolute enter into relationship with the world, the Bible responds with its teaching on the angels. "Heaven" is the sphere of a celestial army of angels. Yahweh is surrounded by a celestial choir which adores, praises and sings to him (as in Isaiah 6 and the Psalms). In its liturgical worship, Israel associated this praise with that of the angels. The Lord himself affirmed that children's angels, their guardians, stand before the presence of the Father (Mt 18:11). St Paul asks; "Do you not know that you will judge the angels?" (1 Cor 6:3). This teaching removes primitive catechesis from all gnostic speculation. According to Heb 1:14 the angels are the *pneumata,* the "spirits" and 1 Corinthians 11:10 stresses their participation in liturgical worship.

The Scriptures tell us nothing about the nature of angels, but speak of them in terms of their office and functions as messengers, guardians and celebrants of the heavenly liturgy. According to the Fathers (especially Clement of Alexandria, Origen, Pseudo-Dionysius), the angels personify the *exousiai*, the heavenly powers, and are placed by God before the nations as their guides and protectors. Even the guardian angel, unique for each person, bears God's thought toward that person and is the image of that individual's projected sanctity. The guardian angel thus is intimately linked to the one with whose protection he is confided. The angels take a very active part in the historical existence of the world. Under the leadership of the archangel Michael, they struggle against the demons, who are the fallen angels and powers of nothingness. After death, the "angel-leader of souls" receives the soul as it leaves the body. According to St Basil, the angels of the Last Judgment "weigh out" souls. Assistants in the action of God, the angels are present most particularly to the martyrs. Origen insists on their liturgical function, surrounding the Holy Trinity and concelebrating the heavenly Liturgy with Christ.

The vision of Jacob's ladder reveals the angels as messengers of God. They are attached to the word and the will of God and personify them. When God decides to heal, his will to do so takes the figure of the angel Raphael, whose very names means, "God's healing." Every time an angel appears, it is in order to transmit and accomplish the will of God. If a human being is free and a creator because of the ability to choose and act, an angel is totally identified with his function. The angels present "heaven" to us because they exist in and enact what is in God's mind for us. In guarding the power of direct revelation, most often God reveals himself through the angels as the bearers of his energies, his light and his revelation. This is why the three angels who appeared to Abraham beneath the oak of Mamre are considered, especially in the iconographic tradition, as the figures of the Three Divine Persons in the icon of the Trinity. The angel is a theophany, a living manifestation of God, for in the angel the Name of God abides and in the Name, God is present.

Traditionally the monastic life has been compared to that of the angels. A holy monk is called in the liturgical texts, "an earthly angel and a heavenly man." Our spiritual life is identical to the angels' action of prayer and contemplation, as God's "second lights." The cult of the angels then is rooted in their liturgical function of intercession, hence the Church addresses prayers to the angels. Along with the saints, we find the angels, especially Michael and Gabriel in the well-known icon of "Supplication," or *Deisis*, of Christ the King of all, flanked by his Mother and St John the Baptist, which becomes an icon of the Church herself, coming to the Lord in prayer. The "Cherubic Hymn," sung during the "Great Entrance" of the Liturgy, invites us to become icons of the angels, images of their adoration. St Basil says that the Holy Spirit is the Spirit of communion and that the angels are especially his servants in their guiding us into the communion of the saints in the love of Christ.

The cult of the Theotokos, the Mother of God

For the Fathers, it is the maternal function of the Church which is the natural passage toward the cult of the Virgin Mary. If the Word, Christ, is sufficient in his objective bearing, the insufficiency is in us and we need maternal protection. We need to find ourselves as children, sitting in the lap of the Church, in order to receive the Word.

"The name of the Theotokos, Mother of God, contains the entire economy of salvation," says St John of Damascus.[23] The analogy established among Eve, Mary, and the Church goes back to St Irenaeus of Lyons and since then, for the Fathers, Mary is the Woman who is the enemy of the serpent, the Woman clothed in the sun, the dwelling-place of the Wisdom of God in his very principle, namely, the integrity and chastity of being.[24]

If the Holy Spirit personalizes divine holiness, the Virgin personalizes human holiness. Virginity, the integrity of the very structure of its being, already triumphs over evil and contains the power that is invincible. The simple presence of the "most pure" is already unendurable for the demonic powers, the spirits of nothingness. Linked by her very nature to the Holy Spirit, Mary thus appears as the living consolation, the Eve-Life who safeguards and protects every creature and who stands as a figure of the Church in her maternal love. According to the Fathers, such an analogy cannot be arbitrary. *Mater Ecclesia* and *Virgo Mater*, Mother Church and the Virgin Mother are both *orantes*, the intercessors in prayer, and both bring forth new life. The icon of the Virgin holding the child Jesus is the icon of the Incarnation, the communion of the divine and the human, which is the very essence of the Church. The icon of the *Orant*, the Virgin with her arms raised in prayer, usually a fresco in the apse of the altar, is the icon of the Church.

"Wisdom has built her house, she has set up seven pillars and prepared her wine" (Prov 9:1-2). This text, at the same time referring to the Wisdom of God, sophianic, and mariological, speaks of the liturgical and intercessory function of the Church. The consecration of the Virgin to the life of the Temple, according to Tradition, and her love of

23 *De fide Orth.* III, 12.
24 *Adv. Haer.* I, III, c. 22, 4.

God, reached such depth in her and such an intensity that the conception of her Son took place in her as the divine response to her transparency to God. [Trans. note: Mary's entrance into the Temple is celebrated in the Orthodox Church on November 21.]

"The Crown of dogmas," the Mother of God projects her light on the Trinitarian mystery reflected in the human, created in the image of God: "You have given birth to the Son without a Father, the Son who was born of the Father without a mother."[25] To the paternity of the Father in the divine corresponds the maternity of the Theotokos in the human, the figure of the maternal virginity of the Church. Thus St Cyprian said: "One cannot have God as Father unless one has the Church for a mother."[26]

Participating organically in the descent of Adam, sharing in the consequences of the Fall, the Virgin nevertheless is protected from all personal impurity, from every evil, which are rendered ineffective in her by the successive purification of the "righteous ancestors of God" [Trans. note: As the Orthodox liturgy calls the holy ones of the Old Covenant, especially the parents of Mary, Saints Joachim and Anna], by the special action of the Holy Spirit and by her own free will. This response is set in relief in the beautiful words of Nicholas Cabasilas, the great lay liturgical theologian of the fourteenth century: "The Incarnation was not only the work of the Father, of his power and Spirit, but also the work of the will and the faith of the Virgin. Without the consent of the Most Pure One, without the cooperation of her faith, this plan of God would not have been realizable except through the intervention of the Three Divine Persons themselves. It was only after having been instructed and persuaded that God took her as his mother and borrowed from her the flesh that she desired to lend him. Just as he willingly became incarnate so he wished that his mother should give birth to him of her own free choice."[27]

In confessing the perpetual virginity of Mary, the Orthodox Church does not accept the idea of her exemption from sin claimed in

25 The *dogmatikon* of the 3rd tone.
26 *De cath. eccles. unitate*, c. 6.
27 *Homily on the Annunciation*.

the Roman Catholic dogma of the Immaculate Conception.[28] This dogma sets the Virgin apart, removes her from the common destiny of humankind, and suggests the possibility of liberation from original sin before the act of Christ's redemption on the cross, that is, solely by the action of grace. In this case, in order for the redemption to occur (through the Son yet to be born of her) it would have had to have taken place already, the Virgin would have to enjoy the effects of the redemption before it actually took place. Such a plan on God's part, who already had made Adam righteous through grace would render the Fall incomprehensible for the Orthodox. For the Greeks, the original righteousness was not a gratuitous privilege but "the very root of being." But God does not act upon us but in us. He did not act upon the Virgin through a gift, a *superadditum*, but he worked beyond even the common effort and the reciprocity between the Spirit and the holiness of the "righteous ancestors of God." Every good thing imposed turns into an evil. Only the free submission of holiness constitutes the objective human condition of the Incarnation which allows the Word to "come home." Grace does not violate or impose itself upon the natural order. Rather grace perfects nature. Jesus was able to take on human flesh because Mary gave him the humanity she herself possessed. In the Virgin all of us say: "Yes, Come Lord." This is why the words of the Creed "born of the Holy Spirit and the Virgin Mary," according to the Fathers, also designate the second birth of every believer, who is born of faith and of the Holy Spirit. The faith of every Christian is rooted in universal faith and courage and action of the Virgin, in her *fiat*.

To the *fiat* of the Creator corresponds the *fiat* of the creature: "Here I am, the servant of the Lord. Let it be done to me according to your word." The angel Gabriel is like a question that God addresses in freedom to his prodigious daughter: do you really want to contain in your womb the Uncontainable One? In the Virgin's response shines the pure flame of one who gives herself and by this act is ready to receive him. The action of the Holy Spirit through the line of the "ancestors of Christ," the righteous ones of the Old Covenant [Trans note: particularly Joachim and Anna],

---

28 In the iconography of the Virgin, she is shown wearing three stars, one on her head, the others on her shoulders, these attesting to her virginity before, during and after the Nativity of Christ.

and the purity of the one who receives God, the one "full of grace," culminate at this point, disarming evil. Sin remains effective but has become inoperative. Humankind brings to the Temple its offering, bread and wine, and God in a royal gesture makes this his flesh and blood. Humanity brings the purest of offerings, the Virgin, and God makes her the one who gives birth to him, and Eve, the Mother of all the living, is fulfilled. At the vigil of Christmas the Church sings, "What shall we offer you, O Christ? Heaven offers the angels, earth offers her gifts, but we, human beings, offer you a Virgin Mother." One can well see here that Mary is not just "a woman among women," but the full arrival of Woman restored to maternal virginity. In the Virgin all of humanity gives birth to God and on account of this, Mary is the new Eve, and her maternal protection which cared for the child Jesus now envelops all the world and every person. Listen to the words from the cross: "Jesus said to his mother: Woman, behold your son. Then he said to the disciple, behold, your mother." These words institute Mary's universal intercession.

It is her humanity, her flesh which becomes that of Christ; his mother has become "one blood" and "one body" with him. She is the first to realize the purpose for which the entire world was created, "the boundary of the created and the uncreated."[29] and through her, "the Trinity is glorified."[30] In bearing Christ, as Eve, she gave birth to him for us all, and she brings him to birth in every soul. The Church therefore is represented here in her mystical motherhood, her continually giving birth, her always being the Theotokos, the Mother of God.

St Maximus the Confessor defines "mystical" as "the one in whom is best manifest the birth of the Lord." "Contemplation," he says, makes "the soul fertile, at the same time virgin and mother."[31] St Ambrose writes, "Every soul who believes conceives and gives birth to the Word of God; by faith, Christ is the child of us all, all of us are his mothers."[32] These words shed great light on the passage in the Gospel (Lk 8:19-21) and remove any pejorative meaning which classic

---

29 St Gregory Palamas, PG 151, 472 B.
30 St Cyril of Alexandria, PG 78, 992.
31 PG 90, 889C.
32 In *Evang. S. Lucae*, II, 26.

Protestant interpretation has given to this passage. The accent is not on the Virgin but on every person: "Whoever does the will of God, this one is my mother." These words signify that every person is given the grace of bringing Christ to birth in his or her soul and of thereby identifying with the Theotokos, Mary the Mother of God.

Christ is "the Way" and "the Door," the God-Man. He is unique. The Virgin is the first. She precedes humanity and all follow her; "the good direction," "the one who shows the way," "the pillar of fire," she leads the world toward the new Jerusalem. She is the first to pass through death made powerless by her Son, and this is why the prayers read at the hour of death for every Christian are addressed to her, for her protection. "In your falling asleep, O Theotokos, you have not abandoned the world," the Church sings and in her the world already becomes the "new creation." Iconography places both icons side by side in synoptic vision, those of the Ascension of Christ and the Dormition of the Virgin.[33] God made man and man makes God and this illustrates the patristic adage quite amply, that God became man so that man could once again become God. The Dormition closes the gates of death. The seal of the Theotokos is placed upon nothingness, it is sealed from on high by the God-Man and from below by the first risen creature.

The Virgin is thus at the head of the Church's holiness and her virginity expresses the very essence of the Kingdom, eternal sanctity, the very epitome of the *Sanctus*. The lesson from Proverbs 8:22-30 read on the feast of the Conception identifies the Virgin with the place of the Wisdom of God and celebrates in her the goal attained by divine creation, according to Dante, *termino fisso d'eterno consiglio*.

The Virgin is the "purification of the world" and "burning bush." She is "the praying one," and she expresses the ministry of prayer, the charism of intercession. With the Holy Spirit she says, "Come Lord!" At the Judgment, the Word of Truth judges and reveals the wounds, and the Holy Spirit, the Advocate and Comforter, gives life and heals. It is this maternal protection of the Holy Spirit which is expressed in

---

33 The Dormition, or Assumption, is not a dogma in Orthodoxy for it does not come to us from the Scriptures but it nevertheless is a reality of Tradition both in the Liturgy and in personal piety.

the ministry of the Virgin together with that of St John the Baptist.[34] The icon of *Deisis*, or supplication, shows them on either side of Christ the Judge, presenting to him the prayer of the Church, the intercession for mercy for all, and this is why the same icon signifies the marriage of the Lamb with the Church and with each Christian soul.

Christ wears the priestly vestments and gives the priestly blessing and is the great, unique priest. At the moment of judgment, he is the eternal Bishop and Shepherd. The Judge, he holds the book of the Gospels as the only and unique interpreter of its meaning. But the Spirit manifests the charism of praying for the Church. The plain and objective truth of the humanity of Christ exercises judgment: "The Father has given him the power to judge because he is the Son of Man" (Jn 5:27). Along with the pure humanity of the Word are the archetypes of holiness, the Theotokos and St John the Baptist. "Do you not know that the saints will judge the world?" (1 Cor 6:2). Holiness shows the "foolishness" or absurdity of love and pleads for those who are being judged. The Word judges but the Spirit-Advocate confronts justice with mercy and the saints are the servants of the Spirit.

The feast of *Pokrov*, of the protection and the intercession of the Mother of God, clearly points to her ministry. The origin of the feast lies in her appearance to Andrew, a "fool for Christ," and his disciple Epiphanius. This vision took place in Constantinople, in the church dedicated to the Virgin of Blachernae. In the account of two witnesses, the Virgin, kneeling, wept for the world and pleaded with her Son for the world's forgiveness. At the end of her prayer, the Virgin lifted up her veil—*pokrov*—from her head, shedding forth light upon the people and the whole world as a sign of her protection. The veil is like the heavens covering the earth. In a fifteenth century icon one sees an astonishing unity between the veil and the saints that it covers. One could almost say that the veil is woven of holiness which forms a wall of protection. This wall surrounds the witness showing the hands stretched out in supplication, the Church praying for the Church and above all these are the hands of the *Orant*, the Praying One, the Virgin who carries the entire universe in her arms, in love. The wall is further

34 In the Semitic languages, the Spirit is feminine. In the Hebrew text the Spirit "broods" over the abyss from which life will gush forth (Genesis 1).

represented by the iconostasis in Orthodox churches, Christ with his saints, and with his Mother at the head. The Orthodox liturgical hymns say: "Indestructible wall." "Mother of Life you have brought joy to the world and this gladness dries up the tears of sin." "All of creation rejoices in you."

The Virgin is this joy and peace which searches for every soul in its solitude and its anguish. Dionysius the Areopagite, in addressing his prayer to the Theotokos, expresses well her ministry: "I wish that your image may be reflected unceasingly in the mirror of souls and keep them pure to the end of the ages, that it will raise up those bent down to the earth by their sorrows, giving them hope and joy, all who venerate and imitate the eternal model of your beauty.

In the school of holiness

The art of the Desert Fathers

The Lord said, "Call no one Father for there is only one who is your father and he is in heaven" (Mt 23:9). Nonetheless the Eastern Church, from the very beginning of Christianity, used the title, "spiritual father," "father" in short, *géron, starets*, that is "elder." The evolution of the Semitic word *abba* is rich in meaning. While it has passed into all languages in one or another form it nevertheless signifies something absolutely new in relationship to the Old Testament. This newness comes from the revelation of the Trinity. "Abba, Father," in the Lord's Prayer (Mk 6:9) expresses a nuance of intimacy with God unthinkable before that time in Jewish prayer. The Gospel reveals the love of the Father for the Son, who implants his fatherhood in all people as his children. It is this same Lord Jesus who taught us to pray, "Our Father." According to the early Christian text, the *Letter to Diognetus* (10, 1) the catechumens, those preparing for baptism, learned above all to know their heavenly Father, "Abba," through the Son and the Holy Spirit. St Cyril of Alexandria in his *Thesaurus* writes that in Christ the relationship of God to man as Master-slave is replaced by that of Father-child.

It is in light of the Trinity then that we must understand the Gospel interdiction mentioned above, namely to call no one "Father." The practice of spiritual fatherhood is a homage rendered to the unique father-hood of God, to its manifestation through different forms of human par-ticipation in it. According to the *Coptic Life of St Pachomius*, for his disciples Pachomius was "after God, their father." It is precisely in this sense that St John the Theologian and Evangelist says in his letters, "my little children," and that St Paul speaks of the sufferings of giving birth to his children in Christ. This spiritual childbearing is always in relation to the cross and Abba Longinus reminds us of the saying of the desert fathers: "Shed your blood and receive the Spirit." a "spiritual father" is not so much a teacher who gives instruction but one who engenders, gives birth, in the image of the heavenly Father. You don't acquire the art of spiritual fatherhood as you learn a discipline or skill in school. The genealogy of the "neptic" or "vigiliant" fathers evokes this charismatic transmission of spiri-tual fatherhood by means of the verb, "to engender."

One should notice the title of spiritual father is not the same as that of "Father of the Church," given to great teachers and theologians who contribute to elucidating the Church's doctrinal and dogmatic truth. There are two traditions for the use of "Father" in a more personal rela-tion. One goes back to St Ignatius of Antioch, that of "functional fatherhood." Every bishop and priest is called "Father" in view of the priestly function he exercises. They baptize and make new children of God by means of the sacraments and the pastoral ministry. The other tradition has no connection with the priestly office or function. St Anthony the Great, the founder of monastic life, was a simple lay person and monk. Here a person is a "father" by divine call, through the charismatic gift of the Holy Spirit, by being *theodidactos*, that is "taught directly by God." Neither age nor function play any role here. The *Sayings of the Desert Fathers* show this. "Abba Moses said one day to Brother Zacharias: 'Tell me what I should do.' At these words the brother threw himself at the elder's feet, crying: 'Is it of me that you should ask this, Father?' The elder told him: 'Believe me, Zacharias, I have seen the Holy Spirit descend upon you and since that time I have been constrained to ask this of you.'"

According to the *Lives of the Desert Fathers*, these spiritual masters are precisely "fathers," and the collection of their words and deeds (*Sayings*) attest to this and are called *Paterika, Works of the Fathers*. It is important to note that even the bishops came to seek counsel and assistance from these simple lay monks who were directly guided by the Holy Spirit. The people regarded them as infallible and the holders of a charismatic ministry distinct from the ordinary authority of bishops.

The essential condition for becoming a "spiritual father" is to be above all *pneumatikos,* that is, "spiritual," oneself. St Simeon the New Theologian said: "The one who is not himself reborn in the Spirit is not capable of giving birth to spiritual children." He added: "In order to impart the Holy Spirit, one must first possess him." He was referring here to the words of the Lord: "It is not you who speak, but it is the Spirit of your Father who speaks in you" (Mt 10:20). A spiritual father is a confidant and a vessel of the Holy Spirit. In order to be the "physician who heals himself," it is necessary to heal the cognitive function of the intellect first. The tradition of silent contemplative prayer, that of *hesychia,* reestablishes the integrity of the human being. "Make your mind and intellect (*nôus*) descend into your heart." The heart is illumined by the intellect and the intellect is oriented by hunger and thirst for God and is opened by the Holy Spirit, showing that "spiritual fatherhood" is not a doctrinal or teaching ministry but one of life and being. St Gregory Palamas insists on this: "Our piety, our faith is in the realities themselves, not in our words."

Among the charisms or gifts of such a "father," the primary one is love and it is the most certain mark and witness, both visible and invisible. "Every ascetic act devoid of love, every one which is not a sacrament of the brother/sister, does not come near to God." St Isaac the Syrian said to his disciple: "My brother, here is the commandment that I give you: that compassion should always be your measure, until you yourself possess the compassion which God himself has toward the world." Again St Paisius the Great prayed for his disciple who had turned from Christ, and when he prayed the Lord appeared to him, saying: "Paisius, why are you praying? Don't you know that he has turned his back on me?" But the saint did not relent in his love and his prayer for the disciple and then the Lord said to him: "Paisius, you have brought him back to me by your love." St Gregory the Theologian said that a spiritual father is a "repository, a treasury of God's love for mankind." St Isaac the Syrian says: "His heart is enflamed with love for every creature, even for the reptiles and the demons." It is this "onto-logical tenderness" that is the cosmic love of the saints. A hermit, after forty years of living in the desert said: "The sun has never seen me eating." But another brother immediately corrected him. "The sun has never seen anger in me." Abba Poimen refused to punish any of the brothers and it is easy to see the maternal dimension of his spiritual fatherhood: "When I see a brother fallen asleep during the prayer offices, I place his head in my lap and let him rest there."

The gift of "fiery prayer" in which one loses the very sense or feeling of his own existence is found in the life of St Anthony. He prayed for three days and three nights, and the next day the demons threw themselves prostrate before God, begging him to stop the saint from further praying, for his fire had become unbearable for them and was imperiling their entire demonic attack on the world. St Isaac and so many others saw, during their prayer, "the flame of things" and were themselves transformed in their prayer into pillars of fire. "If you want to become perfect," said Abba Joseph, "become all fire," and standing he raised his hands up in prayer toward heaven and his fingers became like blazing torches.

There is also the gift of prophecy, the discerning of the plan of God in specific cases, a "diagnosis of the heart" (*cardiodiagnosis*) in which the very heart and hidden thoughts of a person would be scrutinized, in which spirits were discerned and there was clairvoyance, a vision of the future. The Fathers could read the heart of a person, they could know the contents of a message without even opening and reading it. Long before the discoveries of modern depth psychology, they demonstrated the astonishing ability to penetrate the subconscious: "Many passions are hidden in our heart, but when they escape our attention, they reveal themselves." And again: "The one who reveals his thoughts is thereby healed; the one who hides them only worsens his sickness." "Discern your thoughts, ask a father capable of discerning them...."

Terrible *philautia* or self-love closes us in upon ourselves. To fight against this, everyone who is full of such passions and of the spirit of self-sufficiency must become a novice and submit to obedience. The fathers would teach this by example of their own lives and would support the neophyte by their continual prayer. St John Climacus put this in a rather paradoxical sentence: "To obey is to exclude discernment by a superabundance of discernment," that is, an excess of love, not of fear. The search for an authority for formal obedience is a temptation. Spiritual fatherhood has no formal criteria just as it is with truth. According to Abba Anthony, a spiritual father is one who "judges according to the Holy Spirit who is in him." A brother said to Anthony, "Pray for me," and Anthony replied, "I will have no pity on you and neither will God, if you do not take yourself seriously, particularly when it comes to prayer."

The last word in being a child of such a father is beyond obedience. The novice should obey and submit as one would obey Christ himself, in order to conform to him, to become like Christ in his obedience to the Father. To surpass obedience is to totally substitute the will of God for one's own human will and here we come to the very heart of spiritual fatherhood. *There is no other way than this to be led out of the status of a slave into the freedom of being a child of God.* This is why the fathers ceaselessly warn of the danger one risks in looking for human assistance. St Basil the Great counsels us to find a "friend of God" of whom we are certain that God is speaking in and to him. As great as the authority of such a father, even greater must be his humility. A disciple stated very well the purpose of his request: "My Father, tell me what it is that the Holy Spirit suggests to you, so that my soul may be healed." "Give me just one word (*rhema*) so that my soul may live." Only the heart is able to receive and contain such a life-giving word. St Seraphim of Sarov spoke very precisely of this art: "I renounce completely my own will and my own knowledge of souls and I listen only to the movements of the Spirit."

For Abba Poemen, the spiritual father places the soul of another in direct connection with God, and he counsels: "Never order anybody to do anything but always make yourself an example. Never make rules." The path toward holiness is not revealed in rules but in God. It is the fear of deforming the integrity of the person of a disciple that explains the total sacrifice of self on the part of the spiritual father. A young person came to be instructed about the way of perfection but the elder would not say a word to him. The disciple then demanded the reason for the silence: "Am I then your superior, your commander, that I should issue you orders," the elder responded. "I will not tell you anything. If you want to, do what you see me doing." From that point on, the novice imitated his father in everything and he learned the meaning of silence and of *obedience* in *freedom*.

A spiritual father is never a "spiritual director." He does not engender his spiritual child but a child of God, mature and free. Both place themselves in the school of Truth. The disciple receives the charism of spiritual attention, the father the charism of being a channel for the Holy Spirit. Here total obedience is obedience to the will of the heavenly Father, participating in the action of the obedient Christ.

To those well trained in the art of humility Theognostos says: "The one who has realized submission, spiritual obedience, and who has subordinated his body to the Spirit has no need of submitting to another person. He who has submitted to the Word of God and his Law is truly obedient." Further: "The one who wishes to live in the desert and follow its way has no need of being instructed. He himself should be a teacher without which he will perish." Such advice however, is only for the strong. Nevertheless the counsel given here is crucial. There is to be no blind obedience to human authority, no idolatry of a spiritual father, even if he is a saint. Every bit of counsel imparted by a father should lead to freedom before the face of God. True obedience is the crucifixion of one's own will in order to bring to life again the ultimate freedom of the spirit of each person listening to the Holy Spirit.

These "ultimate words" of the fathers for our time constitute an appeal for the powerful take-off of the human heart into the pastures of the heart of God. The "one thing necessary" is to recover again the mature freedom of being a child of God and to be able once more to walk joyously to the encounter with the Kingdom. St Simeon put it this way in summarizing the results of spiritual fatherhood: "For those who have become children of the light and of the day to come, the day of the Lord will not come unless they are always with God and in God...The one who prays without ceasing envelops the entire world in the embrace of his prayer. No more is it merely an obligation to praise the Lord seven times a day." The holiness of such people of the "Eighth Day" is an audacious, creative sanctity. "There is a light within such an illumined person and it illumines the whole world."

Some examples of the holiness of Russian saints

St Seraphim of Sarov

Every nation once baptized, is never simply passive in the manner of receiving, assimilating and living the faith. The spirit of that people personalizes the universal tradition of Christianity, makes it their own. Across the centuries, the religious life produces an ideal type of holiness for that culture, a saint who synthesizes all the belief, character and aspirations of his or her people. Their doctrines, ideas, liturgical and other forms of worship and piety are shaped but it is in the saints of a land that the faith is best incarnated. The saints are the living icons of the spiritual life of a people.

In Russia, one is impressed by a great sense of balance and the absence of extreme forms. One cannot find there any asceticism of pure mortification, that is violence in and for its own sake. Even the word "asceticism" is not very familiar, though its meaning is clear in such simple terms as fasting, work, and prayer. The spiritual life has always been radiant in monastic communities whose spiritual activity has also expressed itself in social ministry. All the saintly heads of monastic communities recognized hospitality to all visitors and all forms of social assistance as conditions of spiritual growth. A constant link between the monasteries and the rest of the country is to be found in the monastics' concern for those who come to them for confession, counsel, and prayer, and thus it evolved that priest-monks became the most usual father confessors to people, rather than their own parish priests. There also was the witness to justice before the powerful in this world as well as the resistance of the monastics to the all too common ritualism of the people and their piety. The spiritual fathers taught the Russian people to see heaven beyond the cupolas of their churches.

The monastics were engaged in intellectual work such as the copying and later printing of liturgical books and ascetical literature. There was an enormous respect for spiritual knowledge and theological learning, yet in the formative period before the time of Peter the Great there were only a few great intellects and theologians: Abraham of Smolensk, Stephen of Perm, Dionysius of the Trinity monastery, and a few writers such as Cyril of Tourov, Luke of Novgorod, Joseph of Volokolamsk and

Nil Sorsky. On the other hand there were far more renowned icono-graphers such as St Andrew Rublev, and among these quite a few bishops.

The mystical type of the speculative sort was not prevalent, yet the essential life of mystical contemplation is firmly linked to the name of St Sergius of Radonezh. In the heart of the primeval forest, where there was "an abundant fragrance of the pines and evergreens," he dedicated his first church to the Holy Trinity. He left behind no writings but in the history of Russian spirituality there is no greater visionary than St Sergius, who was ceaseless in contemplation of the Holy Trinity. As a teenager, he had received the blessing of a mysterious *starets* or elder for the "knowledge of spiritual realities." After his death the Orthodox Church recognized his importance and his blessing on the Russian people.

There are almost no documents from before the fourteenth century, but from that point on, the Hesychast movement penetrated Russia through figures such as Cyprian, the Metropolitan of Kiev, Nil Sorsky and Joseph of Volokolamsk. Never given to speculative analysis, this movement of silent prayer was greatly humanized in Russia and was never separated from active social and charitable work by monastics.

More and more Russian spirituality expressed itself in love for the kenotic, the suffering, self-emptying and self-giving Christ. It remained a simple, humble spirituality, full of joy and always oriented compassionately toward the poor, downtrodden and the suffering. The painter Nesterov captured this in his well-known tableau, the painting entitled, *Holy Russia*. A contemporary historian, George Fedotov, defined Russian sanctity by its "ecclesial evangelicalism." Dostoevsky also said: "Perhaps unique to the spirituality of the Russian people is their love for the image of Christ found in the Gospel, that of his merciful, suffering love."

One can see this very well, even in the beginning. The first canonized Russian saints, Boris and Gleb, have the distinctive title of "passion-bearers," innocently and freely accepting violent death without resistance. It is the image of Christ the Lamb of God, innocent and pure, offered in sacrifice. Among other types of saints, we find the holy elders and "fools for Christ," particularly popular in Russia, although rarer in other lands.

One should also mention the two founders of Russian monastic life, St Anthony and his disciple, St Theodosius of Petchersk. By his name, St Anthony was already linked to the monastic father, St Anthony the Great of Egypt, and he was of the same rigorous school of asceticism as the Egyptian monastics. Strangely enough, however, St Anthony rapidly disappeared from popular memory, which retained rather that of the luminous and gentle figure of St Theodosius, more in the Palestinian school of St Sabbas, a most humane type of asceticism, oriented toward the people and the world.

After Peter the Great, despite the damage done by the schism with the Old Believers and the synodal regime, there was a renewal in the monastic tradition. [Trans. note: Evdokimov here refers to historical periods of decline in the Russian Church, namely the upheaveal caused by the breaking off of "Old Believers" over ritual changes, their subsequent harassment, and the governmental control of the Church through the office of the Ober-Procurator.] At the end of the eighteenth century St Paisius Velichovsky came to Romania where he worked on the writings of St Nil Sorsky and established there a renewal of the Hesychast movement through the Jesus prayer and his translation into Slavonic of the *Philokalia*. The monasteries of Optina and Sarov then became spiritual as well as cultural centers. The well-known *Way of a Pilgrim* witnessed to the expansion and force of the tradition outside the walls of the monasteries in the nineteenth century.

St Seraphim of Sarov lived and thereby revived the experience of the great spiritual fathers such as Sts Macarius of Egypt, Simeon the New Theologian, and Gregory Palamas. He synthesized Russian spirituality but his white simple clothing, his Paschal joy, and his prophetic spirit witnessed to the modern era perhaps in a pre-apocalyptic way. In him one could see lived out the words of the *akathist* for his feast day: "Rejoice in the joy of the Kingdom which you have already tasted on earth."

The life of St Seraphim

St Seraphim lived from 1759-1833, a contemporary of Pushkin. When he died, Gogol was 24 and Dostoevsky was 12 years old. The course of his life appears quite simple, yet it was constantly marked by powerful signs. His birth coincided with the construction of a cathedral on which his father had worked as construction manager. Thus one could say that symbolically St Seraphim came in to the world as a radiant portion of the Temple, as one of its living icons.

In his childhood there were miraculous healings, apparitions of the Mother of God, predictions accompanying them and leading him toward the monastery of Sarov. Tall and strong, a vibrant personality and intelligent, already well instructed by assiduous reading of the Scriptures and the Fathers of the Church, possessed of a wonderful, luminous spirituality, he became a novice at the age of 19. At 28 he made his monastic vows and received the name "Seraphim," the Hebrew name of the first hierarchy of angels, literally the "flaming" or "fiery" ones. The Church sings on his feast day that he was an "earthly angel and a man of heaven." Ordained a deacon on Holy Thursday, during that Liturgy he saw Christ surrounded by the angels. As a priest he celebrated the eucharistic Liturgy every day and found in the Eucharist and in the prayer of Jesus an unalterable source of strength and joy.

After 17 years in the monastery he withdrew to the forest to lead the life of a hermit. His desire was to be alone with God. "I could hardly believe I was still living on earth, so full of joy was my soul," he would say later on. This was a less than communal joy however, since several monks tried to join him as neighboring hermits in the heart of the forest, but none were able to endure the austerity and rigor of such a life. St Seraphim shared his daily ration of bread with the forest animals who would patiently wait for him to return to his log cabin. "How do you have enough for all of them?" he was asked. "Only God knows," he replied, "I surely don't know how."

During these years of isolation and complete solitude, St Seraphim endured a frightful struggle. "The one who has chosen the desert and its silence will thereby feel constantly crucified," he would later comment. He would place himself on a large stone in the depths of the forest, praying the prayer of Jesus continually. This extraordinary spiritual exploit lasted three years, at the end of which St Seraphim became living prayer, prayer incarnate. Only at the conclusion of this fiery experience did the forces of evil finally abate, and God's peace descended upon the hermit.

One day, after having been beaten almost to death by thieves, he was visited by the Mother of God, together with the apostles Peter and John. Having healed Seraphim, the Virgin told the apostles: "He is one of us." Though healed miraculously, Seraphim remained hunchbacked for the rest of his life and had to use a cane. His hair and beard had become white. When they were arrested, Seraphim insisted on pardon for those who had beaten him, threatening to leave Sarov if this were not granted. This episode marked the end of his isolation and his return to the community. Leaving the forest, he lived for five years at the monastery but completely cloistered, with no contact beyond the minimal necessity. Finally, in obedience to the Mother of God's demand, he lessened the rigor of his solitude and opened the door of his cell. People thronged there, even to just hear his voice.

Thus after 37 years of monastic isolation, St Seraphim opened to the world and began his ministry as an elder. In this essentially charismatic ministry he manifested the gifts of a healer, a confessor, and a prophet. As a *healer* he cited the command: "Heal the sick, cast out demons," considering this charism as the expression of his priesthood. As *confessor* he would tell younger priests: "Always remember that you are only a witness and that it is God alone who acts." Taking upon himself the sins of others he would prostrate himself at the side of the penitent, begging him or her to pray to the Lord for poor Seraphim's sins. Here was the communion of saints in sin, the sense of universal guilt, that all are guilty and responsible for all. He was not at all interested in lists of faults being recited to him in confession. He saw rather the whole person, the heart, and there he searched for humility and faith. As a prophet he was constantly giving warning. It was as if he were the guardian angel of the Russian people, his prayer like a lighthouse in the darkness. To be a prophet is not just to foretell the future but it is mostly to be the messenger of God's judgments. "We are invoking God's anger upon us," he would cry out in anguish. He spoke of the times of the Anti-Christ when the crosses on the churches would be torn down, the monasteries destroyed. "It will be a sorrow such as has not been seen since the beginning of the world, the angels will not have time to gather the souls from the earth...." He foresaw economic depression; warning the people, he stopped epidemics, averted storms and predicted many of the events of the Russian revolution.

In 1831 on the eve of the feast of the Annunciation St Seraphim received his twelfth and final vision of the Mother of God. A monastic sister participated in it and later told of the apparition. The Virgin came to warn the saint: "Soon, my dear friend, you will be with us." "What joy awaits the soul when the angels come to take it," the saint would say, completely radiant and joyous for the end. To a monk saddened by his words, "Soon I will leave you," Seraphim added: "This is not the time for sadness, my friend, but for joy." New Year's Day of 1833 was a Sunday and the saint received Holy Communion and bid his farewells to all the brethren present at the Liturgy. In the evening, despite the fact that it was not yet the liturgical season for it, Seraphim could be heard singing the Paschal canon and hymns, the songs of Easter. In the morning they found him on his knees before the icon of the Mother of God called "the Joy of all joys," his hands crossed upon his chest and his eyes closed. A candle which had fallen had singed his clothing. It was the sign predicted by the saint, that his death would be announced by fire. That same morning one of the hermits saw a blazing light in the sky and told his disciple: "That is Seraphim's soul, rising to heaven."

St Seraphim as an icon of Orthodox spirituality

No one saint can ever express the fullness of the spirituality which produced him, but can only be a personalization of it, one of its rays shining forth. The spirituality of the Church engenders the saint, that is, gives birth and nurtures him, and from such an intimate parent-child relationship we can therefore recognize in the child, the saint, many of the distinctive features of the parent, here the mother, the Church which sustains him.

This is all the more justifiable in the case of St Seraphim who neither formed disciples nor was master of a school yet was a master in a much more universal sense. The radiance of his figure, his life, and his teaching thus form a living icon of the very heart of Orthodoxy. His Paschal joy, for example, was not simply a personal trait of his character but the very song and atmosphere of the Eastern Church's tradition.

The art of a spiritual father

St Seraphim above all is a *starets*, an elder, but his counsel excludes any determinism. To a merchant he predicted a fearful death, "if he did not repent and change his ways." This kind of clairvoyance does not suppress any possible future changes but sees ahead to the immanent punishment which comes when the spiritual life is ignored.

St Seraphim, a direct disciple himself of the Holy Spirit, the Paraclete, exercised a ministry of consolation. "Visit the widows and the orphans in their affliction." This affliction was the primary object of his priesthood. His actions expressing this immediately materialized the deep movement of the heart which participates in, takes upon itself the sufferings of the other person. St Seraphim could instantly discern, even in a crowd, those who were afflicted, the despairing, the oppressed. He would often console them by citing the ninth verse of the canon: "Most Holy Virgin, fill my heart with joy, you who destroy all sinful sadness." Such sadness is a sin against the Holy Spirit. In the contemporary philosophy of despair, cares define existence. But according to the spiritual masters, such cares stem from the anxiety over death on the part of one who does not know how to live already here on earth the "small resurrection," an essential gift or charism of baptism.

In greeting people in their afflictions, St Seraphim would transfuse his peace into their souls and would feed them in the image of Christ multiplying the loaves and fish. In distributing to his visitors fragments of bread, he put his tenderness and compassion into material form and symbolically reminded them of the Eucharist. This was an interiorized Eucharist, located in the heart of the relationship between a spiritual father and his children.

A miracle is not magic but the result of synergy, of cooperation, of human actions placed within the divine. This is how the saint worked. He would challenge the afflicted person, vigorously calling forth an act of faith. If such a person truly believed in God, he would believe immediately in the divine power to heal. In this case St Seraphim would say: "If you truly believe, you are already healed." Thus he brought to life the limitless powers of faith and created the situation for their manifestation. "Authentic hope," he would say, "searches for the Kingdom, and then, but only then, hope knows that everything else, all that is necessary for earthly life, without a doubt, will be given, in abundance." Miracles, therefore, are not just supernatural, extraordinary occurrences but are supernaturally natural. They belong to those who are given what they need in abundance. They are but the direct consequence of the "one thing necessary." They accompany the search for this uniquely indispensable reality, the Kingdom. Here, it seems, is a distinctive feature of Orthodox spirituality. Such a hierarchy of values informs the life of a believer that, even if life is full of miracles, these are no longer so astonishing. They are not sought after, but are received naturally, with grace, given in abundance at the moment that the Holy Spirit deems necessary. The liturgical sense protects the mystery completely and at the same time makes this remarkably familiar, intimate, as noted, "supernaturally natural." Often one is amazed at how the Orthodox search out the mysterious side in everything. It is true for them that every empirical situation is transcended by the constant awareness of God and his presence. This is precisely the liturgical and iconographical sense of existence. The icon attests to the nearness of God everywhere and at each moment. The prayer of Jesus immediately draws us to his presence. Even the tiniest fragment of God's creation bears in itself, as a cosmic icon, traces of his light.

The therapeutic understanding of salvation

St Seraphim was often seriously ill and each time he was miraculously healed by the intervention of the Mother of God. He always refused medical attention and rather begged everyone to increase their prayers for him. Healed once after three years of suffering, he began the project of constructing a chapel for the monastery infirmary. This was to show that the infirmary chapel was the sign of the fundamental action of healing. Seraphim built a visible symbol of a spiritual clinic, of healing by God, "the only healer of soul and body." He would repeat a part of the prayer before Communion: "May the Communion of your holy mysteries be neither to my judgment, nor to my condemnation, O Lord, but to the healing of soul and body. Amen." This is the *therapeutic understanding* of the sacraments in the tradition of the Church of the East. The priest who hears a confession does not look for punishments but new conditions in which the penitent will not be so tormented by sin. The prayer before confession makes this clear: "You have come to the physician. Do not leave without being healed." The Council *in Trullo* says the same: "Confessors should act as physicians, intent on finding the right remedy for each patient." Even canon law ought to be used by the bishops as "therapeutic ordinances."

In healing his friend Manturov, who was desperately ill, St Seraphim said: "By the grace given to me I treat your sickness," adding: "It is not my business to give death or life, to lead out of hell or into it, only the Lord, who listens to our prayers." Sinners are terminally ill with a disease that makes life already a hell. However, repentance and faith immediately provide the conditions for healing, leading them out of hell and to the threshold of the Kingdom. Certainly, repentance and faith are gifts of the Holy Spirit, but they require ground in which to be planted, the good soil of humility. Humility is not weakness but the greatest power, for it displaces the existential center of things from the ego to God. The great ascetics saw in humility the art of finding exactly one's place. It is precisely the attitude of the servant of the Lord and the friend of the Bridegroom, namely the Mother of God and St John the Baptist. Salvation-healing reconstitutes order, the cosmos, beauty, the harmony of all things. *Philokalia*, the Greek title of the well-known collection of ascetical writings of the Eastern Church, means "the love of the beautiful." A saint is good but is also beautiful, harmonious, in balance. The saint's human life is beautifully set out and ordered, like the liturgical services, like the architecture of the church building, like the painted icon, all of which teach the art of being "in the very likeness" of the order of the Kingdom of God.

Prayer

In the life of prayer, St Seraphim followed the ancient rule of St Pachomius the Egyptian, but above all he was the disciple of St Nil Sorsky in practicing the "prayer of the heart" or "Jesus-prayer." This prayer opens up and makes free the spaces of the heart and invites Jesus by the incessant invocation: "Lord Jesus Christ, Son of God, have mercy on me, a sinner." Thus all discursive elements are eliminated and prayer becomes, as it were, a single word, the name of Jesus. This name resounds without ceasing in the depth of the soul and in some way becomes "attached" to breathing, becoming the very breath of life, incapable of separation from either the body or the soul. This is an interiorized Liturgy, the ceaseless communion with Jesus present in his name. With Jesus come into the heart, there is the Kingdom of God in the soul at peace and it is from here that the Greek term *hesychia,* or prayer of stillness, comes.

It is in the sense of such prayer that St Seraphim responded to the question of a choice between the contemplative life and one of action: "Acquire peace within and many around you will find salvation, healing." The name of Jesus, repeated incessantly, brings his presence to a person and transforms that person into his presence. Iconographically, as the halo or nimbus shows, the luminosity of the saints' bodies is ontologically normative for them, a very quality of their being. The saints' radiance is a sign of their being of the "new creation."

Trinitarian-centered evangelism and Orthodox spirituality

St Seraphim's evangelical character, his rooting in the Gospel, underscored his historical sense and made any kind of speculative abstraction alien to him. During the first four days of the week he would read the four Gospels in their entirety. He brought the Holy Land to the forest of Sarov by giving biblical names to different paths and places in order to better follow the life and actions of Our Lord and bring the Gospel to life. However this was not the cult of the suffering humanity of Jesus. Rather than a Christocentrism, St Seraphim followed the Trinitarian-centered tradition of the Eastern Church. We find this Trinitarian balance well expressed in the prayer of the holy chrism: "O God, mark them with the seal of the pure chrism. They will bear Christ in their hearts in order to be the dwelling-place of the Trinity." Thus a person, sealed by the Holy Spirit, is a Christ-bearer (*Christophoros*) and thus the temple or abode of the Holy Trinity. In the teaching of the Fathers, Christ is the great Forerunner of the Holy Spirit. According to St Athanasius the Word, "God, the Flesh-bearer," (*sarcophoros*) has assumed flesh so that human beings would be able to receive the Holy Spirit and thus to become "Spirit-bearers" (*pneumatophoroi*). The attention given to the theology of the Holy Spirit inherent in Eastern monasticism makes St Seraphim a spiritual master in the line of Ss Simeon the New Theologian and Tikhon of Zadonsk, also prophetic types who proclaimed the joy of the age to come. The same intimacy with the Holy Spirit was at the source of St Seraphim's extreme asceticism, which was striking in its joyfulness. "Every soul crucified with Christ," he would say, "invokes the Holy Spirit: Our God, give us your peace." In the Matins service the Church sings: "Every soul is enlivened by the Holy Spirit, exalted in purity, illumined by the Trinity, in a sacred mystery."

This vivifying by the Holy Spirit is the exact meaning of the Orthodox understanding of *theosis*, being filled by the Spirit, the penetration of each human being by the energies of God. Fasting, asceticism, these are the horizontal means of purification, as the prayer to the Holy Spirit said at the start of every Orthodox service says, "Cleanse us from every impurity." Prayer, immediate communion with God, is the vertical path, the fire of the burning nearness of God. The same liturgical prayer says, "Come and abide in us." "God is a fire which enflames our hearts with perfect love for him and for our neighbor." Authentic spirituality therefore "adds fire to fire."

Joyful dying

In the Eastern Church, suffering is never cultivated for itself, for it has neither meritory or expiatory value. It is only a means of purification in order to attain joy. The eschatological atmosphere of the first centuries of Christianity, the eager waiting for the Kingdom is experienced again in St Seraphim who taught the art of "joyful dying." To a nun very much anguished by the thought of death he said: "For us to die will be a joy." The sign of the presence of the Holy Spirit is "the experience of his peace and joy, for God creates joy wherever he goes." This was further evident in the well-known greeting of St Seraphim to every person he met: "My joy, Christ is risen!" This greeting was the expression of the permanent state of his soul, a paschal, Resurrection joy that permeated everything and made it gleam with light. According to the Gospel of St John, the believer does not come to judgment, for he or she has already passed from death to eternal life. Death resides in time, which is already behind us. Before us is only the passage to life eternal which we possess now. "The one who eats my flesh has eternal life."

Prayerful theology

The patristic saying, "The theologian is one who knows how to pray" explains quite well the two meanings of the word "Orthodox." It means correct, right doctrine but also true worship or praise. Authentic theology is always a form of prayer, translating into theological terms the direct experience of God, the source of unity. This is why the Fathers would read the Bible in the same way as they consumed the Eucharist, seeking above all the presence of Christ and communion with him.

In reading the Scriptures and works of the Fathers, St Seraphim would enter the texts in a spirit of prayer, an attitude of watchfulness. He would always do his reading before an icon, just as if he were reading the daily prayer office. In speaking to a novice about St Paul's being taken up into heaven, St Seraphim immediately and visibly passed through the same experience. His head inclined, with eyes closed, he looked and listened with a profound and always new astonishment and he confided to the young monk, "If you only knew what joy awaits your soul in heaven. But if even St Paul could not find the words to express it who can say anything about it?" This is why, "if it is good to speak of God, it is even better to purify oneself before him." Theology is proclaimed but also prayed in all the liturgical services. Theology is not essentially an intellectual system but the acquisition of the spirit of the Fathers and in them the apostolic spirit. In St John, St Macarius, St Simeon, St Gregory Palamas or St Seraphim, we experience exactly the same root, the apostle.

St Seraphim's teaching on the Holy Spirit

St Seraphim often quoted the words of Scripture from Ecclesiasticus: "My child, give me your heart, and all the rest I will give you in abundance," and the complementary words of the Gospel: "Seek first the Kingdom of God, and all the rest will be given to you in abundance." These two texts reveal that the human heart for God and the divine Kingdom for the human being are correlative and that their unity is the goal of God's creation. The variant of the text of the Our Father has in the place of "Thy Kingdom come," "Thy Holy Spirit come," thus identifying the coming of the Kingdom with the coming of the Holy Spirit. We therefore are asked only to seek the "one thing necessary," the Kingdom, that is to say, *to seek the Holy Spirit*. And it is in this offering of the heart to God that the Spirit is manifest and leads one into the eternal circulation of love between the Father and the Son—this is the Kingdom. Now it is possible to understand the definition St Seraphim proposed of the goal of the Christian life, the acquisition of the gifts of the Spirit and of the Holy Spirit himself.

According to the Fathers, "God cannot constrain anyone to love him." The offering of one's heart to God is therefore the maximal expression of human freedom. The heart forms the free space, "the pastures of the heart," according to St Macarius, where the human spirit attains fullness by the breath of the Holy Spirit. The Spirit "blows where it wills," and there is created the icon of the Holy Spirit, the human heart.

For St Cyril of Alexandria, the Holy Spirit is holiness hypostasized, made personal, the fulfillment of Trinitarian love as well as that between God and man. This is why the Spirit is called "Gift." At the invocation of the Holy Spirit, the response of the Father is immediate for the essence of being gift is free grace. This is the meaning of the *epiclesis* in the Orthodox Liturgy. Yet it surpasses its eucharistic function, extends universally, to every action. In offering our hearts, we call down the Holy Spirit and receive him. The saying of the desert fathers has it thus: "Give your blood and receive the Spirit." St Seraphim brings us into this circle of fire and communicates this blessing of the Paraclete to his companions on the road to the Kingdom.

His theology of the Holy Spirit is rooted in a philosophy of history and very much connected to the meaning of our existence in time. The inherent conditions of the temporal, the possibilities of change, of evolution, growth, permit one to augment, that is, to nurture the charismatic state, to transform oneself into fire and light. For St Seraphim, the parable of the wise and foolish virgins shows that the foolish ones were "virgins." That is, they were surely quite moral beings, full of moral virtue, in fact preoccupied by morality. But their empty lamps signify the sterility of their efforts in their misunderstanding of the one thing necessary, by their running dry of the charisms, the gifts of the Holy Spirit.

St Seraphim drew attention to the frequency of Gospel images of wealth, treasure, riches and connected all of these to our eternal destiny. His was a striking statement: "Profit from the times, by exchanging temporal paper currency for the hard cash of eternity." Time is the capacity of acquiring that which brings in the Kingdom. The Book of Revelation (2:21) says: "I have given you time to repent." Repentance yields the Spirit without measure. We should understand the Spirit just like the unfaithful steward of the parable who makes use of the property of the Master (of Love) so as to make "friends in Christ," and to make grow in this world the value of communion with him.

The revelations of St Seraphim: the encounter with Motovilov

The revelations of St Seraphim bring alive in our time the experience of the desert fathers. Over against the evolution of consciousness, which has become complex and yet scattered, his teaching underscores the rapid loss of an original and normative simplicity. St Seraphim said: "The passages of Holy Scripture sound very strange to us today...Are we even able, anymore, to see God in a concrete way? We have become distanced from the primitive simplicity of Christian understanding. Under the pretext of 'enlightenment,' we are caught in the darkness of ignorance such that today we find inconceivable what the ancients found perfectly clear, enabling them to speak of the manifestations of God to human beings, realities known by all and not at all strange." This warning is most significant before reading the account of the conversation with Motovilov.

The saint's partner in this encounter was one of his closest disciples, Nicholas Motovilov, who had been healed miraculously by St Seraphim of a paralysis of his legs. The conversation took place during the winter of 1831 in the heart of the forest. St Seraphim was explaining the goal of life, the acquisition of the Holy Spirit. Motovilov asked of him a more precise description of being in this state of grace. The saint then told Motovilov to look at Father Seraphim himself. "I looked at him," Motovilov wrote, "and was seized with fear." St Seraphim appeared to him to be clothed in the sun. When asked by the saint, Motovilov asserted that he himself felt "an indescribable joy, calm and peace." To this state of the soul was joined the external phenomenon observable by the senses—the sight of dazzling light, an unusual feeling of warmth, and a beautiful, perfume-like scent. The conversation ended with these words: "It is not only for you that these things are happening but for the whole world." Thus it was a revelation of the greatest importance, a message addressed to all.

The experience here related was not an ecstasy but an anticipation of the transfiguration of the total being of a person. The participation of the senses was one of the most striking elements. Grace was experienced, coming to the senses as sweetness, joy, peace and light, all this as a foretaste of the life of the age to come. This is neither the suppression of the senses made disorderly by the Fall nor rejection of them but rather their transfiguration, their elevation beyond the normal state. St Gregory Palamas recognized the superiority of man over the angels precisely in our corporeality. The angels, pure spirits, are only messengers. We are artists and creators, both of the matter of this earth and our own bodies. "The body itself participates in sanctification."

The spiritual and the physical are integrated in the historical economy of the Incarnation and of salvation, and the Kingdom of God is manifest in anticipation in the totality of human being. The liturgical music we hear and sing, the icons we see and contemplate, the incense burned and smelled, and the cosmic material of the sacraments consumed and experienced enable us to speak of sight, hearing, smell, taste and touch, all as liturgical actions. Matter is lifted above itself to the level of meta-empirical perfection, revealing that the material of this world is neither autonomous nor neutral substance but in service of the Spirit and the vehicle of the spiritual.

Culture, which is accustomed to the icon, has learned to contemplate the glory of God alive and scintillating in the material world, to sense in this world the very flame of his reality. Ascetical purification, the "fasting of the eyes," elevates our senses, yet without ever yielding to nominalism or a disincarnated approach. Matter is the vehicle, the vessel for divine energies orients our sight toward the light of Mt. Tabor, seen in the transfigured Christ. St John of Damascus writes: "In the Transfiguration Christ appeared to his disciples as he was and in so doing, opened their eyes." St Gregory Palamas said: "Light is not just the object of vision but the very means by which we can see."

During the conversation with Motovilov, St Seraphim revealed this. He said: "Now you too have become as luminous as I am...otherwise it would not be possible for you to see me." St Gregory Palamas writes: "Those who are worthy receive grace and perceive both by their senses and intelligence that which is beyond all intellect and the senses." This is the ascetic rehabilitation of matter to its deepest levels by the resurrected flesh of Christ. In its own transcendence, the uncreated light of God is revealed to *the whole person*. The antinomy is maintained. The divine light is not material, sensible, intelligible, yet it allows itself to be contemplated by the eyes of a body which has been transfigured. God makes himself known to us who have been recapitulated and reconstituted in wholeness in Christ. This is neither the "sensible" mysticism of a sect like the Messalians nor a reduction of the fullness to intelligibility, nor a gross materialization of the spiritual but rather the communion of created human nature as a whole with the uncreated nature of God.

This is the mystery of the Eighth Day, already realized in the sacraments and experienced by the saints. As St Seraphim put it, the "breath of life" which is the Pentecost of Adam, the light of Tabor, the Pentecost of the apostles and of the sacraments, the light of the Liturgy and of the Parousia, these are all identical. It is crucial to understand this for all dimensions of spirituality. Spirituality must be rooted in the most concrete reality and fullness of the Incarnation, must take up the whole of our humanity but also the cosmos entrusted to us in the promise of the Resurrection. Such teaching accentuates the very real, that is, material reality of the Kingdom of God which is already manifest in the beauty of this world and which leads the way to and prepares all to become the heavenly Kingdom.

This is the vision of Christ surrounded by the angels and saints taking part in the heavenly Liturgy that St Seraphim was permitted to see when he was serving at the altar as a deacon. The numerous appearances to him of the Mother of God, the apostles and other saints, along with many other historical events in St Seraphim's life show very clearly that at no point was there ever merely the adaptation of the spiritual realm to human sensibility but rather the elevation of the material, physical dimension to the heavenly without its disappearance. This is precisely how theophanies or manifestations of God occur in the Bible. Thus as St Seraphim distributed the bread which remained after the visit of these heavenly beings, he was also visibly bestowing the fruits of the "new earth," the gifts of the heavenly Kingdom.

All of this sheds much light and explains the localized and concentrated presence of spiritual realities in places of pilgrimage, "holy places." This explains, as well, the communion we can have with those who are absent yet are present in their name or by some other manner, at the place of burial or in their relics. The saints have a particular connection with the earth, not entirely leaving it. They have the gift of hearing and being present where and when their names are invoked.

The name, the places they inhabited, their remains all become an *icon* of their presence. St Seraphim, recalling the words of the Gospel of St John (14:18) "I will not leave you orphans, I will come to you," would say before his death: "For you I will remain alive...come to my tomb to speak your soul to me...speak to me as though I were alive." Death and its separation thus are truly transcended.

The last message

The greatest of the monastics displayed a very easy transcendence of their own state almost as a formula or a rule. At the decisive point of his ministry, St Seraphim abandoned the extreme forms of eremetical life and of the stylite (his time of praying on the stone in the forest) and went out towards the world. Having acquired the Holy Spirit, one could perhaps even say that he had transcended monasticism. He was, in a way, no longer a monk removed from the world nor one simply living there either. As a disciple, witness, and confidant of the Holy Spirit, St Seraphim seems to have transcended both. He said to Motovilov: "As to the fact that you are a layperson and I am a monk, there is no need to dwell on this...the Lord searches for hearts full of love for him and for the neighbor...He listens to the prayers of the monastic and those of the layperson insofar as both have a faith without error, Orthodox. If they truly believe and love God from the depths of their souls...both can move mountains." Both the monastic and the layperson, having the same identity, are a sign and reference to the "wholly other," are witnesses to the "last things." Both are disciples of the Holy Spirit. Monastics leave the world in order to transcend every state of life, every static form and so doing to "reach maturity in Christ." The layperson is called as well to transcendence of his or her situation in an "interiorized monasticism," which is the equivalence of the three monastic vows. These vows are really a great charter of human freedom. Poverty liberates us from the obsession to acquire things. It is the baptismal metamorphosis into the new creature in Christ. Chastity frees us from imprisonment by the flesh. It is the marriage mystery of the love of God. Obedience liberates us from the captivity of the ego's idolatry, our worship of ourselves. It is the new reality of being a child of the heavenly Father. Both the professed monastic and the ordinary baptized Christian must follow the three parts of the

Lord's Prayer: obedience solely to the will of the Father, the poverty of one whose only hunger is for the supersubtantial bread of the Eucharist, and finally the chastity which purifies us from the Evil One.

The Gospel account of the three temptations of the Lord in the desert emphasizes this theme. Satan advances three infallible solutions to human destiny: a three-fold suppression of human freedom, a three-fold enslavement of humanity by miracles, magic and unique power. In his divine response, Christ, on the other hand, offers our three-fold liberation. If Constantine's empire made as its secret substance these three temptations, monasticism was clearly founded upon the three responses of Christ restated in the three monastic vows. At least such was the intent of the first charismatic Christians before the organization of the multitudes under monastic institutions and rules. Those later on who knew how to make of monastic law a grace were responding to the authentic grandeur of monastic life. Beyond the institution, beyond every historical deformation of this life, in every monastic the essence of this vocation was kept alive. A layperson, a member of the universal priesthood insofar as one is an interiorized monastic, is also a person royally, absolutely free and totally consecrated in his or her priesthood to the service of the Lord and of the Church. Here perhaps we have the essential message of St Seraphim and of the entire Eastern tradition as well for the person in the modern age: to recover the freedom of being an adult and yet a child of God, to become a sign of the Kingdom and to walk joyfully in the light of Christ's coming again.

St John of Kronstadt

On the eve of the Russian Revolution the brilliant figure of Father, now saint, John of Kronstadt (1829-1908) emerged. The many healings he did crossed even the frontiers of Russia. Non-Orthodox and Muslims wrote to Father John, asking his prayers and receiving the healing they prayed for. His spirituality was much rooted in the Prayer of Jesus: "To resist constant temptations it is necessary to keep the prayer of Jesus in one's heart," he would say.

Like the great liturgical theologian of the fourteenth century, Nicholas Cabasilas, also a married cleric, Father John called his principal writing, *My Life in Christ*, Cabasilas calling his own volume, *The Life in Jesus Christ*. He saw the Eucharist as the source of these extraordinary charisms for healing. "I would die if I could not celebrate the Liturgy...the Love which is incommensurable is revealed there...You are completely there, Lord. We see you, touch you, experience you here."

A spiritual inheritor of St Seraphim of Sarov, Father John incarnated the words of St Paul: "It is not I who live but Christ who lives in me." His intercession made him priest for all of Russia on the eve of her greatest torment, a prophetic sign, a vessel of the gifts of the Holy Spirit, a light to illumine a new form of holiness adapted to this age by its simplicity, transparency and astonishing power. He was all fire, filled with Pentecostal fire, a shining witness to Love crucified for every human being.

The miracle

Every miracle witnesses to the existence of God and his active presence in the world. The one who, under the influence of "demythologization," speaks of the impossibility of miracles in this age of technology accepts at least the reality of prayer. Prayer, the most powerful form of faith, is at the same time the most enigmatic form, a "mystery" and a perpetual miracle.

God has created the world which runs according to its laws, those of nature established and set up by the Creator. Is not a miracle a fact which contradicts the laws or which appears as a most unusual and unjustified occurrence? "You set the earth upon its foundations, unshakable for ages of ages" (Ps 103:5). But if the world God created is a world in becoming, it is therefore not static but dynamic. God the Creator allowed room for God the Savior who said: "My Father is still working and I too am working." Human beings, superior beings, are created *free*. God enters into relations with humankind, opens us to the energies of his grace but also is open creatively to the cosmic body of the universe. This is why alongside the determinism of necessity and of natural causality there is placed the *spiritual causality of the free creation*.

Does the miracle suppress natural causality with its unshakable chain of cause and effect? The medicine which a physician gives to a sick person, the advice of a psychiatrist, the intervention of the surgeon all stop the natural chain of cause and effect in an illness which quite naturally brings death. All of these introduce a new cause whose effect is sufficiently powerful enough to dominate and change the course of the illness and lead to healing. *Ex nihilo nil fit.* Every violence against the laws of nature is an act *ex nihilo* and unthinkable. But every healing of a purely medical sort and not at all a miracle is already an act where the creative causality of a wholly new situation, and thus freedom, dominates and manifests power of modifying the mechanical causality and hence natural necessity.

One who believes is able to do the same by a spiritual remedy, that of his prayer and intercession and this is indeed a miracle. In both cases we have inspected the creative causality which acts upon nature by introducing a new cause: a remedy or energy, in this case now, of grace. It is a transfinalization which changes the preceding finality and points everything toward a new end. The natural laws are not themselves abolished but reset, one is tempted to say "accomplished," just as Christ's accomplishing of the law was a fulfillment to the extent that the law became something else, namely grace.

The miracle is not supernatural nor is it anti-natural, rather it is supernaturally natural. The world is not a pure machine, the clock of the Deists and the material of the materialist. It is a living organism composed both of flesh and spirit, where everything can become carnal, even the spirit, and where everything can become spiritual, even the flesh. With regard to their power, miracles can proceed from opposite sources: "You will be able to do things greater than I have done," and at the opposite pole, "The impious will appear with all sorts of miracles, signs and prodigious lies...." As master of the cosmos, man can show forth the power of being a prophet of God, the demonic force of a sorcerer and quite simply the art of a physician who shows a creative genius of the human spirit. This is why every miracle demands a spirit of discernment. This is not superstition which confuses the causes, nor is it unhealthy curiosity. A true miracle is never an argument which tries to convert another, violating freedom of conscience. In its coming into being, the world has innumerable possibilities. God conspires to that which is the best but it is never imposed and must be realized freely. This is the meaning of the cross and of crucified Love, themselves not at all spectacular. But the one who accepts them receives the power of faith which can move mountains: "Give your blood and receive the Spirit."

Gratia naturam non tollit sed perfecit. Grace does not remove nature but perfects it. The miracles done by Christ were always out of compassion and were a response to faith, never acts of violence upon the world or human conscience. For one who is superstitious the laws of nature simply do not exist. On the contrary for one who is wise and denies miracles, such a one does not understand nature realistically, scientifically, nature whose mysterious side confounds all great minds.

Christ performed his miracles as the perfect Man. These only took place by a human power transfigured by God and thus belong to that dimension hidden even to nature herself. Man is capable of acting through science or by spiritual force or by the two together in the struggle against sin, suffering and death. Christ's humanity was deified, that is, full of God. The humanity of a saint is likewise full of God by the all-Holy Spirit. Every believer is a *thaumaturgos,* a "miracle-worker," everyone that is, who possesses the power of his own spirit illumined above nature and thus saves it.

Conclusion: holiness today

In our time when we speak of "holiness," a kind of a psychological barrier goes up. Immediately one thinks of the former giants, hermits and stylites, those hidden away in their cave-cells or perched upon their columns, so that such "illuminated ones," those "equal to the angels," seem to no longer be connected to this world. Holiness appears to be out of date, from an age that has long since passed and now seems alien to the discontinuous forms and syncopated rhythms of modern life. A stylite today would not arouse curiosity but would provoke the question of the very purpose of such a feat. Today a saint seems to be nothing more than a kind of yogi, or put more crassly, one who is sick, maladjusted, in any case of no use to us.

The same attitude would exile holiness to the cloister, far from human life, as a useless, cumbersome object, good only for an historical museum. Even within institutionalized, ecclesial religious life, the very thought of striving for sanctity is boring to sincere people. They are bored with archaic ceremonies and services, bored with empty sermons preached in a verbally inflated style, bored with the blaring of hollow and meaningless childish songs, bored with a community closed in upon itself, the key to its liberation hopelessly lost. Such a domesticated, trivialized and democratized religious existence barely conceals its most unattractive features. The intellectual content of such a religious life is terribly low, simplistic and full of unwanted apologetics. Such religiosity merely reinforces those hostile or indifferent to it. Under careful scrutiny it is clear that these religious forms, by their metaphysical indigence and very limited perspective, only function to make religion appear irrelevant and outdated, an immanence inverted upon itself, empty of any real substance.

History teaches by handing down various forms of witness. Formerly the witness of the martyrs was passed down through monastic life. This preserved the value of the witness indefinitely, however the crisis of our time has made us particularly open to a spirituality rooted in the universal baptismal priesthood of the laity. The witness to the Christian faith in modern times calls for the universal vocation of interiorized monasticism, and this determines the forms that holiness will take.

According to the great masters of the spiritual life, the monastic is only one who "wants to be saved," one who "intends to follow the life of the Gospel," one who "seeks the one thing necessary," and who "does violence" to his own will and preferences. This describes perfectly the situation of every Christian, every layperson today. Both the monastic and the layperson are a sign referring to the "wholly other." St Tikhon wrote to the ecclesiastical authorities, his own abbot in fact: "Do not be in a hurry to make too many monks. The black monastic habit itself does not save anyone. The one who wears the white habit, that is, ordinary clothes and who has the spirit of obedience, humility and purity of heart, such a person is a true monastic, one of interiorized monasticism." [Trans. note: In Russian, the expression is "untonsured" (*nepostrizhenniy*) monasticism.]

Monasticism is centered on the "last things" and by this "eschatological maximalism," in former times, transformed the world. Today it makes its appeal to all, to the laity as well as to monastics and offers a universal vocation. Everyone, celibate or married, can find the personal equivalent of the three vows of poverty, chastity and obedience. This vocation is hardly the expression of mystical romanticism but obedience to the direct and realistic meaning of the Gospel. It is not just for great saints and extraordinary chosen ones. Our faith is able to work miracles and God's call, whose power is accomplished in our weakness, is addressed to me and to each of us. Kierkegaard saw this perceptively: "It is necessary to read the Bible just as a young lover reads a letter from the beloved. It is written *for me*." To become the "new person in Christ," that is, a saint, depends on the immediate, firm decision of our spirit and of our faith which says "Yes!" but which then simply, humbly and joyfully follows Christ. Then the flowers will bloom and miracles occur very easily in our world.

Throughout the tradition of the Fathers of the Church, it is possible to delineate the characteristics of a certain "type" of Christian, this layperson who responds to his or her appropriate form of holiness. This is above all a person of prayer, a liturgical being, the person of the *Trisagion* or "Thrice-Holy Hymn," the one of whom the psalmist says: "I will sing to my God as long as I live." Abba Anthony spoke of just such a person of holiness who worked in his profession as a physician. He gave to the poor all that he had that exceeded his needs and every day said the *Trisagion* together with all the angels who thus constantly praise God. He practiced medicine therefore as a form of his universal priesthood, as a lay "priest."

In Marxist countries, under tragic situations of persecution, more than anything else the Church taught people how to pray, how to participate in the combat of silent witness, how to "listen to the Word's silence" and thus to give a witness more powerful than any word of compromise. The Church encouraged Christians in such contexts to become living temples of God, to make of their lives a Liturgy, to present to others who have no faith a face radiant with liturgical joy...In such a climate of silence and of martyrdom an astonishing prayer, a splendid doxology circulated among believers, appealing to them to "console the Consoler" by their surrender and love. The prayer further says: "Forgive them all, the thieves and the Samaritans, those who fall on the roadside and the priests who pass by without stopping, all who are our neighbors: the executioners and their victims, those who murder and those who are murdered, those who rebel against you and those who prostrate themselves before your love. Take all to yourself, Holy and Righteous Father...."

During the Liturgy, the bishop, when presiding, receives the prayers and gifts of the faithful and carries these offerings to the Father, pronouncing the *epiclesis*, asking for the descent of the Holy Spirit upon all. Yet every believer in the world makes this same request perpetually, making every bit of this world holy, building up the peace of which the Gospel speaks. Following the liturgical litanies, the prayer of every Christian brings this peace to the coming day, to the earth and all that is in it, to the struggles of every person. In the immense cathedral which is God's universe, each human being as a priest in his or her life, whether a worker or a scientist or scholar, makes of everything in human life an offering, a doxology, a song of praise.

During the vigil service on Pascha night, every one of the faithful is an eyewitness of the resurrection of Christ. Hence each layperson is also an "apostolic being" in his or her own way. For the great spiritual teachers, such a Christian is responding to the final words of the Gospel of St Mark, treading serpents underfoot, healing every sickness, moving mountains, bringing the dead back to life if such is the will of God. For St Isaac the Syrian this person has recollected an attitude of silence, of humility, but is also suffused with passionate tenderness. St John Climacus would say that one should love God as one loves his or her spouse and then to extend this love toward all of creation, discerning everywhere the presence of God, to realize that one cannot but see the wisdom of God in the apparent absurdity of history, which then becomes light, revelation, and prophecy.

Marveling then at the existence of God—"the world is full of the Trinity"—a believer is something of a fool in the sense in which St Paul spoke of foolishness, the paradoxical foolishness of the "fools for Christ," the only thing capable of breaking the serious, ponderous religious character of doctrine.

A layperson is one whose faith frees him from the greatest fears of our century, the fear of the nuclear war, of cancer, of communism and of death. Such faith is marked by a perpetual love of the world and the ultimate following of the Lord even to his descent into hell, for it is only in the depths of hell that a shining, joyous hope is able to be born and to act.

In the grandeur of her confessors and martyrs, in the royal dignity of each believer, Christianity is messianic, revolutionary, explosive. In the kingdom of Caesar we must seek and find what cannot be found there, the Kingdom of God. This command rightly signifies that we must transform the world, change it into the icon of Christ. To change the world is to give it what it does not possess. (For this reason it is still the world.) It will be transfigured by becoming something else, the Kingdom of God.

The Gospel's basic appeal invites us to that Christian violence which is the only means of bringing in the Kingdom. To be a true layperson, a believer, is to be the one who by his or her entire life, by that which is already present in oneself, announces the One who is coming; to be the one who, according to St Gregory of Nyssa, is full of "sober enthusiasm," calling to all who pass by: "Come and drink"; the one who St John Climacus describes winged in joyfulness: "Your love has wounded my soul and my heart cannot endure your fire, I come to you singing...."

One of the sure signs of the coming of the Kingdom is the unity of the Christian world. In its waiting for the final fulfillment, hope, the great Christian hope, comes to life. The prayer of the Churches rises to form and to pronounce the ecumenical *epiclesis*, to invoke the Holy Spirit and his descent upon the possible miracle of unity. It is the ardent desire and the prayer of all. The world's destiny depends on the Father's response to this prayer, but it is also depends on the transparency of our sincerity, on the purity of our hearts, *on our holiness*. St Peter says: "How many do not become saints to hasten the day of the Lord...."

Jesus Christ, by the complete gift of himself, has revealed the perfect priesthood. Himself the image of all perfection, he is the unique Bishop, the supreme Pastor, also the unique Believer, the unique Saint. This is why his high priestly prayer bears the desire of all the saints, to glorify the Holy Trinity with only one heart and soul and to reunite all in the one, single chalice.

The Father, the Lover of man, waits for us to share the joy of which there is no greater in the world, the joy which already has begun the feast of the Kingdom.

6

PANAGION AND PANAGIA: THE HOLY SPIRIT AND THE MOTHER OF GOD[1]

The unique Paraclete

The Holy Spirit descends on the world but only reveals himself in his gifts and charisms. His images are blurred and fleeting: a breath, a flame, a perfume, anointing, a dove, the burning bush. St Simeon the New Theologian put it this way: "No matter how much your name is desired and constantly proclaimed, no one knows what it is."

The Holy Spirit, however, in all his manifestations is always a movement "towards Jesus," so that Christ is revealed and made present. The Spirit's presence is hidden in the Son as the breath and the voice which retreat before the Word, which is made audible by them. If the Son is the image of the Father, and the Holy Spirit is the image of the Son, the Spirit, so the Fathers tell us, is the only one who does not have his image in another Person of the Trinity. The Spirit is essentially mysterious, hidden, incapable of being seen. He is the second Paraclete.

Inseparable and distinct

The two Paracletes show us that the Church is founded both upon the Eucharist and Pentecost. The Word and the Spirit, the "two hands of the Father," are inseparable yet ineffably distinct. The Spirit is not

---

[1] "Panagion and Panagia: The Holy Spirit and the Mother of God," in *La nouveauté de 'Esprit: Études de Spiritualité*, (Bégrolles: Abbaye de Bellefontaine, 1977), pp. 253-278. Originally published in *Bulletin de la Société Français d'Études Mariales* (Paris: P. Lethielleux, 1970), pp. 59-71.

subordinate to the Son, he is not just a function of the Word. He is "another Advocate." Fr Hans Urs von Balthasar says it so well: "He [the Spirit] is the Unknown beyond the Word."

The Fathers saw in these two economies reciprocity and mutual service, but Pentecost is not a simple consequence of the Incarnation. It has a value in itself, for it is the second action of the Father. The Father first sends the Son, and then he sends the Holy Spirit. His mission accomplished, Christ returns to the Father so that the Holy Spirit can descend in Person. *Paraklitos*—"the one who is called alongside," the one who keeps himself "near us," as our defender, advocate and witness, he "consoles" us in the visible absence of Christ.

Pentecost thus appears as the culmination of the Trinitarian economy of salvation. Following the Fathers, one could even say that Christ is the "great Forerunner" of the Holy Spirit. St Athanasius wrote: "The Word assumed flesh in order for us to receive the Holy Spirit." God put on flesh so that man could put on the Spirit. For St Simeon the New Theologian: "Such was the aim and destination of the entire work of our salvation, that believers receive the Holy Spirit." Nicholas Cabasilas put it this way: "What is the result, the consequence of Christ's work?...It is nothing but the descent of the Holy Spirit upon the Church." The Lord himself said: "It is better for you that I go...I will pray the Father and he will give you another Paraclete." Thus Christ's ascension is the *epiclesis* par excellence, In response to the Son's supplication, the Father sends the Spirit and unleashes Pentecost. Without diminishing the mission of Christ in the least, the central place of Christology in the work of salvation, the vision of the Fathers defines the order of the events and shows that both the Son and the Spirit each have their own glory.

The interiorized presence of Christ and the Three Lordships

During Christ's earthly mission, the relationship of humanity to the Holy Spirit occurred only through Christ himself. On the other hand, after Pentecost, the relationship with Christ is made possible by and in the Holy Spirit. Pentecost returns to the world the interiorized presence of Christ and reveals him now, not in front of but beyond his disciples. "On that day [Pentecost] you will know that I am in you." This interiorized presence is shown precisely by the Holy Spirit. St Paul says, "The love of God is poured out in our hearts by the Holy Spirit" (Rom 5:5). It is by the Spirit that we are able to say: "Abba, Father," and pronounce the name of Jesus. Thus Pentecost opens up the history of the Church. The Acts of the Apostles is a veritable Gospel of the Spirit inaugurating the *Parousia*, Christ's coming again, and anticipating the Kingdom. He, the Spirit, makes us "sons in the Son," and in the Son we find the Father.

"We are transformed," St Paul writes, "by the action of the Lord, which is the Spirit" (2 Cor 3:18). The Spirit is called "Lord," the very same title as Christ. Alongside the Lordship of Christ there is the Lordship of the Spirit. A variant of the Lord's Prayer has, in place of "Thy kingdom come," "Thy Holy Spirit come." This identification of the Spirit with the Kingdom, made frequently by the Fathers, indicates the last action of salvation, the return to the Father and his supreme lordship: the Son "will return the Kingdom to God the Father." In this progression of events, the Holy Spirit is the great Forerunner or Precursor of the Father, of his revelation at the threshold of the Kingdom.

Panagion

The Spirit is "completely holy," not by appropriation, but by his very nature. If each of the Divine Persons is holy, St Cyril of Alexandria points out, the Spirit is holiness itself, the very holiness of God. For St Basil, "Holiness is the essential element of his nature," the special character of the Holy Spirit is the very quality of divine holiness. Thus for the Fathers, the Spirit is holiness hypostasized, holiness personified. This is why the Fathers distinguish between the gift, grace and the Giver of grace. It is this character of the Giver that conditions the Church's prayer, the *epiclesis*, the call for his personal coming. This is also why the *epiclesis* is always wondrously answered, for the Spirit is both the Giver and the Gift, by his very nature. God hears all prayers without guarantee of their fulfillment, all except this call for the coming down of the Spirit. The Lord said: "If you know how to give good things to your children, how much more will your heavenly Father give the Holy Spirit to those who ask him for this" (Lk 11:13). To refuse such a request would be to deny the very nature of the Giver.

St Cyril of Alexandria insisted on the personal presence of the Holy Spirit in the soul sanctified by him: "It is not only his grace but we also possess the Spirit who dwells in us." The prayer addressed to the Spirit: "O heavenly King, the Comforter, the Spirit of truth," used in the Orthodox Church, further begs: "Come and abide in us." In the Lord's Prayer, "Thy Kingdom come," Evagrius of Pontus explains, "the Kingdom of God, this is the Holy Spirit and we pray the Father that he will make the Spirit descend upon us." In this sense, to "seek the Kingdom of God," means to seek the Holy Spirit as the one thing necessary and this is why, according to St Seraphim of Sarov, the goal of the Christian life is the acquisition of the Holy Spirit. To see is to find. This is true for all of the scriptures and all of Christianity.

St Irenaeus of Lyons said, "Where the Holy Spirit is, there is the Church," and it is here that we find the meaning of the assertion in the Gospel that the sin of blasphemy against the Holy Spirit cannot be forgiven. It would be a contradiction of the very economy of salvation, for the Holy Spirit is himself the Giver of all the Trinitarian energies which deify and actualize salvation.

The Spirit, the interior reality of the human being

The Spirit accomplished the work of Christ in becoming the inner reality of the human being. Because of the Fall, the action of God had become external to human nature. The Spirit would touch the prophets of the Old Testament for the brief time of their inspiration, but then would leave them. At the Epiphany, the Spirit descended upon the humanity of Jesus and rested upon him. On the day of Pentecost the Spirit descended upon the world in Person and became active within human nature, as an internal reality. In sanctifying us, the Holy Spirit gives to us something of his own nature. The Spirit becomes a co-subject of our life in Christ, closer to us than we are to ourselves. The Dove which rested upon the Son now rests upon each of us as a "son in the Son." This is a return to what St John of Damascus calls the "normative state of nature, that which is its real existence." The Church's prayer during the Sunday Office sings, "All of creation is renewed by the Holy Spirit, returned to its original state." "Every soul is enlivened by the Holy Spirit," made dynamic, alive in every sense.

"Unless one is born again of water and the Spirit he cannot enter the Kingdom of God" (Jn 3:5). According to Dionysius the Areopagite, the baptismal font is a "womb" by which we become children of God. In the "second birth" spoken of by the Gospel of St John, we are restored to the Father as his children. Here in such images we can see the idea of the Holy Spirit's bringing us to birth.

St Basil insists that the Spirit is the source of communion, above all, it is the communion of the Divine Persons in their one nature, and it is by "the light of this Trinitarian unity that the Holy Spirit illumines each soul." "Since Pentecost," says Origen, "the Church is filled with the Holy Trinity." On the Sunday after Pentecost, the Orthodox Church celebrates the feast of All Saints, known or unknown, those of the past as well as those of the future. The Church, full of the Trinity, is fulfilled in the Church filled of saints, of *pneumatophores*, Spirit-filled beings "united in the communion of the one Spirit." The eucharistic prayer or *anaphora* of the Eastern Church is addressed to the Father in order that the Holy Spirit might reveal Christ and in him the plenitude, the fullness of the "Three Unique Persons" of the Trinity. The eucharistic *epiclesis*, the calling down of the Holy Spirit upon the eucharistic gifts and upon the assembly of the faithful, teaches that vertical love, the love of God, is constitutive of the human being, just as is the horizontal love, the "sacrament of the brother." The Church of the end-time offers to the hungry neither the "ideological stones" of systems nor the "theological stones" of textbooks, but as Origen again puts it, "the bread of the angels." "The heart of the brother or sister offers pure food," heavenly, divine food. In its prophetic mission, the Church initiates dialogue with all people in the light of the "metastasis of existence," and the "eschatological earthquake of the end," in St Gregory the Theologian's forceful expression.

Hypostatic maternity, or the Holy Spirit's birth-giving function

The Greek Fathers reject every dyadic formulation and affirm rather, relationships that are always Trinitarian, the *threefold* character and action of the Trinity both internally and externally (*ad intra, ad extra*). The Eastern formula *per Filium*, "through the Son," with the Creed's expression that the Holy Spirit, is "worshipped and glorified *with* the Father and the Son," places the procession of the Spirit in the light of the participation of the Son.

The monarchy of the Father signifies that he is the subject of Trinitarian revelation, for as Source and Principle of divine life, he, the Father, assures the unity, consubstantiality and perfect equality of the Three Divine Persons. This does not concern only the relationship between the Father and one of the other two Persons, but always, explicitly or implicitly, it has to do with the relationship of the One who reveals himself with the other two, of those who reveal him, always in a triple or threefold unity. In this perspective the formula *per Filium* signifies that the Latin Church's *Filioque* cannot be Orthodox except with the corresponding formula *Spirituque*.

The meaning of these two formulas is in the affirmation that each Person of the Trinity should be able to be contemplated simultaneously in relationship to the other two Persons. The formula *per Filium* signifies that the Spirit proceeds from the one Principle who is the Father but that the Son is not alien to or removed from this procession insofar as the relationships are always threefold. The corresponding formula, *by the Spirit*, has the same meaning, the Trinitarian repercussion of every hypostatic action, of the action of each Person.

Thus the Son, in his generation, receives from the Father the Holy Spirit, from who he is eternally inseparable. He is born of the Father and the Spirit: *ex Patre Spirituque*. Likewise, the Spirit proceeds from the Father and rests upon the Son, which corresponds to *per Filium* and to *ex Patre Filioque*. The Father begets the Son with the *participation* or presence of the Spirit, and the Father breathes the Spirit with the *participation* or the presence of the Son. This reciprocal, Trinitarian participation excludes any dyadic or twofold unity in the divine nature. The Greek Fathers strongly affirm the innascibility, the generation and the procession as strictly *hypostatic* actions, actions of the Persons.

In Semitic languages the Spirit (*ruach*) has two genders. It can be feminine, as one sees in the Letter to the Hebrews or in the homilies of the Syrian writer, Aphraate. None of these texts introduce a feminine principle into the heart of the Trinity, but they designate that which corresponds in God to the feminine aspect of the image of God in humanity, that image being both masculine and feminine together. In Andrei Rublev's famous and admirable icon of the Trinity, the angel who represents the Holy Spirit has in character, profile, and coloring something of the ineffable grace and delicacy that we might call the beauty of the feminine. This aspect is reflected very mysteriously in the manifestations of the Spirit.

In the intra-divine life, the Holy Spirit reveals the Son to the Father. His presence in the eternal nativity of the Word conditions his function in the economy of salvation, where he manifests visibly the "birth-giving," or generative function. Thus, in the Creed, Christ is "born of the Holy Spirit and the Virgin Mary." The descent of the Spirit upon the Theotokos made her able to conceive Christ. It is the Spirit who engenders, gives birth to Jesus in the hearts of all the baptized. At the Epiphany, the Spirit descended on the Son in the form of a dove, at the moment when the Father said to the Son: "Today, I have engendered, have begotten you." It is this presence or participation in which the Spirit is involved. The breath of giving birth, in the expression of Fr Sergius Bulgakov, is the Spirit's "hypostatic maternity." This is why the virginal maternity of the Theotokos, according to Tradition, is a figure of the Holy Spirit, the Advocate.

The Meaning of the Assumption for Jung

This is the theme which the great psychologist Jung examined in depth in his remarkable study, *The Response to Job*. There he analyzed the evolution of the idea of God in human religious consciousness. The terrifying Yahweh-God's almost monstrous omnipotence crushes Job and his revolt impels the humanization of God, the transformation of Yahweh into the God-Man. Except in God the Trinity, it is not possible that the Lamb immolated from the foundation of the world is the sign of the eternal nativity or birth in sacrificial love. The Word is already there in the struggle of Job, for on the cross he will be abandoned by the Father. This humanizing of God in the Incarnation is articulated mariologically, that is, through the person of the Mother of God. The Catholic dogma of the Assumption is, for Jung, the response to Job. The Theotokos is the predestined location of *Sophia*, the eternal, not feminine, yet virginal and at the same time maternal, Wisdom of

God. The Virgin holding the child Jesus in her arms reveals the divine philanthropy, God's love for mankind. Finally, Job has found his defender, advocate and witness in the heavens. He has found the Paraclete who has made Mary the Mother of God, source of the energies of maternal protection. The Assumption makes the Theotokos eternal in the bosom of the Trinity as a living icon of the philanthropy of the Father. This theme of paternity, or fatherhood, is important for understanding the feminine ministry in the light of the archetype which is the Theotokos, the New Eve, and her role in the life of the Church.

Theandric (Divine-human) motherhood, a figure of Divine Fatherhood

"I believe in God, the Father almighty," says the Creed. God's fatherhood shapes his relationship with man who is his child. Man is created in the image of God, his fatherhood is projected into man, but there is nothing in the masculine side of humanity that can reproduce spontaneously the religious category of fatherhood, there is no paternal instinct equivalent to that of the feminine maternal. An ancient liturgical text, a *Dogmatikon*, expresses the motherhood of the Theotokos in the light, one could say even the image, of divine fatherhood: "You have given birth to the Son without a father, the Son whom the Father begot before the ages without a mother." The analogy underscored in the text is rich in meaning. *The motherhood of the Virgin is a human figure of God's fatherhood.* If fatherhood is the expressive category of divine life, motherhood is the religious category par excellence of human life. The feminine soul is more sensible to the spiritual, closer to the source, to its genesis. This is why the Bible presents woman as the epitome of human receptivity to the spiritual. Even the Fall was conditioned by woman not as the "weaker sex," but as a being more open and receptive to suggestions without discerning whence they came. However the promise of salvation was given to the woman, to Eve: she is the New Eve, Mary, who receives the Annunciation. It is to a woman, Mary Magdalene, that the risen Christ first appeared. It is a woman clothed in the Sun who symbolizes the Church and the heavenly City in the Book of Revelation. It is the image of the Bride and the Spouse whom God chose to express his love for mankind, and the conjugal nature of this communion with humanity. And most decisively, the Incarnation is accomplished in Mary's feminine being. She gives to the Son of God her flesh and blood. And there are many other ways and forms in which Christianity takes on the maternal image. Near the walls of Jerusalem Jesus laments, "How many times I have wished to gather your children as a hen gathers her chicks under her wings!" St Paul employs the same image in speaking of the goal of his pastoral ministry: "I suffer all the labor pains of your birth so that Christ may be born in you." In the tradition of the Eastern Church, the essential charism of the priesthhood is "maternal tenderness." One finds the same theme in the spiritual fathers and mothers in the *Sayings of the Desert Fathers*. Abba Poemen expressed it when he said, "When I see a brother overcome with sleep during the vigils, I place his head on my knees and let him rest there."

If in history woman is a being considered inferior to man, in the charismatic dimension of the economy of salvation, men and women are perfectly equal. Women are not the Fathers of the Church, they are spiritual mothers, just as the spiritual fathers of the desert and certain women are given the title: "equal-to-the-apostles" for their proclamation of the Gospel. *The Teaching of the Twelve Apostles* gives this idea precision in a most significant way. "The deacon has the place of Christ, and you must love him. The deaconesses should be honored, for they have the place of the Holy Spirit." This affirmation synthesizes the tradition of the Church. Man is ontologically connected to the Word, woman to the Holy Spirit. This is why in the symbolism of the liturgical assembly woman is called the *altar* and represents prayer. Woman is the *orant*, the one who prays, the image of the soul in adoration, the human being becoming prayer, the complete and pure offering of oneself (just as the image of the Virgin *Orant* in the apse of the church.) She is the sign of the Spirit, who in the account of creation, "hovers" over the surface of the world. By her prayer-being, woman hovers over life with her maternal protection. She takes life into her hands and raises it to God.

The Eastern Church tradition never has conferred upon the Theotokos the dignity of priesthood. If on certain icons she enfolds the world with an *omophorion* (the bishop's liturgical stole) over the world, this is not a sign of episcopal power but the charism of her protection, as in the feast of her maternal protection, in Slavonic, *Pokrov*. Sacramental priesthood is not among the charisms or spiritual gifts of woman, for her archetype, the Theotokos, is the head and expression of the new humanity and is above the priest and every hierarchical order. She is "more honorable than the cherubim, more glorious beyond compare than the seraphim," as we hear in the Eastern Church's principal hymn to the Theotokos.

In Heraclitus one finds an image of astonishing depth, that of the bow and the lyre. The Greek word *bios* means both life and the bow, whose arrows signify death. The bow is a cord under tension. The bow of many strings, sublimated one might say, becomes a lyre. Thus in place of the death-bearing arrows, the bow become a lyre brings forth music, harmony, beauty. The masculine instinct for destruction, "the father of war" can be brought into concord, harmony, transformed by the feminine, the "mother of life," given the instinct for life, for a constructive and positive cultural existence. Man limits his being, makes of the cosmos the external projection of his body, fills it with his accomplishments and technical power. But woman, "the glory of man," according to St Paul, is like a mirror which reflects the face of man, revealing him to himself and thus correcting his tendencies. She is a "helper" (Gen 2:18). She assists man in deciphering intuitively his destiny, his dignity and his truth. St Peter's words, (1 Pet 3:4) define this essential charism or gift of woman, to bring to birth the hidden man in the heart, *homo cordis absconditus*. Over against the fragmentation of human life by science and technology, the relationship of woman to the Holy Spirit challenges men to pose the question of truth about themselves. It challenges them to stop at the edge of the abyss and to prevent the destruction of history and humankind. Man as warrior and engineer of the universe dehumanizes the world. Woman on the other hand, watches over every form of human life as if it were her own child.

But woman will not accomplish her task unless she accepts the ministry of the "wise virgins" of the Gospel parable, whose lamps were filled with the gifts of the Holy Spirit. If she does, then *gratia plena*, "full of grace," she will follow the Mother of God and become the "great seductress," in Kierkegaard's sense.

An astonishing prayer, a marvelous doxology inspired by women circulated among believers in Soviet Russia. It spoke of "consoling the Consoler," the Holy Spirit, by our surrender and love: "Forgive them all, bless them all, the robbers and the good Samaritans, those who fall along the way and even the priests who pass them by, all who are our neighbors: the executioners and their victims, the murderers and those who are murdered, those who rebel against you and those who prostrate themselves before your love. Take all of us to yourself, just and holy Father!"

In a church in the north of Russia, a fresco from the twelfth century represents St George as usual, on his horse. But he has neither armor nor his lance and the dragon is not slain by him. Rather, a queen, who represents both the Theotokos and the Church, holds the dragon on a small leash, and the dragon follows her, in quite a docile fashion. How relevant this vision is to us. Evil is not destroyed by a man but is converted by a woman.

Mariology

Mariology is a chapter within Christology, but one without which the latter would not be accomplished. On the other hand, the pneumatological accent of Mariology links it to ecclesiology. The teaching of the icons is most important here. Nearly all the icons of the Virgin represent her with the child Jesus. What we see in this is that such an icon is not so much one of Mary but of the Incarnation and of the most intimate communion between the divine hypostasis of the child Jesus and the human hypostasis of his Mother, who gave him her own human flesh. The icon composition called *Eleousa*, "the Virgin of Tenderness." reveals the ultimate tenderness of this communion between God and mankind. Another icon, called *Hodigitria*, "She who points the way," presents Mary, whose right hand points to the Savior, representing thus the Christological dogma.

The dogmatic precision of the subject of Mary shares in a certain silence, the same mystery with the Holy Spirit. Both are relatively late and belong to nearly the same period.

The only dogmatic reference to Mariology is the name of Theotokos proclaimed by the Third Ecumenical Council. It may be small but according to St John of Damascus, "Only the name of the Theotokos contains all of the economy of salvation." This name, alone adequate to the mystery, is more than sufficient and avoids the all too human multiplication of kinship ties which confuse without any purpose.

In the conciliar acts, from the Fifth Council on, one finds the term *ai parthenos*, "ever Virgin," and although discussed in the Eighth Council, it has never been explicitly defined in conciliar declarations. In her icons, the Virgin bears upon her head and shoulders three stars which attest to her virginity *ante partum, in partu et post partum*— before, during and after birth. The Eastern Church exhibits the greatest sobriety and reserve which prohibit physiological questions about her virginity, a curiosity completely inappropriate to such a mystery. Mary's virginity means, as she herself witnesses, that she "did not at all know man." It is essential to note that virginity is not so much a state but the very essence of Mary's being as the "new creature," "the boundary of the created and the uncreated," in the words of St Gregory Palamas, in which the created is totally *deified*. Mary's physiological structure is that of a creature of the "new creation," one which transcends the fallen human order and thus every question of "how" is completely surpassed and cannot be asked. The miracle expresses spiritual realism over against any Docetic tendencies. It is not at all against nature, for the miracle of Mary's virginity refers back to the condition before the Fall, when giving birth was not a function of sexual activity.

The lack of explicit dogmatic precision is however compensated by the Patristic and liturgical tradition which is striking in the richness and the praise of Mary.

The dogmatic fact

We have here therefore, not a dogma but the "dogmatic fact," which has not received the imprimatur of an ecumenical council but expresses the truth experienced liturgically. The Church's devotion is rooted in the experience which unites doctrine and worship. This is realm of certainty and evidence disengaged from a philosophy of revelation and remains inaccessible to discursive thought. It is the intuitive and discrete grasp of the non-demonstrable first principles of an axiomatic nature.

All which is most evident (for example, both the physical and the divine light) is always the most incomprehensible: "Unglaublich ist immer die Rose, Unglaublich ist die Nachtigall," "Ever unbelievable, the rose and the nightingale," as the poet Goethe says.

St Gregory Palamas also affirms this. "Every word is able to dispute another word, but what is the word that is able to dispute life?" Here, it is the life of the Liturgy. The Liturgy confers upon Mary a title beyond boldness: *theoprepis doxa*, "the glory appropriate to, which belongs to God." Certainly this refers not to Mary, a creature of God, but to Mary the Mother of God, the locus of the Incarnation where divine glory bursts forth and it is this glorification which has become a sure element of the Church's Tradition. St Basil the Great, in his treatise *On the Holy Spirit* (XXVII), directs attention to the certain content of Tradition which presents "a teaching incapable of being published or even expressed, preserved by our Fathers in a silence inaccessible to every curiosity and indiscretion...A certain obscurity...which is the way in which silence is maintained."

The liturgical veneration of the Theotokos underscores this esoteric, mysterious, hidden character, and the lack of explicit scriptural references to her explains her absence in the apostolic preaching. The "apocryphal" origins of the feasts of her Presentation in the Temple and her Dormition are analogous to the iconography which beyond all historicism and naturalism, point to the mystery which only prayer-filled contemplation can discern.

The reading for the feast of the Dormition of the text from Philippians 2:5-11 proclaims the *kenosis*, the emptying of one's self, which the Mother of God shares with her Son. The veneration of the Mother of God is the effort of the interior consciousness of the Church. The festal icon contains a detail concerning a Jewish priest, Athonius, who seeing the bier upon which the apostles had placed the body of the Theotokos, wanted to overturn it. He is struck blind, and the icon further shows his hands being severed by an angel. Receiving the apostles' teaching, however, he cries "Alleluia," and is restored. This is clearly a symbolic manner of teaching that the cult of the Virgin can only be explained from within the interior liturgical life and Tradition of the Church.

Tradition

The deacon Philip asked of the Ethiopian eunuch, who was reading the book of Isaiah, "Do you understand what you are reading?" (Acts 8:26-40). The eunuch replied, "How can I, if there is no one to guide me?" The apostolic guide is the Tradition but the unanimity of Tradition is not a formal principle. The definition of St Vincent of Lérins: *quod semper, quod ubique, quod ab omnibus*, taken in the horizontal of duration is absurd. However vertically it indicates the dimension of depth where through time and space, the *consensus omnium patrum*, of all the Fathers, coincides with Truth and shows the perfect agreement of all, always and everywhere. The paradox of the Tradition is to express in the present the agreement of the past with the future but, as Alexis Khomiakov said, this is not a human but a divine definition.

Few of the texts which speak of Mary are difficult ones. In its spiritual, interior manner of reading them, the Tradition makes explicit the glory of the Theotokos. Thus if John the Baptist is called "the greatest among those born of woman," he has never been placed above the seraphim, and his icon is not of the same rank as those of Christ and his Mother on either side of the royal doors of the iconstasis in the Eastern Church sanctuary. The text: "Blessed are those who hear the Word of God and keep it" is read in the Gospel at the Divine Liturgy on the feasts of Mary. In an apparently negative form, this text glorifies her. "My mother and my brothers are those who hear the Word of God and accomplish it"—the Lord says this in the immediate context of the parable of the sower. "The good earth, that is those who, having listened to the word, keep it in a pure heart and bear fruit in silence" (Lk 8:5-15). It is this manner of hearing the Word which the Lord exalts and places above physical parenthood. "Blessed is the womb that bore you and the breasts that nourished you." This is why the Gospel of St Luke rightly says of Mary: "And Mary kept all these words, pondering them in her heart." Christ's words here, while seemingly very hard on his Mother, actually exalts the unique quality of her purity of heart and obedience and likens this to the heart of the Church. The unique relationship of a Mother to her Son and her ceaseless sanctification by the Holy Spirit raises her consciousness to the fullest level of revelation, to that of a being completely deified, filled with God. St John the Baptist is still in the economy of the Old Covenant and at the very border between it and the New. Mary is the summit of both covenants and it is because of this that she is "glorified by all generations."

Panagia

The Eastern Church's Tradition forcefully emphasizes the perfect synergy of Mary's holiness with the action of the Holy Spirit and the effort of all the righteous "ancestors of God," the uninterrupted succession of the saints of the Old Testament. If the Holy Spirit—*Panagion*—hypostasizes, personalizes divine holiness, Mary is *Panagia*. She is the personification of human sanctity.

Ontologically, by her very being which is linked to the Holy Spirit, Mary appears as life-giving consolation, as Eve-Life, the one who safeguards and protects every creature. Thus she becomes a figure of the Church and her ministry of prayer. According to Tradition, the Virgin's consecration to the life of the Temple and her love of God attained such depth and intensity that the conception of the Son took place in her as the divine response to the deepening of her life of prayer, to her transparency to the energies of the Holy Spirit.

Sharing organically in the descent from Adam, participating in the common destiny of all mankind, Mary, however, was kept from all personal impurity. Every evil was rendered inoperative in her. It is this dynamism, this human reaction so royally free, that Nicholas Cabasilas stressed in synthesizing the Patristic tradition. A human being cannot be saved without the free agreement of his own will. "The Incarnation was not only the work of the Father, of his power and of the Holy Spirit, but it was also the work of the will and the faith of the Virgin. Without the consent of the most Pure One, without the agreement of her faith, this plan would not have been realizable except through the intervention of the Three Divine Persons themselves. It was not until after having instructed and persuaded her that God took Mary to be his Mother, and took from her the flesh that she was willing to give to him. Just as he wished to become incarnate, so too did he wish that his Mother would give birth to him of her own free will." The objective action of her motherhood coincided with the action of her personal, active holiness. This is why she is eternally *Theotokos*, bearer of God and *Panagia*, the Most-Holy. In her saying *fiat*, "Let it be done," she has become Mother, not only in external obedience but also inwardly, by her love of God who came to her. With the Holy Spirit, she was made Theotokos.

The idea of Mary's exemption from original sin is foreign to Orthodoxy. In the Orthodox marriage service, Mary's birth from Joachim and Anna is mentioned along with a series of other births considered common to the natural order. Original righteousness, for the Eastern or Greek Fathers, was not a gratuitous privilege but "the very root of being." *Vulneratio* does not follow *privatio*. It is just the opposite. Vulnerability to sin, as an immediate consequence of being deprived of grace, becomes a lesion which destroys the nature inherited from Adam. God does not act *upon* but *within* a person. God did not act upon Mary as something added (*superadditum*). Rather, he works within the very synergy of the human and the divine. Only the free, active submission of personal holiness could present the objective human condition for the Incarnation. This gave permission to the Word, Christ, to come to her, to become her own. Jesus was able to take on human flesh because Mary freely offered her humanity to him. And in the Virgin, all say: "Yes, come, Lord." This is why, according to the Fathers, the words of the Creed, "born of the Holy Spirit and of the Virgin Mary," correspond to the mystery of the second birth of every baptized Christian, born *ex fide et Spiritu Sancto*, of faith and the Holy Spirit. The faith of each Christian is rooted in Mary's exploit of courage, in her universal *fiat*, her "Yes" to the Lord. The Annunciation, which St John Chrysostom called "the feast of the Root," inaugurated the new age. The entire economy of salvation stems from this "mariological root," and this is why Mariology is an organic part of Christology.

The angel Gabriel represents the question posed by God to Mary, his wonderful child. "Do you want to contain within in you, the One who cannot be contained, to give birth to your Savior?" In Mary's response burns the pure flame of one who gives herself, and is thereby ready to receive. The sanctification of the Holy Spirit and the personal purity of the one who receives him coincide and culminate here, disarming the power of evil. Sin remains effective but becomes inoperative. The sinful inheritance has lost its grasp upon the "Most Holy," the Mother of God.

We bring our offering of bread and wine to the temple, and, in a royal gesture, God transforms them into his body and blood. Humanity brings the most pure Virgin as its offering, and God makes her the place of his nativity and the Mother of all the living. On the eve of Christmas, at the vigil service, the Church sings: "What shall we offer you, O Christ? The heavens offer you angels, the earth brings her gifts, but we human beings, we offer you a Virgin Mother." One can clearly see that Mary is not at all "a woman among women," but the pinnacle of Woman, restored in virginal motherhood. The protection which she gave the child Jesus now covers the entire universe and every human being. The word from the cross: "Woman behold your son...Son, behold your mother" is the institution of Mary's ministry of maternal intercession.

In giving birth to Christ, she did the same for all. She gave birth to him in every soul. As a figure of the Church, she has precisely this ministry of mystical or spiritual motherhood, of continuously bringing to birth, of forever being Theotokos. To everyone given the grace of giving birth, as St Ambrose said, "each of us has become the mother of Christ," each receives the grace of being identified with the Theotokos in her personal giving birth.

Christ is "the Way" and "the Door." The God-Man is the unique one. Mary is the first, she goes before all of mankind and all of us follow her. In the names given her liturgically, "good direction," "guide," "column of fire," "gate to the Kingdom," she leads all to the New Jerusalem, to the Orient, the liturgical name of Christ. She is the first to pass through death, rendered powerless by her Son to hold her. This is why the prayers at the time of death of a Christian are addressed to the protection of the Mother of God: "In your falling asleep, O Theotokos, you have not abandoned the world." Her Dormition closed the gates of death. The Theotokos has placed her seal on death's abyss. Death has been sealed from above by the God-Man and from below by the first creature raised from the dead, the Mother of God.

The Deisis

"We do not know what to ask for or how to pray, but the Spirit himself intercedes for us," says St Paul. Mary is united to the Holy Spirit in this ministry of prayer, each and every prayer becoming "her own." Her presence at Pentecost signifies that she participates in prayer in every descent of the Holy Spirit. At the last judgment, Christ, the Word and the Truth, judges and reveals the wounds, while the Holy Spirit, the "life-giving" Giver of life, heals them. It is this aspect which is expressed in the ministry of the Virgin, together with St John the Baptist. The *Deisis* icon, of "supplication," depicts them on either side of Christ, the Teacher and Judge, and they offer the prayer of the Church, the intercession to him for mercy. This is why this very icon is placed in the iconostasis above that of the Mystical Supper, to show the wedding feast of the Lamb with every Christian soul. The Divine *Hypostasis*, or Person, of Christ judges, but the human person, his Mother, is compassion incarnate, motherly tenderness. Through her, the Holy Spirit manifests his ministry of being the Consoler and the Advocate and gives the love of the Father, the smile of his love that we will have all eternity to sing of and to contemplate.

The ultimate mystery

One may conclude here with a final statement, not speculative in nature but contemplative, iconographic. The Holy Spirit has no place, no location of incarnation except the unique, most extraordinary person to receive his presence, and that is Mary. According to the Christological dogma defined by the Seventh Ecumenical Council, in Christ, the God-Man, we affirm the duality of nature in which the human manifests the divine. Christ's humanity, according the Fathers of that Council, is the epiphanic icon of his divinity....

[Trans. note: The text edited by Paul Evdokimov on September 15, 1970, just on the eve of his death, stops here. But one can present the rest of the "ultimate mystery" of which he wished to speak on the basis of notes he had prepared for the conference for which this essay was prepared.]

The Father is enveloped in the silence of *apophasis*, of what cannot be said. It is the hidden face of the Father that the Son and the Spirit reveal to the world. The absolute subject, the Father, reveals in his Son the meaning which becomes life through the Spirit. Now, the Theotokos in her motherhood, translates this Trinitarian mystery into the human dimension as a faithful and authentic image. It is in this sense—which itself rests upon a hidden revelation—that Mary is the mysterious icon of the Father. The iconographic canons forbid any representation of the Father, who is the Inconceivable and Indescribable One. The Theotokos receives the breath of the Spirit, and her maternity enables us to contemplate in silence the divine Paternity, the face of the Father. A Marian hymn exalts her as the human being who, as the deified new creature, fully participates in the divine being according to grace: "Let us the faithful sing the Glory of the universe, the door of heaven, the Virgin Mary, Flower of the human race and Theotokos, she who has become heaven and the temple of the divine."

7

God's Absurd Love and the Mystery of His Silence[1]

The fact of atheism

The suffering of the innocent places before us the dilemma in which God's silence and the absence of his intervention are raised as evidence of his complete failure as God. In Sartre's writing, Goetz raises the cry, "Have you heard me at all, you deaf God?" If God is silent, how then can we listen to him? Is not God's silence in history a sign of his absence, better yet, of his lack of existence? All the "unaccomplished promises" seem to witness to religion's existential ineffectiveness.

Having come of age, our critical spirit muses on the destiny of man and finds in religious aspirations an alibi for our own miserable failures. Tormented by solitude and insoluble problems, man becomes a storyteller, a maker of fiction, invents God and creates a "stop-gap" of human ignorance and tosses out the hypothesis of a final or ultimate explanation. Cast into an apparently hostile and absurd world, man resigns in desperation and seeks to escape to more consoling settings. Freud describes the escapism of affective, fearful daydreaming in the face of reality, escape to the womb, to the archaic and prelogical. "I am like a child in my mother's womb and I do not wish to be born. There, in the womb, I am sufficiently warm," affirms the Russian writer Rosanov.

God appears as the projection of the image of a "foolish Father," who protects us from risk, from collision with reality and hard choices. This is a truly "useful" God, a solution to boundary situations and insurance for eternity in the sense of Pascal's wager. A lack of energy results from the

1 Originally published in *Oecumenica, Jahrbuch für ökumensche Forschung* (1969), pp. 287-302 and reprinted in *L'amour fou de Dieu* (Paris: Éditions du Seuil, 1973), pp. 11-39.

juxtaposition of this world with the other world of the sacred, a lack of energy for building the human city here below. In Nietzsche's ironic words, isn't Christianity a "Platonism for the masses," that famous "opium," which consoles and deadens our sensibilities to life here and now?

It is necessary to recognize the massive advance of atheism, now a worldwide fact which determines the new face of our age by permeating all sectors of public life. The cognitive and affective structure of our era is decisively atheistic. In Geneva, the day after the end of World War II, Sartre declared, "Gentlemen, God is dead. From now on, the true humanism is atheism." What need is there of God? Malraux said, "God is dead, and thus man is born." "Moral conscience died because of contact with the absolute," added Merleau-Ponty. Real human dignity obliges us to "move from heaven to the thoughts of human beings here on earth."

The pressure of a secularized culture and social milieu is such, quite simply, that religion no longer has any interest for us. "What's said from the depth of heaven has nothing to do with us," claims Simone de Beauvoir, and Françoise Sagan so easily admits, "God... I never think about that."

The essential motivation is rooted in the primal sense of life, in its apparent absurdity. In his films, Ingmar Bergman transposes the silence of God into human relationships. In *Smiles of a Summer Night*, Maria, who has lost her fiancée, is defiant: "If God is not interested in me, then I am no longer interested in him." For Antonioni, the world is most definitely closed. In *Blow Up,* everything appears for an instant as petrified, immobilized by the camera's lens, and then it all suddenly disappears, leaving man in his solitude, accompanied only by illusions.

In our modern mentality, post-Christian, desacralized and secularized, God has no place and the Gospel no longer has any force. That there are believers does not impress anyone. Faith appears to accomplish nothing in such a world as ours, one in which there is no trace of miracles. Religious faith appears as an infantile stage of human consciousness, now being efficiently replaced by technology, psychoanalysis and social solidarity.

Civilization in reality is not so much against God as being able to exist perfectly well without him. Sociologists tell us that "atheism has become widespread," without any further repercussions. We live on a superficial plane where, by definition, God is absent. To become an atheist today is less to choose, even less to deny, anything, as it is simply to follow everyone else, to follow the culture, the society, the world. To be religious, indifferent, or an atheist is, for the average person, almost completely a matter of temperament or more often, a political option.

Atheism's insufficiencies

Atheism proposes a classical argument. The knowledge of God presupposes the gift of faith and atheism does not have this. Now the Gospel words, "The light of Christ illumines every person coming into the world" (Jn 1:9), respond to this objection. These words signify that the simple refusal to grant to reason absolute power makes other things possible for the human spirit. At the very least, it allows an opening for the mystery of the "wholly Other." According to Pascal, the rupture of the equilibrium stems from the "two excesses: excluding reason and admitting nothing but reason." In *The Sphere and the Cross*, Chesterton notes that "the fool has lost everything, except reason." If one uses only reason and refuses intuition, imagination, and the contemplative consciousness, the negation of God is then only cognitive. It is only an objective reality at the conceptual level. Cognitive abstraction never can attain to the Transcendent, to the living being of God. It does not deny anything but a theological doctrine, a philosophical system, a concept which is without any real relevance and quite short of the divine mystery.

The atheism of fact, spineless but practical, has no metaphysical content of its own, no constructive explanation sufficient to deal with existence. This is why atheism of the academic kind is not located at the end of reflection but at its beginning as a gratuitous affirmation. Philosophic contestation does not intervene except *a posteriori*, in order to justify its positions, to create an alibi.

In such an ambiance, the ancient distress in the face of death has nothing to say to modern people much more concerned with political and economic issues. Prenant writes, "At times I have been aware of being in imminent danger of death and I never for a moment dreamt of the immortality of the soul."[2] Yes, it seems to be a matter of temperament but also the reflection of an extreme secularized perspective.

---

2 *Recontres internationales de Genève* (1947), p. 377.

Thus oversimplified, stripped of any real metaphysical investigation in spreading to the masses, scientific atheism deals with the world without the need of divine intervention. In discerning the secrets of nature, we do not really prove that God does not exist, we simply no longer have any need of him.

But a certain difficulty arises in ethics. It is that of the moral foundation of imperatives. Also, following depth psychology, the resistance of the subconscious to every order of the will, what St Paul referred to when he said: "I want to do good and I do evil" (Rom 7:18). According to Georg Simmel, the legalistic morality of Kant and his ethical autonomy conditioned, that is, led to Nietzsche's amoralism. The profound bitterness of Freud's last works witness to the erosion of his humanist utopia. Sartre, in his *Critique of Dialectical Reason*, claims "I do not want to end up in nothingness, but my thinking does not allow me to construct anything...."

After the dead end on the subjective level, the moral problem is shifted to that of the social. Feuerbach's thesis (*homo homini deus est*—man is god for man) seems to conclude that if the human person is only an individual then the human totality must be divine. Francis Jeanson sees it in the same way: the individual is nothing but the human community is everything. But if the individual is nothing, a zero, would the sum of all individuals then turn out to be divine, would it not be rather a large Zero?

The closed circle of the human condition is not surpassed by the outright "mystical" ideology of the Marxist vision, by the substitute for religion of its own non-religiosity. In its own terms, such militant atheism is only the preliminary phase of the struggle, for contrary to Marx's claim,[3] that in "integral socialism there would no longer be the need for God," it places itself beyond antitheism. It would suppress the very conditions which have permitted access to this state of fullness and, with them, any dialectical return from behind and thus all possible verification of its own foundations. Just like God, absolute humanity would no longer be able to ask any questions about its own reality.

Therefore the negation of God in Marxism is useful for the given

3   *Gesamtausgabe*, I/III, p. 125.

moment, so that the revolutionary conscience of the proletariat can be formed. Consequently, this negation is not valuable in itself at any other moment. The gap between rights and actions makes it impossible to appeal to one or the other and this flagrant defect of true dialectic deprives the Marxist perspective of any authentic philosophical force. Marxism resolves the problem of God without having raised it correctly, and replaces it by its own *credo*: "I believe in matter sufficient to itself, infinite, uncreated and moved by an eternal movement." In philosophical terms, the idea of automovement is one of the most absurd.

The indoctrinated, because of their simplistic optimism, do not grasp how difficult, tragic, and inconsistent atheism is. Péguy writes: "Really, it seems to be impossible not to believe...." Only systematic demythologization of atheism would be able to render it somewhat less certain of the nonexistence of God.

Existentialist philosophy seem more nostalgic than aggressive. "Man is a powerless god," Heidegger claims. Kantian rigorism, as adapted by Sartre, inverts the ontological argument, but with the same failure: God contradicts the absolute of the ethical exigency, therefore God ought not to exist.

Every atheism which obeys its own immanent law in the absence of absolute certitude, without having denied the Absolute, God, consequently becomes an illicit negation. In order to adorn its defiance, it constructs its own myth. Its internal logic gives to militant anti-theism a passionate, but clearly pathological quality. The Bible offers a lucid vision of the reality that it is not religion which alienates the human spirit, rather it is atheism which does this. In the etymology of the Hebrew term, not to believe is not to say *Amen* to God, to refuse His existence. We have here a medical diagnosis: "The fool says in his heart, there is no God" (Ps 14:1). "Atheism, this madness of a very few," St Augustine would say. Yet it is imposing because of its massive quantity. If for psychologists madness is the loss of reality, atheism is precisely the loss of transcendent reality.

According to St James, even "the demons believe and tremble" (Jas 2:19) they tremble because they believe they are opposed to God. It is not God whom they oppose, but in reality it is an object of their imagination, for God could never be known as an enemy or an adversary. In the prayer of Manasseh, "God has closed the abyss of the demons." They find themselves entrapped in the absence of God. We are able to enclose ourselves in the same absence of the Transcendent and the tragic emptiness of our hearts becomes more and more violent and insensitive as we sink further into the negation of God.

The insufficiencies of historical Christianity

The great theologians along with the fathers of Vatican II have said that the theology of the last decades has lost the sense of mystery, that it is built upon speculation *about God*, and has thereby ceased to be a dynamic thinking *in God*. Marcel Moré put it in his own way: "The words of people who have found the means of sitting down, one does not know how, in a manner comfortable with the Cross, are no longer able to have any resonance...."

For Renan, in his *Prayer on the Acropolis*, religions are mortal. One can add that theological systems are also, this is also the case with the formula we find spread worldwide today: "God is dead." [Trans. note: "today" here is 1968.] The God of a certain theology is dead. It is the death of the current conception of God as an object almost physically situated on the periphery of cosmic space, pure exteriority, and therefore only a fearful Master.

St Cyril of Alexandria replaced the Greek dialectic of master-slave with that of the Gospel: Father-Son. F. Boulard, in his study on problems in mission work, cites the account of a missionary priest: "My Christians...think of God as faraway, One to whom it is necessary to submit as far as one is able, not out of love but out of fear of hell. God is not the Father...No, God is the one who has given the ten negative commandments: *Thou shalt not*...The conclusion: God is the one who keeps us from being happy." In another study published in *Réalités*, "God is sadness," says an engineer, "it's everything we do not have the right to do. It's the dark places with the little vigil lights, women with veils, the Jesuits' condemnations..."

The distorted image that Christianity itself has made of God has fueled the revolt of people against the Church. The image of God has become that of an earthly monarch and his attributes: dignity, majesty, power. Throughout the Middle Ages, whole peoples were often converted *en masse*, as cultural or political communities, at the orders of their prince, or even at the point of a sword. The idea of God became a guarantee of the social and political order. The unbelief of the 1700s affirmed the scandal of a God imposed and an enforced religion.

In scholastic theology one sees the fossilization of divinity and eternity dangling over the future as a secure nook, beyond time. Philosophers posed their troubling questions: "If everything is already decided beforehand, why pray, what good could that do?" The graciousness, the freedom of salvation, this marvelous mystery of God's love that the Reformation saw so clearly in the Bible and in the Fathers, once posed in terms of causality and then conceptualized, became the terrible doctrine of double predestination. If in our time one tried to correct this, speaking of the salvation of all and showing that only one is culpable, namely God himself, then one would see how this doctrine cannot in any way serve humanity.

Every misreading of freedom of choice—*compelle intrare*—"to force them to enter" of St Augustine—justifies both the Inquisition and the politics of the sword. One forgets here the words of St John Chrysostom: "The one who threatens or forces a heretic commits an unforgivable sin." It is the "nightmare of good imposed" in which everything good imposed turns into evil. Official Christianity has looked like a religion of law and punishment which translates itself into prohibitions and taboos. The dominating forms were denounced by Freud under the name of the "sadistic Father." Such regressive religion forgets the Trinity, God's sacrificial fatherhood which does not dominate but gives birth to freedom. Such regression presents God as the jealous Judge, the fearful, terrifying magistrate who prepares punishment and hell for all eternity. With reason, we are hardly fearful of being alienated from such a hell. Such "penitential theology," in Fr Sergius Bulgakov's words, with all of its prohibitions and hell, such a "terrorist" religion is one of the actual causes of atheism.

On the other hand, over against a scientific worldview, even in a cultural context of belief, God finds himself exiled to heaven. One finds instead the boring, moralizing stance of the average person. The second birth in light of the Resurrection, the bursting forth of the new creature, these amazing realities find themselves replaced in history by the hierarchical institution of the Church, empty of anything dynamic since everything has been reduced to obedience and submission. This is the tragedy of the "closed world" of which Bergson spoke, the "closed heaven" too, of mediocre, average Christianity.

Atheism: the need for purification of faith

Kurt Marek, one of those arguing for the death of God, in his *Provocative Notes* says: "The atheism which once was the breaking crest of the wave of progress is no longer in vogue. For several generations to be an atheist has seemed backwards..."

The surpassing of atheism among the intellectual elite, even if little understood at the moment, is affirmed however in the qualitative level of the spirit. The poet Osip Mandelstam in the Soviet Union declares: "In our time, every truly cultured person is a Christian." The young intellectuals in Russia, after being saturated with ideology, look for the meaning of life and aspire to that "revolution of the person and of the spirit" which Berdiaev preached. They react against all rigid ritualism and are profoundly hungry for the infinite and the transcendent. The greatest of the Russian scientists say quite simply that real science leads ineluctably to religious questions. Waiting for a new St Paul before the Athenians (Acts 17:22) they even have formulated an astonishing prayer to the "unknown God."

A genuine respect on the part of such specialists for the competence of others makes ridiculous any opposition between science and religion. Science does not evaluate the metaphysical opinion of a sage who in turn would find this absurd. But if the world is closer than ever to the Transcendent, the spiritual thirst of mankind where the problems are raised at the global level has become more critical.

The chief obstacle, perhaps surprising, perhaps not, comes from the amorphous mass of believers. It is not only the Christians who live in an atheistic world but that atheism lives within them, within Christians themselves. There is no pit to which the fruit clings more tightly than the thick ignorance about God in this mediocre group. This is why according to Lagneau, "atheism is the salt which prevents belief in

God from being corrupted,"[4] and for Simone Weil, atheism purifies the idea of God from every theologically and sociologically bound context and raises the necessity of a "holiness born of genius."

Such a purification necessitates an "ecumenical dialogue" with those who are atheists, who have never approached the living content of the faith in which the historical expressions are put in question. If a religious court session could encompass all of past civilization, it could not encompass the future except in surpassing every mode of representation to which modern man is a stranger. Our period of history is one of human maturation, of passing into adulthood, and it refuses any knowledge of God which is not at the same time knowledge of man and of him as an epiphany of God. This is, in fact, God's own wish and the actual meaning of the Incarnation.

Biblical eschatology is qualitative, qualifying history by the ultimate, the *eschaton* and shattering every concept that is closed and static. This is the wonderfully rich theme of the Exodus. "Abraham left without knowing where he would arrive" (Heb 11:8) and without any possible return to the point of his departure: "The one who looks back is not fit for the Kingdom of God" (Lk 9:62). Biblical time breaks the cyclical time of eternal returns, Ulysses returning at the end to Penelope. "I am..the Way...the Light...the Bread...." These names of the Lord summarize the Exodus of Israel nourished by the manna, and led by the pillar of fire towards the Promised land. But now in Christ all of history takes on the figure of the Exodus centered upon *homo viator*, man the pilgrim, humankind on the way. The Church in the historical situation is the Church of the *diaspora*, the eschatological community on the march towards the Kingdom, towards its own fullness and precisely in this through the earthly city. To lack the presence of the world is identical to lacking the faith of the Gospel.

The reality and relevance of the Christian message can only be revealed through the Church's engagement as an eschatological partner in the world and within the experience of humanity today. Historical life is never a means for the age of the future. If the world is finalized by the Kingdom, it is because the Kingdom is already "among men."

---

4   "Cours sur Dieu" in *Célèbres leçons et fragments*, Paris: PUF (1964), p. 284.

The *deus ex machina*, a compensation to human weaknesses and inadequacies, is therefore quite dead. But he is very much present as the creative source when we are the masters of ourselves. God clings to us when we are strong and forceful, and this is why the Gospel should be present in all the decisions and risks of the human condition.

The Church need not take charge of the many specific tasks of the human city, but a Christian consciousness is called to be fully at work even in the most technological situations. Politics, economics, development, these are spheres common to both believers and nonbelievers alike. The immense task of bringing the world to completion in the qualitative "catholicity" of all is planted in culture by the light of the transfigured Christ on Mount Tabor. "There is a light which enlightens the hearts of men and which illumines the whole world." A survey recently in Russia (in the 1960s) quotes a young believer: "Christianity is everywhere. It is the very heart of existence, in the holiness of motherhood, in the events of everyday life, in the goodness of love and friendship."

Asceticism without love, the "sacrament of the brother," is empty and pointless, so the great spiritual teachers witness. Speaking of the Eucharist, St John Chrysostom said: "Here is that same upper room where the disciples were then, and from here we depart for the Mount of Olives. We also depart to find the hands of the poor, for these belong to us. Yes, the multitude of the poor is like a forest of olive trees planted in the house of the Lord. From this place there flows that oil which we need in order to go out with the wise virgins whose lamps are full, to meet the Bridegroom...."

The Church of the last times will offer to the one who is hungry not the "ideological stones" of systems, neither the "theological stones" of catechisms but the "bread of angels," and "the heart of the human brother offered as pure food," in Origen's beautiful words.

The Christian response

Negative theology and the symbol

Today we witness everywhere a shaking of the foundations. Even theologians are unsure of what they believe. In demythologizing, Christianity has been emptied of its evangelical content. One can easily go beyond a cosmology limited to three stages or levels. It is essential not to confuse or merely connect the absolute otherness of transcendent truths with the processes of nature. Electricity has nothing to do with the reality of miracles. The Cross remains a scandal and foolishness, and it is necessary to accept it as a most exact expression of the truths of faith in history. "Under the pretext of 'light,' we engage ourselves in a darkness of ignorance such that today we find inconceivable the manifestations of God to human beings understood by the ancients as common and known to all and not at all alien," St Seraphim of Sarov would say.

Paul Tillich's insistence on the encounter with God in the horizontal dimension, Bishop Robinson's refusal to apply spatial categories to God, Rudolph Bultmann's demythologization—these are all reactions of theologians who can no longer convey the Gospel to a desacralized, secularized world, in a radically immanentist culture. These reactions, based in their critiques of religion, are at the same time ineffective because of their lack of understanding of apophatic or negative theology.

Through the negative way, the Fathers teach that God has no equivalent in the absolute sense, no name can adequately express him. *Adonai* replaces the unspeakable name of God, *Yahweh*, the name one cannot pronounce. Classical positive theology is not devalued but placed within its own limits. It cannot apply anything other than revealed attributes, manifestations of God in the world. This theology translates them into an intelligible mode of expression but they remain ciphers, symbols, for the reality of God is absolutely original, transcendent, and irreducible to any system of thought. Around the deep abyss of God, the flaming sword of the cherubim drew an impenetrable circle of silence.

The negative way is not a negating way. It has nothing in common with agnosticism, for "negativity is not negation." It is not merely a corrective or an appeal to prudence. By means of negations, it leads to a mystical knowledge-beyond-knowledge and to a most paradoxical grasp of the Inconceivable. By an "intuitive, primordial and simple approach," it knows by piercing through all knowledge. What is most important in this method is that it is a transcending, but one which never detaches itself from its historical and biblical footing. It is not the iconoclasm of abstract art. The vertical coordinate of transcendence is raised high and yet is even more rooted in the horizontal of immanence. What is essential is in this way to place the human spirit in the experience which generates unity, just like the mystery of eucharistic union. God is more unknowable in the transcendence of his Being and is more capable of being experienced in his immediate proximity as the Existing One. Now the actual problem is not precisely that of the being of God nor that of his own existence, but that of his presence as the Existing One in human history.

When the Fathers touch upon these mysteries they resist the powerlessness of words and turn rather, to the antinomic expressions of symbols. Thus "One hopes in that which already exists," or "One remembers that which is coming," or again, one quenches one's thirst at "wells of living water." Today, under the impulse of the great philosophers and of depth psychology, the symbol has become a dimension of avant-garde thought. The profound formulation of Paul Ricoeur, "Hope is the same thing as reminiscence," illumines the symbol in the patristic sense, namely that every hope is an *epiphany*.

The *symbol* (from the Greek word "to throw together") implies the putting together of two halves, that which symbolizes and that which is symbolized. It exercises the expressive function of meaning and at the same time acts as an expressive receptacle of the presence. It is then *epiphanic*, witnessing to the coming of the Transcendent.

The Liturgy is centered on the descent of the Holy Spirit, the epiclesis which makes the remembering, or *anamnesis, epiphanic*, that is, makes present the event remembered. This is why the only efficacious argument for the existence of God is the liturgical argument of prayer-filled adoration. Prayer witnesses to the One who hears it. This is important for the subjective weaknesses of a believer do not at all affect the objective value of his faith. The true subject of faith is not the isolated individual but his "liturgical self," the transsubjective place of faith and revelation. Some modern exegetes thus translate Genesis 2:15:"Yahweh Elohim took man and placed him in the garden of Eden *for worship* and for its preservation." In such pronounced symbolism, paradise becomes a sanctuary and the first man is its *priestly guardian*. In our very origins we are *liturgical beings*.

Proclamation is inseparable from the Liturgy. According to Bultmann, Jesus is risen in the *kerygma*, in the proclamation of salvation. But the Resurrection has no other meaning without the historical event, and in no way can it be the subjective vision, for example of a St Paul. In refusing with Bultmann every objectivizing of this mystery, it is necessary however to preserve its objective character, that of the event as a whole. The Resurrection is in the *kerygma*, but the Resurrection is also in the Eucharist. This is the living memorial of the Resurrection and is the most immediate proclamation of it, for in the Eucharist each communicant is integrated with the Risen Christ and the Eucharist makes of all an "assembly of immortals." St Irenaeus put it well: "Our doctrine is conformed to the Eucharist and the Eucharist confirms our doctrine." The past event is even more real and efficacious today. St Isaac the Syrian (in his *Sentences*, 118) makes it clear that the only true sin is to be "insensible to the Resurrection." What an astonishing prophecy from the seventh century and one which brings judgment upon the indigence of every spirit which is critical of the historical reality of Christ's Resurrection.

Apophatic theology and the idea of the symbol are the keystone for every ecumenical dialogue and for all dialogue with the world as well. This is the most effective approach to "depetrify" contemporary theology, avoiding any break between the heavenly vertical and the earthly horizontal in their intersection which is the *mystery of the Cross*.

The New Testament presents the different "views" (*synoptics*) of the witnesses of the same faith, different perspectives which determine their different theologies and spiritualities: Johannine, Pauline and Petrine. Such pluralism of theology is most legitimate. On the contrary, however, dogmas are intentionally placed on the level of liturgical affirmations: in the Nicene Creed, the Holy Spirit is "worshipped and glorified," which reflects the mystagogical function of the Spirit, the function of the liturgical and doxological order. This prohibits any separating of the intelligible aspects of dogma from their liturgical content. Every dogmatic affirmation comes from the positive theology which the Fathers characterize as "symbolic." The rapport between that which symbolizes and that which is symbolized reveals in every dogma a verbal icon, an intelligible icon of the Truth. But every icon is, above all, epiphanic, witnessing to the presence of the one represented there. It is therefore necessary to grasp, through the dogma, the real presence of truth and not confuse the formula with its presentation in a particular cultural milieu, nor to separate the dogma from its *experience* in the Liturgy.

The ecumenical dialogue and movement are ultimately and in an interior way oriented toward a great council of all the churches. Such a gathering would be convened in order to revisit together the sacred deposit of the apostolic faith, always discerning the Truth in its many iconic expressions, comparable to the diverse iconographic compositions of the same theme, diverse but converging on the one and the same Subject.

Faith and its proofs

St Gregory of Nyssa saw in Abraham the image of one who, without posing questions, journeys into the deepest mysteries of God. We however, do ask questions and above all, demand proofs. But proofs wound the Truth and the Lord rejects them. Pascal noted contemplatively: "Revelation signifies the veil removed, but the Incarnation once more veils the face of God." The former optimism of proofs for the existence of God has disengaged itself from our "fundamental boredom." Such naivete ignores the fact that God is not evident and that silence is a quality of God. It further overlooks the fact that every proof which constrains violates human consciousness. This is why God limits his omnipotence, withdraws all signs and encloses himself in the silence of his suffering love. He has spoken by the prophets. He has spoken in his own earthly existence. But after Pentecost, he does not speak, except through the breathing of the Holy Spirit. It is in this silence, Nicholas Cabasilas says, that God declares his love to us, *manikos eros*, the foolish, absurd love of God for us and his incomprehensible respect for our freedom. "The form in which God gives us his hand is the same by which his hand becomes invisible."[5] The hand of the crucified Christ covers our eyes, but having been pierced by the nails, our eyes can see through it.

5   Joseph Malègue, *Pénombres*, p. 98.

Faith is the response to God's kenotic, that is, self-emptying attitude, of which we read in Philippians 2:7. It is because we are able to say no that our yes takes on full resonance and enters the same key as God's yes. And this is why God also accepts being refused, misunderstood, rejected, even expelled from his own creation. On the cross, God takes our side, against God, according to Péguy, "God has been one of us."

Nicholas Cabasilas has put it admirably: "God presents himself and declares his love...pushed aside he waits at the door...For all the good he has done for us he asks nothing in return but our love, in exchange he excuses all our debt to him."[6] The Christian may be a miserable person but he knows there is Someone even more miserable, suffering even more, this Beggar of love at the door of his heart: "Here I am, I stand at the door and knock, if anyone hears my voice and opens the door I will enter and dine with him" (Rev 3:20). The Son came to the world to sit at the "table of sinners." Love can only be a sacrifice until death. God dies so that we may live in him.

Faith is the reciprocity of the two *fiats*, the two yeses, the encounter of the love descending from God and our love ascending to him. The voice of God is silence, exerting a pressure that is infinitely light, never irresistible. God does not give orders, he makes an appeal: "Hear, O Israel!...If you would be perfect...." To a tyrant's decree comes the response of secret resistance but to the invitation of the Lord of the banquet in the Gospel comes the joyous acceptance of the "one who has ears to hear," of the one who has himself made a choice by closing his hand on the gift offered by his King.

That we should be free does not at all mean that we should be the cause of our own salvation but that God himself is not able to constrain us to love him. Faith says: "Give up your puny reason and receive the Logos, the Word...shed your blood and receive the Spirit." The experience of faith is at first the response. The simple invocation of God's name makes immediately present the One who, though unrecognized, is always intimately known.

Proofs are insufficient, because God is the only criterion of his truth.

---

6   *The Life in Christ*, Carmino J. deCatanzaro, trans., (Crestwood NY: St Vladimir's Seminary Press, 1974), p. 163.

In every thought of God it is God who is already thinking in the human spirit. This is the true sense of the ontological argument. It means that faith does not invent itself, that its origin is not arbitrary, that it is a gift, but also that it is offered to all, so that God is able to make every soul his dwelling place. According to the Fathers, the Holy Spirit is the hypostasized or personalized Gift and this is why the prayer to the Father that the Spirit come can never be refused, for this would contradict the very nature of the Spirit: "How much more will our heavenly Father give the Holy Spirit to those who ask him," says the Lord.

Freedom and hell

To the atheistic formula, "If God exists, then man is not free," the Bible responds, "If man exists, God is no longer free." We are able to say no to God, but God is no longer able to say no to us, for according to St Paul, "there is only yes in God," (2 Cor 1:19) the yes of his Covenant which Christ has given on the Cross. Then, "I am free" means "God exists." It is God himself who guarantees the freedom of doubt, so as to not violate human conscience.

God has created the "second freedom," and he takes the supreme risk of a freedom which is capable of stopping him, of obliging him to descend into death and into hell. He freely allows himself to be assassinated in order to offer pardon and resurrection to the assassins. His omnipotence is to make room for human freedom, to veil his presence in order to be in dialogue with "the other," to love with an infinite patience which waits for the free response, a free creation of a common life of God and his child. A patristic saying states it this way: "God can do everything, except constrain us to love him." The omnipotence of God is to become the life-giving Cross, the unique response to the case of atheism on freedom and evil.

"The Kingdom of God has come among you," means that hell has also come among us. Marcel Johandeau puts it in his own way: "On my own, I am able to set up before God an empire in which he can do nothing, and this is hell...if we do not understand hell it is because we do not know our own hearts...."[7] It is the hell of all those who despair

---

7   *Algébre des valeurs morales*, p. 229.

and who explore the depths of Satan and cast towards heaven their empty blasphemies.

Now even the despair of hell is wounded by Christ, who as a person has experienced God's silence: "My God, my God, why have you forsaken me?" (Mt 27:46). Here we see the connection of hell with the freedom of loving God. Human freedom can create hell because we are always able to say: "May your will not be done," and not even God can control these words.

The freedom to refuse God is his wish for us, without limits. The suspended power of human choice renders our destiny conditional. And it is hell, therefore, to speak of divine love, the heavenly dimension of hell, the divine vision of humanity immersed in the night of solitude.

It is of the greatest urgency to correct the "terrorist" and "penitentiary" ideas of God. It is no longer possible to believe in a heartless God incapable of suffering. The only message which could reach atheism today is that of Christ descending into hell. As deep as the hell in which we find ourselves, it is even more profound to find Christ already there waiting for us. God does not ask of us virtue, moralism, blind obedience but a cry of assurance and of love from the depth of our hell. We ought never to fall into despair. We can only fall into God and it is God who never despairs. St Anthony the Great said that hell surely exists, but only for himself, which is to say that hell is never "for the others," that it is never the object of our discourse.

The powerlessness of an all-powerful God

The idea of an omnipotence blocks every passage to the future. Evil becomes an inevitable corruption of creation that God tolerates, without being responsible for this evil. Darkness, it would seem, is allowed to overshadow the light.

It is the passage from Philippians 2:6-11 which is the key, the one which speaks of the veritable alienation of God himself: "He lowered himself, taking on the form of a servant...making himself obedient even to death on a cross." God's omnipotence is freely annihilated. God renounces all power, above all the will to power. "I am among you as one who serves" expresses a total otherness with respect to our human conceptions of God.

God is more than truth, for he incarnates it in himself in making himself "other," in emptying himself of himself. In the omnipotence of *manikos eros*, of his "absurd love" for us, God does not simply destroy evil and death but takes them upon himself. As the Liturgy sings, "He has destroyed death by death." His light shines from Truth, crucified and risen.

It is this light which confronts the suffering of the innocent, of handicapped and deformed children, of senseless catastrophes. Here is the most paradoxical reality of God, who is invincible weakness. The only response to such suffering is to say that "God is weak, powerless" and that he can only suffer with us. We can only say that suffering is "the bread that God shares with us." God is powerless, certainly not in the omnipotence of his being, but in his love which freely renounces his power. It is in this weakness that Nicholas Cabasilas saw God's "foolish, absurd love for man."

The fearful God who is incapable of suffering, this God beloved of some theologians, misguided in their understanding of the Old Testament, turns out to be the suffering Father, in the words of St Filaret of Moscow, "The Father is the love which crucifies, the Son is crucified love, the Spirit is the invincible power of the Cross." The mystery of crucified Love streams from the light of Easter morning, the "weakness victorious" over death and hell.

This mystery was already present in the mysticism of the Judaic tradition. Rabbi Baruch searched for the way of explaining that God is our companion-in-exile. Alone and abandoned, he is a stranger unknown and unrecognized among us. One day, the Rabbi's grandson was playing hide-and-seek with another little boy. He hid himself, but the other child refused to look for him and went away. The boy rushed in tears to his grandfather. Then himself in tears, Rabbi Baruch exclaimed, "God says the same thing: I have hidden myself but no one seeks to find me...."[8]

Here is another, even stronger statement of this God's abasement: "Divine compassion is God's turning from himself." You could say it is God's weakness. A saint said to a child, "Look here, if you were able to play with the Lord, it would be the greatest thing anyone could ever do. All the world takes him so seriously that it has become horribly boring...Play with God, my child. He is the best playmate."

8   Martin Buber, *Tales of the Hasidim*.

God's weakness corresponds to our own. St Paisius the Great prayed for his disciple who had denied Christ. The Lord then appeared to him and said "Don't you know that he has turned from me and denied me?" But St Paisius did not cease to have compassion for the disciple and he prayed even more intensely for him. Then the Lord came back and said: "Paisius, you have brought him back to me, by your love."

The mystery of silence

What can one say to the atheist, to the non-believer who demands proofs of God's existence? Only this: When we enter into ourselves, we recover true silence, and we sense ourselves waiting for the coming of the "Father who is present in secret" (Mt 6:6). The Father speaks through his Son, his Word. He does not overcome, but he witnesses to the immediate proximity: "I am here at the door, knocking" (Rev 3:20). There is something here infinitely greater than any demonstration or proof, greater than overwhelming evidence, greater than certitude without any doubt: God exists, he is present, "the friend of the Bridegroom hears his voice and his joy is great." Jesus told his disciples be to be joyful with an immense joy whose roots were beyond humanity, in the objective existence of God, in the joy of the Trinity. God said: "See, I have loved you with an eternal love" (Jer 31:3). "As the lover is the joy of his beloved, so you will be the joy of your God" (Is 62:5).

The silence is the Advent, the time of waiting " while it is night." It is waiting for the unexpected, and, as Heraclitus put it, "If one does not hope, one will not encounter the unexpected."[9] It is the lack of hope that fills our mouth with negativity, but despair is the threshold of hope. "Keep your soul in hell and do not despair," Christ said to a contemporary elder (St Silouan of Athos).

Only in silence can we comprehend the saying of St Maximus the Confessor: "The love of God and the love of man are but two aspects of only one, total love." In an immense sigh, God's silence shadows the world with peace: "All is yours, Lord, I am yours, receive me." To the question of whether to pursue a life of contemplation or action, St Seraphim of Sarov responded: "Find peace within and silence, and a

9   Alain Entralgo, *L'Attente et l'Esperance.*

multitude of people will find their salvation near you." God created the angels "in silence," as the Fathers said. God guides those who are silent. Those who remain agitated make the angels laugh.

"The Lord fights for you, remain in silence" (Ex 14:14). This is a singular silence, one which assures the purity and transparency of hearts capable of welcoming and rejoicing in the victory of God.

"The Lord God closed the door on Noah" (Gen 7:16), his silence prepares him to become a sign of the Covenant. Thus Jonah or Job, who "places the hand on his mouth" (Job 40:4) and awaits the *Rhêma*, the life-giving Word of God. The Book of Revelation (8:1) underscores the silence of all the powers of heaven before the announcement of the ultimate revelations. It was when Zachariah the priest became silent, deaf and dumb, that the people understood he had received a revelation (Lk 1:20-22). In the description of ordination to the priesthood in the text of Bishop Hippolytus, during the laying on of hands silence is imposed on all assisting because of the descent of the Holy Spirit, all keeping silent during his coming down.

The great silence seized the earth on Good Friday. After having announced the death of God, it seemed that the world entered into the silence of the Great Sabbath of Holy Saturday. According to the Fathers, before listening to the words of God it is necessary to listen to his silence, "the language of the world to come," according to St Isaac the Syrian, and *silence here signifies that one finds oneself within the Word*. It is only in our own silence that we are able to do this.

It is in a like silence and in the royal freedom of our souls that we are all invited to respond to the most simple question: what is God? St Gregory of Nyssa lets the answer slip out so easily: "You, the love of my soul...."

8

CULTURE AND FAITH[1]

God and humanity

If the biblical idea of "in the image and likeness of God" is fundamental for a Christian anthropology, it must be said most paradoxically that it is again decisive for an atheistic anthropology. Actually, the resemblance between God and man has never been denied by atheism. For Nicholas Hartmann, Feuerbach or Karl Marx, the human person is defined by attributes which are properly divine: intelligence, freedom, creativity, prophetic clairvoyance. For Sartre, man is essentially "project," thus freedom, which means that his existence both precedes and surpasses his essence. St Gregory Palamas affirmed precisely this on the subject of God: "I am the One who is, for I am the One who embrace in myself all being."[2]

In *The Faith of an Unbeliever*, F. Jeanson affirms: "The universe is a machine for making gods...the human species is capable of incarnating God and making him real." For Heidegger, more the pessimist, man is a "powerless god," the god only of himself. Everywhere we think of ourselves in relation to the Absolute. To understand man is to decipher this relationship. Both believers and atheists are able to advance to this same point, namely that the problem of man is one that is both divine and human. God is the archetype, the limiting ideal of the human self. Certainly, the human person bears within himself something of the absolute. In his own way he exists *en soi* and *pour soi*, in and for himself, and Sartre's entire philosophical system pivots on this. Therefore, God

1 "Culture and Faith," in *L'amour fou de Dieu*, pp. 109-137; originally published as "La culture à la lumière de l'orthodoxie," in *Contacts* XIX (1967), pp. 10-34.
2 *Triads*, III, 2, 12.

and man resemble each other. Neither the Greek poets, nor the skeptic Xenophanes, nor Feuerbach and Freud have ever denied this. For all the questions, the basic one is really knowing who is the creator of the other, God or man.

The atheist vision possesses a singular methodological significance. In reality, atheists identify God and man and do not pause before the enormity of such an identification. It is necessary to admit that they are infinitely more consistent than are Christians, faced with the affirmations of the Bible and the Fathers of the Church, which are no less astonishing.

The thinking of the Fathers goes back to the relation between God and his creation. The biblical idea of the "resemblance" is what makes revelation possible in the first place. If God the Word is this Word that the Father addresses to man, his child, then there is a certain conformity, a correspondence between the *Logos* who is divine and the *logos* who is human. This is the ontological foundation of all human knowledge. The laws of nature are proposed by the divine Architect. God is the creator, poet or maker of the universe and man, who resembles him, is also creator and poet in his own way. St Gregory Palamas makes this more precise: "God transcendent of everything, incomprehensible, unspeakable, consents to become a participant in our intelligence." What is more, Clement of Alexandria says: "Man is like God because God is like man."[3] God forms the human being observing, in his Wisdom, the heavenly humanity of Christ (see Col. 1:15, 1 Cor 15:47, Jn 3:13). This is predestined "to reunite all things, those that are in heaven with those on earth" (Eph 1:10), the "mystery hidden in God before all ages" (1 Cor 2:7). We are created in the image of God in view of the Incarnation, placed in this state because it implies the ultimate degree of communion between God and man. The icon of the Theotokos, the Mother of God (especially that called *Eleousa, Umilenie*—tenderness) holding the child Jesus, admirably expresses this. If God was born in man (the Nativity) there is also a birth of man in God (the Ascension).

It is necessary to be attentive to this vision of the Fathers, the deification of mankind is a function, a result of the humanization of God:

3   PG 9, col. 293.

"Man is the human face of God," said St Gregory of Nyssa.[4] This is why "man, destined for the enjoyment of things divine, ought to receive in his very nature a relationship, a kinship with God, with whom he ought to share."[5] The human soul is not fulfilled except in the "divine milieu." "To contemplate God is the soul's very life," says St Gregory of Nyssa.[6]

The Fathers build their anthropology on the divine level, and their perspectives are incisive, paradoxical, bold in the extreme. It will suffice, at some small risk, to select but a few of their most astonishing and well-known theses:

"God became man so that man might become God by grace and share in the divine life."

"Man is a being who has received the command to become God."

"Man must unite created nature and uncreated divine energy."

"I am human by nature and God by grace."

"The one who shares the divine light becomes himself a sort of light."

A microcosm, man is also *microtheos*, a "little God." It is in our very structure that we bear the theological enigma, that we are mysterious beings, what St Peter calls "man, hidden in the depth of the heart" (1 Pet 3:4). This is an apophatic definition and one which shows the Fathers' interest in the content of the *imago Dei*, the image of God in man. For St Gregory of Nyssa, the richness of the image reflects divine perfection, the convergence of all good things, and underscores the human power, properly divine, to freely determine himself.

When we say, "I exist," something of the absoluteness of God is translated into the human: "I am the One who is." For the Fathers these formulas were "essential words," words of life received and experienced. Sadly, in history, these lofty summits of experience and expression experienced a fall toward the flatness of scholastic theology, where these images of fire became clichés without life, common places where this or that theological position was reinforced, cerebral, abstract, polemical, without any revolutionary or cataclysmic power any longer for the life of the world.

4   PG 44, col. 446 B and C.
5   *Catec.* V, PG 45. col. 21 C and D.
6   *De infant.*, PG 46, col. 176 A.

Within current piety, asceticism poorly understood becomes obscurantism. Humility becomes formalized and a passport of good orthodoxy leading to an orthodox Barthianism, where man reduced to something insignificant is able to do nothing except to revolt and negate himself. Monophysitism has never been surpassed in certain currents of piety, taking the form of the "transcendent egoism" of individual salvation. It is the monophysite contempt for the flesh and for the material world, the flight toward the celestial realm of pure spirits, the misunderstanding of culture and of the human vocation or callings in the world, a hostility even a hatred for woman and beauty. According to Nicholas Cabasilas, God's "foolish love" (*manikos eros*) for us or in the magnificent words of St Filaret, Metopolitan of Moscow: "The Father is the Love which crucifies, the Son is crucified Love and the Spirit is the invincible power of the Cross.[7] This religion of crucified Love has been the victim of widespread alienation. It has been transformed into a religion of paternalistic clericalism, or one of a "sadistic Father" (the juridical theory of satisfaction, the Son "satisfies justice," "quenches the Father's anger"), or a religion of law and of punishment, of obsession with hell, a "terrorist" religion where the Gospel is reduced to a purely moralistic system. Again in the nineteenth century according to the then prevalent theology, the "rich" represented divine Providence, and the "poor" blessed God for having sent into the world such worthy, affluent people. When one considers wealth and poverty as divine institutions, one is only able to oscillate between the Father as fearful tyrant and the Father as the generous and reassuring patriarch.

Now authentic Christian Tradition teaches an authentic dialectical tension, so powerfully stressed by St Gregory Palamas: not by one thing or the other, but by the one and the other at the same time. It is the tension between subjective humility and the objective fact of being co-liturgist, co-creator, co-poet with God. It is necessary to relearn these antinomies, formerly so familiar to the Fathers and to the Church, now foreign to us.

We say, "I am imperfect," and God responds, "Be perfect, as your heavenly Father is perfect" (Mt 5:48). We say, "I am dust and nothing,"

---

7   *Oraisons, homélies et discours*, trans. A. de Stourdza, Paris, 1849, p. 154.

and Christ says to us, "You are like gods and my friends" (Jn 15:14). "You are children of God" (Acts 17:28) affirms St Paul, and St John, "You have received the anointing and you know everything" (1 Jn 2:27). "I bear the marks of my sins but I am in the image of your unspeakable glory" we hear in one of the *troparia* of the Orthodox funeral service.

Man is created and nevertheless not created but "born of water and the Holy Spirit." We are of the earth and also of heaven, creatures yet God-in-becoming. A "created god" is a most paradoxical notion, just as a "created person" and "created freedom." The Fathers' boldness deepened these maxims and sayings so that we might "not at all be saddened" and not "stifle the Holy Spirit."

Certainly the Eastern Church's understanding of *theosis* that is, "deification" or "divinization," is not a logical solution nor a concept but a solution of life and grace, an antinomic solution, as is every charism of the Holy Spirit which leads us back to the antinomy of God himself. The Fathers recognized this in saying that the Name of God is relative with respect to the world. How is God able to be, at one and the same time, relative and absolute, the God of history and the God in history? This is a mystery of Christ, of his Love, which transcending his own absoluteness, is leading us toward the Father. How also can the saying of St Ephrem the Syrian be true: "The whole Church is one of penitents and those who are perishing?" How is this statement able to agree with that of St Simeon the New Theologian: "Truly it is a great mystery, God among men, God in the midst of gods, by deification!" But this is one and the same mystery.

The Church and the world

The Second Vatican Council, in its schema XIII, has approached this mystery by dealing with the immense question of the Church in the world. Here is the point of departure for such a topic: the Lord has placed the Church in the world and charged her with an apostolic mission of witness and evangelization. But this is only the beginning of the mission, for its fulfillment it is necessary for the Church to reverse the terms, to catch a glimpse of the result, to trace out the vision of the world in the Church, and this requires a very precise evaluation of human creativity and culture. Such reflection is required of theologians in order to construct an authentic theology of the world. It is precisely eschatology which invites us to deepen the vision, to grasp all of reality in an absolutely new way, in the image of God, redeemed in Christ, to reveal also the exact nature and role of angels and demons in human life, to restore the value of the phenomenon of sanctity, of the witness of martyrdom and of charismatic prophetic witness in the actual context of history. It is an engagement with the world and its destiny in the light of creation and of God's plan for it.

In history, "Christian" empires and states, like the theocracies, have crumbled under the pressure of a world which pure and simple refused submission to ecclesiastical authorities. Every good that violates and forces consciences becomes evil and is, in Berdiaev's words, "the nightmare of good by compulsion" in which human freedom, willed by God at the price of his death, is abused. This is why domination of the world, its submission to the power of the Church, is directly opposed to the central message of the Gospel to those "captive to the Kingdom of God," to the authentic Christian force which "tears apart the heavens."

History and eschatology penetrate each other. The one exists within the other. The meaning of Pentecost and the gifts of the Holy Spirit, the universal significance of the Spirit's *epiclesis*, is above all eschatological, pointing to the *Parousia*, Christ's second coming. This reveals, according to St Maximus the Confessor, the fundamental vocation of Christians "to unite created nature (the world) with deifying uncreated energy" (of which the Church is the living source). The Church in the world qualifies time and existence by the *eschaton*. This qualification by the Kingdom of God judges all closed existence, turned in upon its own immanence, and shows us the shape of the priestly vocation of the world itself. The world does not become the Church, but rather enters a "symphonic" accord with the Church, "without confusion and without separation" (in the Council of Chalcedon's words), accomplishes its own tasks by means of its own charisms or gifts.

A "responsible society" has become conscious of being the active subject of its destiny, and conscious as well, of the universal dimension, of the communion of all mankind. This is why the Church, in speaking to society, is not addressing something alien and separated from herself. The texts of Vatican II are addressed, without distinction, both to believers and nonbelievers alike. The Church's word is the salt and the yeast which finally will determine her reach into the heart of today's civilizations. She seeks to touch not only individuals but nations and peoples in order to move these to responsible choices and to turn their attention toward the problems of wealth, of the Third World and of technology.

There is no ontological dualism between the Church and the world, between the sacred and the profane. The only dualism is ethical, that of the "new creation," and the "old man," of the sacred (redeemed) and of the profane (demonized). For the Fathers, man is a microcosm but the Church is a *macroanthropos*. It is this cosmic, pan-human dimension which, by means of *diakonia,* or a ministry of service (the archetype of which is the Good Samaritan), builds bridges across the chasms and suppresses all division (emancipation, secularization, and on the other hand, the tendencies of Nestorianism and Monophysitism), while at the same time preserving the distinction of vocations. The world in its own way enters into the *macroanthropos* of the Church. This is the place of the ultimate accomplishments, of the *apocatastasis,* or the restoration of all, the sphere of the *Parousia* and of the "new earth," coming in power.

False sacralizations are replaced by authentic consecrations. In the Eastern Church, every baptized person, in the sacrament of anointing/chrismation, passes through the rite of tonsure, which consecrates the baptized completely to the service of God. This rite, analogous to that of monastic tonsure and profession, invites each person to recover the sense of an *interiorized monasticism*, which the sacrament confers upon all. On the other hand, it is time to desacralize all that is petrified and immobilized in the closed circuit of the ecclesial ghetto that has grown up in the Church. And it is also important to desacralize Marxist materialism, for it is neither sufficiently rationalistic nor logically materialistic. If atheism can contribute to purifying the understanding of God among Christians, Christian faith can likewise purify atheism of every trace of illegitimate metaphysics, and this applies to demythologizing as well, all of this in order to make possible an authentic dialogue among the parties clearly defined.

"To bring the earth into submission" means to make it the temple of God. To consecrate the world is to make it pass from a demonic state to its nature as a creature conscious of God. No form of life or culture escapes the universal reach of the Incarnation. The image of all perfection, Christ took on the priesthood and the laity, all vocations, professions and trades in the world. "God so loved the world," even in its sinfulness. The cosmic dimension of Christ's victory, which destroys all barriers, is revealed by his descent into the very reaches of hell. *Theosis* is an essentially dynamic process in which the action of sharing in God's life has repercussions for the whole of the cosmos, just as praise of God projects his glory to all that is human.

In the cosmology of the Fathers, which has nothing in common with natural ethics, the universe is moving towards its fulfillment in the full view of creation, even fuller because of the Incarnation. Christ takes up and fulfills, makes full that which was arrested by the Fall and manifests the saving Love without imposing his plan on us, who are concelebrants of the cosmic liturgy, co-workers with him.

God is present in the world in a different way than he is present in his own Body. The Church has his explicit presence, the world has this implicitly. The Church's task is that of St Paul in Athens when he discerned the "unknown God" and the name of Jesus Christ (Acts 17:22-31). The work of spreading the Gospel must permeate civilization, turning it towards the Orient from on high, Christ himself.

Baptism, as well as the Eastern Church's Great Blessing of Waters at Epiphany, further reveals the cosmic dimension of the Church's reach. The feast of the Cross has all the universe blessed by the holy cross and marked by its sign, that of the Risen Christ. The world is once more found placed within the primordial blessing of God, reaffirmed at the Ascension by the blessing of Christ the Great High Priest as he ascended: "Lifting his hands he blessed them." This consecration places all that is human in relationship with Christ: "All is yours and you are Christ's" (1 Cor 3:22-23).

The Fathers struggled against the gnostics who had nothing but contempt for earthly life. God is not the "wholly other," separated from the world but Emmanuel, "God with us." This is why "All creation waits with eager longing for the revelation of the children of God"

(Rom 8:19). A baptized person is not different from the world, he or she is simply its truth. The world is a royal gift to man in which the horizontal must find its vertical coordinate.

The dignity of mankind and our charism of creation

St Gregory Palamas energetically opposed every deviation from tradition and in his teaching boldly argued for the primacy of humanity over the angels. It is exactly our double structure of soul-body, which makes us complete beings and at the summit of creation. What differentiates us from the angels is that we are in the image of the Incarnate Word. Our soul is incarnate yet completely penetrated by the creative and "life-giving" energies borne by the Holy Spirit. An angel is a "second light," a pure reflection, a messenger and servant of God. Only God as absolute spirit is able to create *ex nihilo*. An angel has no creative power whatsoever but with the human condition it is completely otherwise. According to the Bible, God is more than absolute. He is Absolute and he is his Other, the God-Man. This is why God gives his image to man, in order to make the imperishable gush out of the material of this world and to make manifest divine holiness in the human body. We do not reflect light, as do the angels, we become light. We see this in the luminosity of the bodies of the saints: "You are the light of the world." The haloes of the saints on their icons express this luminosity. The royal position of man determines the ministry of the angels in our service. According to the *synaxarion* or feastday reading of Pentecost Monday, the day of the Holy Spirit, each of the nine ranks of angels comes to adore the deified humanity of Christ during the nine days between the Ascension and Pentecost.

In a homily, St Gregory Palamas defines one of the objectives of the Incarnation: "To venerate the flesh so that the proud spirits would not be able to think themselves higher than man."[8] With astonishing vigor, this text becomes a hymn to the creative spirit of man. It is a full benediction given without reserve to human creation, to the edification of culture and which carries with it the whole authority of the patristic tradition.

---

8   *Hom.* 16, PG 154, col 201D and 204 A.

The Kingdom germinates the seed of paradise, made dormant by the pathology of sin which Christ comes to heal. Salvation consists in the fact that God brings us back from the abyss of the Fall. In the Gospel, salvation actually means healing. "Your faith has made you well." Christ comes as the "great healer," and offers us the Eucharist as the "medicine of immortality." Healing requires ascetic *catharsis*, the purification of our being of every demonic virus, but this is accomplished in an ontological *catharsis*, the restoration of the original human form in the image of God and the real transfiguration of nature.

In the biblical sense, creation is like the seed that produces a hundredfold and then continues to produce. "My Father is working until now, and I too am working" (Jn 5:17). The world was created *with* time, that is to say, incomplete, embryonic, in order to raise up the prophets and "workers for good" across time and to lead therefore to the cooperation of divine and human action until the Day when the seed would be brought to its final maturity. This is why the initial commandment, to "cultivate" the garden of Eden, opens onto the immense perspectives of culture. Stemming from worship, cult, and monasteries, following the typology used in the Scriptures, culture with its own elements reconstitutes the "cosmic liturgy," a prelude already here on earth, to the heavenly doxology.

In our own nature, we are predestined to this ministry, it is a "musical composition, a hymn marvelously composed by the all-creating power."[9] "Your glory, O Christ, is man whom you have created as a singer of your shining brilliance."[10] Illumined on earth, man becomes a miracle. With the heavenly powers, we raise the ceaseless hymn. Though remaining on earth, like angels man nevertheless leads every creature to God...."[11]

Christ gives to mankind the power to act, this is the essential charism, or gift, of the sacrament of chrismation. St Gregory of Nyssa insists upon this human power to rule divinely (PG 44, col. 132 D). These charisms reveal man as king, priest and prophet, almost a god in a human manner.

9   St Gregory of Nyssa, PG 44, col. 441 B.
10 St Gregory Nazianzus, PG 37, col. 1327.
11 St Gregory Palamas, PG 150, col. 1031 A and B.

The ideal preexistence in God of cosmic essences, of archetypes of all that exists, gives particular value to the action of those who are "workers with God," namely to "hasten the Day of God," (2 Pet 3:9-12), to "seek the Kingdom of God" means to "prepare" its way by secret germination. This is our "bringing to birth" of the Kingdom through the faith that belongs to each of us. We then reveal and set in motion the march of history perceptible to all and direct the world, thus prepared and formed, towards the coming of the Lord.

Intense love, purified by authentic asceticism, is our true destiny. The "ontological tenderness" of the great spiritual masters such as Ss Isaac and Macarius, a burning compassion for all creatures, even reptiles and the demons, is accompanied by what we might call an iconographic manner of contemplating and understanding the world, of disclosing there the transparency of God's mind, of penetrating the cosmic shell to the core, full of meaning. This is the source of the cosmic joyousness of Orthodoxy, its inexhaustible optimism, its maximal evaluation of human being: "After God, consider each human being as God" (an unwritten saying of Christ, reported by Clement of Alexandria).

St Maximus tells us, "The divine Master, in a eucharistic manner, nourishes us with the knowledge of the world's ultimate destiny" (*Quaestio* 89). As an immense parable, the world offers a reading of the divine "Poetry" inscribed in its flesh. The images from the Gospels' parables or the cosmic matter of the sacraments, these are not fortuitous. The most simple things are conformed very precisely to their ultimate ends. Everything is an image, a likeness, a participation in the economy of salvation. Everything is song and doxology. "Finally," says Paul Claudel, "The purpose of things is not to provide materials a prison, but a temple."

The gifts and charisms determine the vocation of man, to "cultivate" the immense universal fields, to inaugurate the whole gamut of arts and sciences, to construct that human existence willed by God. This cannot be founded on anything except loving service of the neighbor, biblically more so than social service, the action of healing and restoration of balance in human existence. It is also the communion of all people, grafted onto the absolutely new and desirable reality of which the Book of Revelation speaks to us.

The thinking of the Fathers develops a magnificent philosophy of creation. This is more than a simple justification of culture. When culture becomes a ministry in the service of the Kingdom of God, then it is culture which justifies history, humankind and our priesthood in the world.

Culture, its ambiguity and its destiny

The Lord said: "Go and teach all nations." The Church is concerned with individual souls but she also is concerned with whole nations and peoples. In the formation of cultures and civilizations, the Church has a prophetic word of witness she wants heard. She presents the transcendent in its own eucharistic reality and her paschal message of the Resurrection makes her more than relevant, for she is beyond every age. The Church proclaims that Christ has come to raise the dead who are sleeping and to awaken the living.

Every people appropriates to itself a historic mission, and in constructing itself sooner or later encounters the plan of God. The parable of the talents speaks of this normative plan proposed by God for the freedom of mankind. The ethics of the Gospel are characterized by freedom and creativity. It demands all the maturity of an adult and requires infinitely more of ascetic discipline, of freely accepted constraint and of risk than any ethics of the Law.

History is not at all autonomous, for all events refer to the One who has "all power in heaven and on earth." Even a saying such as "Render to Caesar the things that are Caesar's" (Mt 22:21) has no meaning except in the light of the belief that Caesar is not even Caesar except in relationship to God. "If God did not exist, would I still be captain?" asks an officer in Dostoevsky's *The Possessed*, one who wanted to prove that God did not exist. History cannot escape its normative destiny which will judge it. Here we find the meaning of the inherent "crises" of every civilization and these are eschatological judgments, providential moments, irruptions of the transcendent which attracts the attention of "those who have ears" to hear.

Every Manichean dualism, every Nestorian or Monophysite separation of the divine from the human, all are condemned by the fundamental formula of the Council of Chalcedon: the divine and the human are united without confusion and without separation. This formula determines most accurately the relationships between the Church and the world, between the Church and history, between the Church and culture. Normatively, social life and culture should be built upon this dogma, the application of the principles of a theological sociology, for "Christianity is the imitation of the very nature of God."

Now if a laicized, secularized eschatology is deprived of the biblical eschaton and dreams of a communion of saints without the Holy One, of the Kingdom of God without God, it results in nothing but a Christian heresy, sustained by the weaknesses of Christianity itself. Its poles are the abandonment of the Kingdom for the city completely enclosed and installed in history, or, at the other extreme, a flight from the world and forgetting it in the contemplation of heaven. In our time Marxism has posed anew and violently the problem of the meaning of history and has obliged Christian consciousness to affirm a mysterious continuity between history and the Kingdom of God.

The final revolution cannot occur unless the Church becomes charged with the energies of the Holy Spirit. By her very nature, the Church cannot sanction any canonized social norm and this is why she acts with the greatest flexibility in regards to local circumstances. Yet, if the Word of God consoles, it also judges. This explains the certain detachment of the Church's clairvoyant witness. She condemns all compromise and conformism, but her penetrating realism unmasks and confronts the demonic elements. The universal and most pertinent task before us is to place the goods of this earth at the disposal of all people, without depriving them of religious and political freedom. It is the problem of wealth and not really the poor who covet this wealth. In a technological and free-market civilization, a poet, a thinker, a prophet—all of these are considered useless beings. Artists and disinterested intellectuals already constitute a new form of the proletariat. For sure, above all, by an obligatory international taxation, it is necessary to suppress material hunger. It is also necessary to consider those who hunger and who know that it is not by bread alone that mankind lives. It is most urgent to affirm the primacy of culture and the spirit of finesse. Modern society needs to protect poets and prophets, and while accepting demons out of respect for freedom, we ought equally to reserve a place for the angels and the saints who are just as real as other people and the demons. To doubt that we human beings might be capable of mastering not only the cosmos but ourselves, would be to renounce the dignity given to us as children of God. It is precisely to this world of ours, closed to everything but itself, that the assurance of faith is given in order to penetrate the walls and manifest the invisible presence of the Transcendent One, to raise the dead and move mountains, to cast the fire of hope for the salvation of all and to connect this world and its emptiness to the "Church, full of the Trinity."

No theology which denies the humanity and the Incarnation of God can change the magnificent rule of faith of the Fathers. Neither can minimizing nor watering down the most explosive texts of the Scriptures accomplish anything. It is evident that precisely the eschatological maximalism of monastics has most forcefully justified history. The one who does not participate in the monastic renunciation of the world, the rigorous monastic passage into the world to come without procreation, such a person assumes the entire responsibility of building history in a positive way, that is to say, to open it to all the fullness of humanity: "Prepare the way of the Lord, make straight his paths." This way and its paths manifest human maturity, the dynamism of mankind's fullness.

The theology of the last things and the end presupposes raising thought to its own cross. It has no direct continuity with speculative philosophy: "We proclaim what eye has not seen, nor ear heard, nor the human heart conceived, what God has prepared for those who love him" (1 Cor 2:9). Such theology provides the magnificent definition of every Christian as "the one who loves the *Parousia*," the second coming of Christ (2 Tim 4:8). It is in the light of this coming that the saints, heroes, and geniuses culminate in the same unique reality, that of the Kingdom, when in their own manner they touch what is true and ultimate.

But humanity is never a means for God. If the existence of humankind presupposes the existence of God, the existence of God presupposes the existence of humankind. The human person is an absolute value for God. The person is God's "other" and the "friend" of the One who awaits a free response from this friend in love and creativity. The solution here is both human and divine, the coincidence of the two fullnesses in Christ. This is why the person who is truly eschatological does not remain in passive attentiveness but consecrates himself to the most active and dynamic preparation for the Parousia. Christ comes "among His own," (Jn 1:11), "God among those made gods by deification," the gleaming radiance of divine Fullness in deified human fullness.

"Whoever receives the one I send, receives me" (Jn 13:20). The world's destiny rests on the inventive, creative attitude of the Church, upon her skill in presenting the message of the Gospel in order to gather all to herself and to God. Culture, in all its aspects, is the sphere of this confrontation. But the ambiguity of culture is what complicates this task.

Historically, culture was employed for the preaching of the Gospel without always being accepted as an organic element of Christian spirituality. On the other hand, there is an inherent difficulty in the very nature of culture. The principle of Greco-Roman culture was the form of the perfect in the limits of temporal finitude which was opposed to the infinite, to limitlessness, to the apocalypse, the revealing of what is hidden. By its aversion to death, culture opposed the eschaton and closed itself in upon the duration of time, of history. Now in the "figure of the world passing away," of which the Scriptures speak, it is necessary to heed the warning not to create idols, not to fall into the illusion of earthly paradises, not even the illusion of the utopia of the Church identified with the Kingdom of God. "One waits for the Kingdom and it is the Church instead which comes," Loisy would say. The image of the Church militant passes as does the image of this world.

It is the end of history and its accounting that illumine and reveal its meaning. Historicism, however, does away with this end of history all too simplistically, negating the eschatological perspective which projects this end beyond, out into history. Historicism removes what is human from history, thereby depriving it of its value.

The Christian attitude before the world can never be just that of negation, be it ascetical or eschatological. The Christian attitude is always an *affirmation* but an *eschatological one*, a constant surpassing, which rather than closing, opens completely to the beyond.

In effect then culture does not have an infinite development. It does not have an end in itself. Objectivized, it becomes a system of constraint and, in every way, enclosed within its own limits, the problem becomes incapable of solution. Sooner or later, thought, art and social life reach their own limits and then a choice is imposed: to be located in the infinity of their own immanence, to be intoxicated by their own emptiness, or to surpass their strangulating limitations and, in the transparency of clear waters to reflect the transcendent. God desires this. His Kingdom is not accessible, except through the chaos of this world. It is not the transplanting of something alien into the being of the world, but the revelation of the hidden depths of the world itself.

Art needs to choose between living in order to die, and dying in order to live. Art, abstracted to an extreme, discovers freedom again, pure of every prejudged academic form. External, figurative form is defeated, but access to the interior form, bearing a secret message, is barred by the angel with the flaming sword. The way cannot be opened except by baptism of the Holy Spirit. This is both the death of art and its resurrection, its birth into an epiphanic art, whose culminating expression is the icon. The artist will not find his or her true vocation except in an art that is priestly, in art which creates a sacrament which is also a theophany. To draw, to sculpt, to sing the Name of God, to be one of the places where God descends and makes his dwelling. This has nothing to do with perspective or schools. St Gregory of Nyssa says, "The glory of the eyes is to be the eyes of the Dove, the Holy Spirit."[12] One looks "in advance," for Christ who "is not on high" but before our face, in the watchfulness of the encounter. That which is absolutely new comes from an eschatological return to the sources: "One remembers that which is coming," says the same St Gregory of Nyssa, echoing the eucharistic *anamnesis*, the remembrance in the eucharistic prayer.

St Bonaventure has a formula for this: *si Deus non est, Deus est*: if God does not exist, God exists. Every negation of God, every false absolute, every idol does not exist except in relation to the only true and unique Absolute. For the West, it is the world which is real and God doubtful, hypothetical, and this gives rise to the need to forge

12   PG 44, col. 835.

proofs for his existence. For the East, it is the world which is a matter of doubt, illusory, and the only argument for its reality is the self-evident existence of God. The philosophy of evidence coincides with the philosophy of Revelation. Evidence, with its certitude, in the meaning of Pascal, is the very type of the true knowledge passed through the fire of *apophasis*, of negation.

If we think of God, we will already find ourselves at the interior of divine thought, for it is God who thinks himself in us. One cannot go towards God except by parting from him. The content of all thought about God is epiphanic, it is accompanied by His very presence evoked by such thinking.

The mystery of perverted will, "the mystery of iniquity," however, remains in its entirety. If "ethical resemblance" can pass into radical lack of resemblance, nonetheless, the ontological resemblance of man "in the image" of God remains intact. Freedom, even in ultimate revolt, becomes arbitrary, remains real, and transgressions can even reach the evil limits of madness. Evidence does not at all force our will, just as grace cannot touch or affect us except freely, if we allow it. To a tyrant's orders corresponds the hollow resistance of the slave, while to the invitation of the Master of the banquet corresponds the free consent of the one who makes himself chosen. If one reflects upon the action of the Holy Spirit in the last times, perhaps one can see precisely there this action of the "Father's finger," of the Witness: a suggestion, a decisive invitation addressed to all forms of culture in order to grasp their original intentionality and culminate in the ultimate option of the Kingdom.

St Paul posed the criterion of the unique foundation, which is Jesus Christ: "The work of each will become manifest...and it is the fire which will test the quality of the work of each...." (1 Cor 3:13-15). The same applies to us: "He will be saved, but as one who passes through fire." There are "works which resist fire." This has nothing to do with the destruction of this world pure and simple, but with its being tested. The one who endures possesses the appropriate charisms and becomes a constitutive element of the "new earth." In the past Noah's ark was saved "through the waters." The symbolic image of the ark enables us to see those who are destined to survive and in this prophetic vision is prefigured the great passage to the Kingdom, "through fire."

The Revelations of St Seraphim of Sarov speak of transfigured senses which can already grasp light, warmth, and fragrance as manifestations of the heavenly dimension in this world. St Seraphim himself was clothed in the sun and gave his disciples fruit and flowers which had matured beneath the "new heavens," in anticipation of the "thing in itself" just as a saint reveals "man in himself."

Culture, at its limits, is a like penetration of things and beings as God has thought of them, the revelation of the *logos*, the essence of beings and their transfigured form. The icon also accomplishes this but it is situated beyond culture as a "guiding image," for already in the icon there is a direct vision, a window open to the Eighth Day.

Berdiaev centered his reflection on the apparent conflict between creation and holiness. He was struck by the coexistence in the nineteenth century of the greatest of recent saints, Seraphim of Sarov and the greatest of writers, Pushkin, who, though contemporaries, were unaware of each other's existence. Berdiaev found a solution in the passage of symbols to realities. The government minister, the general, the professor, and the bishop are the keepers of symbols, of functions. A saint, on the contrary, is a reality. A historic theocracy, a Christian state, a republic, all are symbolic. The "communion of saints" is a reality. Culture is a symbol when it collects all the works and is essentially a museum of petrified cultural products, of values without any life. Those with genius know the profound nightmare of the distance between the fire of their spirit and their objectified accomplishments. Perhaps even a Christian culture is in this sense an impossibility. In actuality the great successes of creatures act as the great checks upon creation, *for they do not change the world.*

The paradox of Christian faith stimulates creativity in the world. But in the final phase, true culture, in its eschatological dimension, makes the world shine, obliges history to leave its boundaries. Here it is not the way that is impossible, it is the impossible which is the way and the charisms of the Spirit help to realize it: "Divine power, capable of creating...a way through the impossible."[13] These are the radiant irruption of the "Wholly Other," coming from the very depths of the same.

13   St Gregory of Nyssa, PG 44, col. 128B.

All the forms of culture should lead to this border of the two worlds where they meet, relating the one to the other. This is the passage of the earthly "having" to the heavenly "being" of the Kingdom. The world in the Church, this is the Burning Bush located at the very heart of existence.

A great mind, a thinker, an artist, a social reformer, all ought to be able to rediscover the charisms of the royal priesthood, and each, as such a "priest," can make of his or her work a priestly action, a sacrament transforming every form of culture into a place of theophany. This is to sing the Name of God in the midst of science, of thought, of social action (the "sacrament of the brother"), or of art. Thus in its own way, culture joins with the Liturgy, rendering it a "cosmic liturgy." Culture itself becomes doxology, praise of God.

In former times, the holy princes, such as those of ancient Russia both in the Kievan period as well as under the Mongol domination, were canonized as saints, not just due to their personal holiness but for their fidelity to the charisms of royal power exercised in the service of the Christian people. We, however, have entered in the last times of the Holy Spirit: "The last days, says God, when I will pour out my Spirit upon all flesh...," where we can better imagine the canonization as saints of great minds, scholar, thinkers, artists, those who have given their life and showed their fidelity to their charisms of the royal priesthood and who have worked in the service of the Kingdom of God. Thus the prophetic charism of creation does away with the false dilemma between culture or sanctity, and suggests rather culture-creation and sanctity. Even better, this charism suggests a particular kind of sanctity of the culture itself. It is that of the "world in the Church," the ultimate vocation of its metamorphosis into the "new earth" of the Kingdom.

An even more fallacious dilemma appears: Christ in the Church, or Christ in the world? It is not at all a matter of simply adapting the Church to the mentality of the world, but of adapting both the Church and the world of today to divine Truth, to God's own thinking about the actual world. Christ sends his Church into history to make it, at different moments, the place of his presence, so that all can live the "today" of God in the today of humanity. God is not further removed from our time than from any other age. His presence is even more particularly sensible in every true encounter between people, for this is how we are made human and joined again to the Church.

The presence of Christ is universal. However, the Church is the Body of Christ and Christ calls her to transform the symbolic forms into the explosive reality of the Gospel, to become before all this shining doxology borne by the liberating dynamism of the Holy Spirit of which the Book of Revelation speaks and which none will be able to ignore.

Culture and the Kingdom of God

St Paul said "We are workers with God" (1 Cor 3:9) and the Book of Revelation asserts that: "The nations bring their glory and honor" (Rev 21:24). No one enters the Kingdom of God with empty hands. We can believe that all that the human spirit has to say of truth, all that is expressed in art or discovered in science, and all that we live with the accent of eternity, all the summits of genius and of holiness, will enter into the Kingdom and there recognize their existence in truth as the image is identified with the Original, God.

Even the majestic beauty of snowcapped mountain peaks, the caress of the sea, or the gold of the fields of grain become the perfect language through which the Bible often speaks to us. Van Gogh's suns or the nostalgia of Botticelli's Venus and the sadness of his Madonnas find their serene fullness when the hunger of the two worlds is filled. The purest and most mysterious element of culture, music, in its point of culmination, disappears and leaves us in the face of the Absolute. In Mozart's *Mass,* or his *Requiem,* one hears the voice of Christ and the elevation reaches that of the liturgical reality of his presence.

When it is true, culture may be said to lead us to cult, to worship, to rediscover its liturgical origins. It its essence, culture is the search for the one thing necessary which leads us beyond the immanent boundaries in which we find ourselves. By means of this world, culture lifts up the sign of the Kingdom, a shining spire pointed toward the one who is to come. With the Bride and the Spirit, culture says "Come, Lord!" As St John the Baptist, her star fades into the brilliant light of the *Parousia*'s noontime. As each human being, created in the image of God is a living icon, so earthly culture is the icon of the Kingdom of Heaven. At the moment of the great passage, the Holy Spirit, the "finger of God," will touch this icon and something in it will remain forever.

In the eternal Liturgy of the age to come we, with all the elements of our culture passed through the fire of the last purifications, will sing the glory of our Lord. But already here below we of the one community, the great thinker, artist, all as priests of the universal priesthood celebrate our own Liturgy in which the presence of Christ is manifest according to the measure of the purity of those who receive and contain him. As skilled iconographers, we delineate with the matter of this world and in the light of the Transfiguration an entirely new reality in which slowly the mysterious figure of the Kingdom is made transparent.

9

FREEDOM AND AUTHORITY[1]

Freedom, central mystery of existence

Today we can detect a certain malaise concerning the issue of authority, which will not simply be reduced to its abuse, to authoritarianism. Historically, we see the frequent conflict between obedience to God and obedience to one's own human will. The actual crisis relates not only to a better adjustment of the reciprocal relationship of these two kinds of obedience. It goes much deeper, questioning the legitimacy of the Church's justifying her authority by requiring obedience to the faith. We know very well the violent reaction of the prophets, the martyrs, and the saints in the face of the abuse of theocratic power. St Paul does not cease to exhort us not to lose Christian freedom, to not extinguish or sadden the Holy Spirit by a blind obedience.

There is no doubt that for us today, it is not only with respect to the Church that there is a problem of obedience. Secularized man resents God as the enemy of freedom. In the Hegelian-Marxist dialectic, it is the relationship of master and slave. For Freud, it is the symbol of the "sadistic Father" which gives rise to the "murder of the Father." For Nietzsche, God is the "heavenly Spy" whose glance constrains and transforms me into a thing. The idea of God's omniscience and omnipotence reduces history to a puppet theater. As a philosopher puts it, "The drama is written, including the last act, and no actor can change what will happen." In such a terrible determinism, only God is free and thereby appears to be the only one guilty of the existence of evil. This is what Proudhon affirms when he says: "God is evil itself." "If God

---

1 "Freedom and Authority," in *L'amour fou de Dieu*, pp. 139-158, originally "La dialectique de la liberté et de l'autorité," in *Klêronomia* II (Thessalonika, 1970), pp. 259-271.

exists, I am not free. I am free, therefore God does not exist." Such is the atheistic syllogism on the lips of the anarchist Bakunin and Jean-Paul Sartre.

Without justifying it, one can nevertheless understand this reaction, for the idea of God has undergone an astounding distortion in history. The fearful judge of the Old Testament sacrifices his Son to appease his own wrath. He is omnipotent and manifests himself in all kinds of prodigious actions and miracles. He is omniscient, foreseeing and orchestrating the whole of existence by his "providential" interventions throughout history. According to Shakespeare, history in this light is "a tale told by a fool, signifying nothing."

The conflict

In the Western Church, the situation is complicated by a variety of theologies which produce internal ecclesial conflicts. At the two extremes we have, on one hand, the formalist conformity of the integrists and on the other, the excessive taste for anarchic contestation by the progressives. In the progressive Christian milieu, one does not preach the Gospel anymore but a theology of revolution and violence. In place of "rending the heavens" which is the only use of violence of which Christ speaks: "The Kingdom of heaven has suffered violence and the violent take it by force" (Mt 11:12), for these progressives violence must be directed against the structures of a consumer society, against capitalism insofar as this is an economic system. Certainly the Gospel demands "justice" in human relations and in the construction of the human city of this world, but this demand is articulated in a "hierarchy of values," the summit of which is sacrificial love. The ideal of a comfortable life, clean, relaxing, and abundant is not at all envisaged by the Gospel. Between the suppression of hunger and of injustice that cries out from the Third World and a comfortable, bourgeois life turned in upon itself, there is an abyss. Now the Gospel does not say anything about portioning out and limiting comfort, but much about opening the human city to the presence of God, to the miracle of his Incarnation in which the goal is not simply a "happy" humanity but humanity that is truly "blessed," matured in the sun of the beatitudes even if persecuted and given to martyrdom. "Blessed are those who are persecuted for righteousness sake, for theirs is the Kingdom of heaven." Everything is subordinated to the Kingdom, not solely by natural exploitation of the earth nor by a tranquil spot in history but by the transformation of all into the "new earth." There is no rapture or flight to the beyond, but a profound change of objective. There is the movement from penultimate values to those which are ultimate.

An intelligent faith is an adult action and not that of a child. The Church is established by the second birth of the Spirit and not by the first or human birth. Now only the Church recruited by this first birth is able to listen to certain aspects of the "new theology" and to thus fall into a religious infantilism.

The tiresome opposition between "faith" and "religion" preached by the theology of secularization and the "death of God," makes of Tradition a *tabula rasa* in all that is positive within it, in the doctrine of the deification of man and the emphasis on the "new creature." Such newness comes only from the death and resurrection of Christ which has transformed the ontological conditions of human existence. One asks if, on one side or the other, it has to do with the same God, the same Gospel, the same mystery of Christ, the suffering servant. There has been a dangerous Marxist distortion of Christian consciousness. It poses the option: fidelity to the Word of God and his will, or fidelity to the will of humanity which has inaugurated the millenarianism of the Left and which is rooted more in the Old Testament than in the New. It is symptomatic that the currents of a new ideology claim the inspiration of the profound thought of Dietrich Bonhoeffer. This Lutheran pastor and theologian, admirable in so many ways in his thinking, observed at the tragic and premature end of his life: "I have noticed just how much all that I am thinking and feeling is inspired by the Old Testament, which I have been reading more in these months than the New."[2] The progressive movement is very much engaged in political, economic and social struggle, rightly inspired by the prophets of the Old Testament. It is committed to creating, out of perennial struggle, the myth of violent, revolutionary action. However, the only authentic revolution comes in the Gospel's *metanoia*, the transformation of a

---

2   *Résistance et Soumission*, Geneva: Labor et Fides, 1967, p. 76.

person into a man or woman of the Eighth Day, of God's Kingdom, for whom "everything is new," for "Christ has placed all things beneath the sign of his Cross."

Without neglecting the demands of justice, the organization of the human city, according to the prophet Isaiah (40-53), is subordinated to the vision of the suffering Servant and the presence of God among men. The world, such as it is, is radically confronted by the Gospel. The capitalist world as well as the socialist or Marxist is confronted in the name of the world which is beyond them both. Man works here below and constructs history through the earthly path and all its values, not for an ideal, immanent city but for a "new earth," the new city of the Kingdom of God. Our strategy should share in that of God. In this transcendent strategy, the Gospel promises no material success. In actuality, every age in history experiences defeats, but these are great achievements for they extricate history from its boundaries and lead it toward its own transfiguration. It is Christ who battles this world and this is why his saving energies are unleashed at Pentecost. Christ confronts death by his own death and he descends to hell in order to emerge "as from a bridal chamber." He contests his executioners in order to offer them pardon and resurrection. Christ offers to all not an opulent life but divine sonship and immortality, beginning here and now.

All the activity for justice and social renewal has no absolute value in itself. It is not authentic except in Christ, in whom it witnesses to the love of the Father. This activity is destined, from the here and now, to find its eternal dimension. This is the "today" of God in our today, which only appears when we transcend our existence, moving toward the "wholly Other." The announcement of the "death of God" opens the door to the violence which seeks to appropriate to itself the love of God, according to human standards, and which declares that this love will not be arrived at except through politics and by means of the neighbor. Direct relationship with God is questioned. Prayer and contemplation are considered useless, since it appears that it is through violent revolution that relationship with God becomes accessible once more, for it is through political action that God is risen again!

In the face of such an aberration, it must be said, with the Fathers, that love as "the sacrament of the brother" means welcome of and hospitality for the other, through, in and with Christ present in my soul. Only Christ allows me to recognize others as "brothers and sisters," as my brethren. Theologies of violence, then, lack evangelical roots. In them we do not realize that Christ calls us to overcome the passions which assail us. If an extreme, surgical solution is imposed in a concrete case, we must be aware that such violence risks the unleashing of demonic powers.

God's paradoxical attitude, according to the Fathers

The Fathers of the Church counsel a negative approach to the mystery of God. They warn of the danger of anthropomorphism which embezzles the concepts of power and omniscience. The Fathers claimed that these categories do not apply to God. He is the "wholly Other," the "mysterious One," the One "eternally sought." The dogma of the Trinity shows that the Father is not Father because he renounces all superiority in relationship to his Son and the Holy Spirit. In a dignity of equality, the Father gives to the Son and the Spirit all that he has, everything that he is. According to St John of Damascus, the Three are united not to be lost but in order to be distinct in each other reciprocally. Each divine Person is present in presenting the others, containing the others, offering everything to the others in an eternal circulation of Trinitarian love, of the kind in which divine freedom is identified with love.

The creation of man ("Let us make man in our image") places him in an intimate relationship with the Trinitarian mystery, at the heart of divine sacrificial love. This creation, the masterpiece of the Trinity, implies a certain risk on God's part by a free and sacrificial limitation of his omnipotence. God made us and waits for our free response: "I desire mercy more than sacrifice" (Hos 6:6). This is why God "withdraws himself" in order to allow us the pastures of our own hearts, space for our own freedom, for "God is able to do everything except to constrain us to love him," as the patristic saying puts it. He wishes to establish a free reciprocity with us in which he becomes vulnerable, "weak." He gives up his omnipotence. He shares with us the bread of suffering in wishing to also share with us the wine of joy. But this divine "weakness" is actually the apex of his omnipotence. It gives rise not to a passive, puppet-like submission, but gives birth to a "new creature," free in the image of divine freedom, that is to say, without limits, someone capable of loving God for himself because he can refuse, say "No" to God as well. This is why God does not manifest himself in thunder and lightning but in the soft breeze, purely interior to our hearts, as the almost secret waiting of a friend (1 Kings 19:11-13). According to the great mystics, God is a beggar of divine love who waits at the door of our hearts: "See, I am at the door and I knock, and if anyone hears me and opens the door, I will come in and dine with him" (Rev 3:20). According to St Maximus, God has made himself a beggar because of his bending down low as a beggar towards us, suffering until the end of time, along with each and every person who suffers.

The orders of a tyrant always evoke deaf resistance. On the contrary, the Bible emphasizes the multiplicity of God's appeals and invitations: "Hear, O Israel" (Deut 6:4), "If you wish to be perfect..." (Mt 19:21), "The king sent his servants to call those who were invited to the wedding banquet" (Mt 22:3). God is the king who makes such an appeal and who waits "in suffering" for the free response of his child. God's authority is not an order which is imposed from on high upon us. God's authority is a secret action, one that takes place within us. God is "closer to us than we are to ourselves," as St Augustine says, for he is infinitely beyond everything that we are able to imagine of him. "I am who I am." God is the Incomparable One, the Imperceptible One. His authority is in his being the shining truth of love, and this is evidence one can neither prove nor demonstrate but which one simply receives, saying with Thomas, "My Lord and my God" (Jn 20:28).

The prophets never substituted themselves for God but rather transmitted his word. Even the apostles are ministers because they are servants. "But you are not to be called Rabbi, for you have one Teacher and you are all students. And call no one your father on earth, for you have one Father—the one in heaven. Nor are you to be called teachers, for you have one teacher, the Christ" (Mt 23:8-10). Christ is the only Master and Teacher, the Son who transmits to us the Father's love and our divine sonship. The Gospel applies no juridical terms of authority to this "suffering servant," to the "child Jesus." Rather what is implied is the obedience of a spouse. Where authentic love rules, the relationships between spouses are such that obedience becomes truth experienced as reciprocal and open to the presence of Christ. The Church follows the example of the Lord. She is nothing but the servant of the Truth so as not to place an obstacle between people and the Gospel, between children and their Father. The spiritual fathers and mothers do the same in their complete humbling of themselves, making their "spiritual children" not only their own children but children who are free and mature adults in the Lord himself.

"Whoever hears you, hears me" (Lk 10:16). If one places the accent upon "hears you," then this is a juridical concept of authority and the delegation of powers of a sovereign lawmaker. But the one, unique will of God is to unite himself to us in a love that is free. To the pyramidal concept of the Church, with the delegations of power cascading hierarchically, is opposed the figure of the concentric circle, with God as Love at the center radiating out, and as the rays approach each other, they converge towards the divine center. There is no questioning of the Church's authority here, insofar as she is the location of the Word and the divine presence. Rather, we must not confuse God with the ministries and the human functionaries in the Church.

Authority and freedom in their historical evolution

In the West since the Reformation, this problem has been posed in terms of the relationship between authority and freedom, with the accent migrating from one to the other of these realities in ecclesial life. It is very much a problem of how much. What is reciprocal in both authority and freedom? For Rome, it is the question of how much freedom for the people is legitimate, with the order and authority of the clergy protected. Protestantism emphasizes freedom and asks what is the legitimate amount of authority that can protect the freedom of each believer. One can see clearly that this conflict views authority and freedom as correlative principles, freedom being defined in connection with its limit which is authority, and authority being defined in connection to freedom, which it ought to limit. Through the ages, the limit has travelled from one pole to the other.

In anarchist movements, the limit is moved to its outmost boundary. This is the elementary demand of a radical freedom which does away with every constraint. In its own logical terms, freedom is not able to remain "moderated" with a little more or a little less. It is all or nothing. Sooner or later, the shadow of Nietzsche's "Superman" emerges, Feuerbach announces the liberation of every alienation, Dostoevsky finally writes up the account and states the final truth of the arbitrary revolutionary: "Freedom or death." The circle has closed in on itself and the conflict is without resolution concerning the balance of these terms. It exteriorizes them and opposes them to each other, and this leads to the loss of a *deep interiorization*, their rooting within the person, which is the only means to a solution. The external correlation of these two terms, their objectivization, is explosive. All through history, freedom undermines authority and authority imprisons freedom under the hypocritical pretext of inviting to do freely that which is actually dictated by authority. "The underground man" of Dostoevsky rises up violently against the formal logic and argues: "What if we send all this 'two and two are four' to all the demons." We know well what this means concretely.

Before presenting the interior problem, it will be useful to recall several classical definitions. According to Littré, authority is the power of making oneself obeyed, of imposing oneself and of ordering. Authority, legitimate or not, is invasive, it does easily resign itself to not being omnipotent. If it uses power and knowledge which it possesses in order to subordinate others to its own particular ends, it is coercive. The philosopher Alain radically distinguishes the authority of power, reversing the terms and warning: "If authority feigns love, it is most hateful and if it really loves, it is without power." Karl Jaspers explains in a penetrating analysis: "The idea of authority comes to us from Roman thought. *Auctor* is the one who sustains a thing and develops it, the one who gives it growth. *Auctoritas* according to etymology is the force which seeks to sustain and give growth," which keeps watch not in defense but in belief. It is apparent that it has nothing to do with making someone obey but to make one flourish, bloom. Lafay is precise: "Authority differs from power. The one inspires the sentiment of respect and veneration, the other fear. Authority has to do with dignity, power with force." But it is Father Laberthonnière who goes the furthest: "Authority which subordinates itself to those submissive to it and which links its situation to theirs, achieves with them an exquisite communion and this is liberating." In this case, authority is the guardian of freedom, her guarantee. As Bishop Dupanloup says: "All authority whose principle is not that of self-sacrifice is not worthy of this great name." Such self-sacrifice the scriptures call *diakonia*. "Authority," Father Laberthonnière continues, "which is uniquely conceived as a power imposing itself by constraint or by entitlement, finds itself, by its very essence, irremediably exterior and alien to the one upon whom it is enforced...But it can assume another character, even one absolutely opposed to this." This would be the interior character. In the Gospel of St Luke (9:54 ff), "When his disciples James and John saw it, they said, 'Lord do you want us to command fire to come down from heaven and consume them?' But he turned and rebuked them. 'You do not know the spirit by which you are given life.'" In a manner very close to that of the Eastern Church, Fr Laberthonnière expresses well his principle of interiorized authority, which completely changes authority's nature.

The Tradition of the Eastern Church

St Paul draws for us the map of the freedom of the human soul proper to Christianity. The maximalism of the Gospel does away with the moderation of justice nicely weighed and dispensed. "God does not require so much...," says the commonsense of an honest person, yet, God demands everything and more.

The desert fathers posed no theoretical problems. On the contrary, they quite simply lived a freedom without limits. Their example always teaches us this same interiorization. Every person finds the same expanse of interior freedom in placing himself before God. This had been the experience of Epictetus and was St Paul's teaching, that even a slave is within, royally free. It is in God that such a limitless freedom is found, for his limitlessness never limits but is the unique source that satisfies our hunger and is the object and content of the freedom beyond all constraint. We must submit ourselves to God's will and it will not do to submit purely and simply. God wants his will to be accomplished, yet he does not wish us to be slaves but his children in freedom and friends of Christ.

The classic definition of freedom is the ability to choose. St Maximus the Confessor however, affirms just the contrary. The need to choose, he says, is itself an impoverishment, the consequence of the Fall. True free-dom is a total impulse oriented completely toward the Good, without question or hesitation. At the level of holiness, choice ceases to condition freedom. The one seeking to be perfect follows the Good immediately, spontaneously, beyond any option. In its highest form, freedom is an activity producing its own reasons rather than submitting to them. Free-dom raises us to the level where the most free actions are the most perfect. God does not choose, and in his image, a saint acts in a way surpassing all personal preference. To hesitate and to choose, to look for authority and its commands, is the nature of a will which is still divided by contradictory desires ceaselessly colliding with each other. Perfection is in the simplicity of a convergence supernaturally co-natural to the divine will. One cannot attain this except by overcoming all exteriorization of relationships.

Authority is the truth that sets us free

If one follows the false dialectic (here, the power of the bishops, and there the freedom of the people of God) everything is distorted, objectivized and exaggerated by the anxiety of quantifying. We have al-ready seen that authority conceived of as an external reality deforms its very nature. On the contrary, when interiorized, it appears as the most contradictory of values, namely as authority which denies its own au-thority, which refuses the power of coercion and thereby raises itself to the point where it is identified with the Truth. This is confirmed in the Tradition of the Eastern Church. The Church is not an authority, nei-ther is Christ or the Gospel, for authority is always something *external* for us. The Church, Christ, the Gospel are *not authority* which places us in captivity but *the Truth* which makes us free.

Every image we derive from politics sees freedom as a choice. Thus we are free insofar as we are able to choose, but since choice is a fact, a reality, it is no longer free. Rather one has here chosen a principle which sets up in authority that to which one submits oneself. Here we have a paradox. Freedom is a choice which limits and in the end suppresses itself.

The Gospel speaks in a completely different way about freedom. We are called by the Gospel to know and then to choose Truth, and this sets us free and makes us truly free. This means that every opposition between authority and freedom is outside the Church where the victory of the one or the other does not free us at all, in the sense of the Lord's words. Scholastic theology is always tempted by its own need for measurement. The bishop has the fullest, the priest somewhat less and the layperson the least measure of grace, of authority? But the Spirit blows where he wills and who can contain him? We know his presence but we ignore his absences, perhaps even where they do not exist.

One of the most ancient "symbols," or confession of faith says, "And in the Holy Spirit, the Church," a mysterious identification which signifies that to believe in the Church is to believe in her superabundance, her "grace upon grace," without measure. "The Law [authority] was given by Moses, grace and truth come through Jesus Christ" (Jn 1:17). "God gives the Spirit without measure" (Jn 3:34). The thirst for true freedom is the hunger for the Holy Spirit who makes us free without measure. Simone Weil described this thirst very well: "To call upon the Spirit purely and simply, an appeal, a cry, as when one is at the very limits of thirst, sick from it, when one can no longer imagine oneself drinking or even action in general. One can only think of water, water itself, but this image of water is like a cry of one's whole being...." To this thirst responds the Church, experienced as a continual Pentecost: "Whoever thirsts, come and drink! The one who desires it freely receives the water of life" (Rev 22:17). This is the very essence of the Church, not authority but the source of superabundance, grace upon grace, freedom beyond freedom, doing away with every "objectivizing" conflict, every slavish cowering.

The Fall was precisely the perversion of the interior relationship established by God. But even before this, it was the serpent who perverted the state of paradise, suggesting the false idea that there was a prohibition, hence a law before the Fall. The serpent insinuated: "God said, 'You must not eat from all the trees of the garden'" (Gen 3:1). Now God had actually said exactly the opposite: "You can eat from all the trees of the garden" (Gen 2:16), but with different consequences. If St Paul says: "Everything is permitted but not everything is useful" (1 Cor 6:12), the serpent would say "Everything is forbidden but everything is useful." God thus is transformed into a law, into a prohibition. But God did not say: "Do not eat of the fruit, otherwise you will be punished." Rather he said, "Do not eat of the fruit, otherwise you will die." This is not an order but the announcement of a destiny freely chosen in one meaning or in another. It has nothing at all to do with simple disobedience but with inattention to living communion with the Father, with the drying up of the thirst for his presence, for his love and truth which is life, in the absence of which there is only death. At the moment of temptation we see God as an authority dictating orders and demanding blind obedience. Such a suggestion comes from Satan. It comes from the first revolt against an objectified, and therefore impoverished and perverted authority, one which ceases to be liberating truth. We have "objectified" God and set up a distance between ourselves and him, an external space wherein we seek a dark place to hide ourselves, in which we fashion our captive existence. This is why Christ came "to proclaim freedom to the captives...to free those who were oppressed" (Lk 4:19).

The consequence of original sin is to transform God into an external authority, into the Law, and the logical step following is the transgression against this Law-God, placing us outside of God. The Incarnation was necessary so that we could once more find ourselves within God. Only the "child Jesus" could again reveal the true face of the father in the parable of the prodigal son, where authority and justice are not the obsession of the father but of the older son, the "good boy." The father could only run to the encounter with his lost child.

"Leave the dead to bury the dead" means to bury dead authority and dead freedom, both perverted of their very identity. "You know that the rulers of the Gentiles lord it over them, and their great ones are tyrants over them. It will not be so among you; but whoever wishes to be great among you must be your servant and whoever wishes to be first among you must be your slave" (Mt 20:25-26). St John the Baptist is the " greatest among those born of women," because "the least in the Kingdom of heaven is greater than he" (Mt 11:11). St Paul's words (2 Cor 1:24) "I do not mean to imply that we lord it over your faith; rather, we are workers with you for your joy." This magnificently defines what is in the Eastern Church the "authority" of the bishop.

In the New Covenant, the "new commandment" replaces the law of Moses and sets up a reciprocal relationship: "The one who loves me...I will love." The messianic authority of Jesus is the power of forgiving sins and of healing, saving. Everything is interiorized. The Law and the prophets have become the new commandment of love. The authority conferred upon the twelve Apostles and their successors has been placed within the community of the Church and never above it. The identification of the Church with Christ, the Body with the Head, makes impossible all human authority over the People of God, for this would be to place a human authority over Christ himself. Since the time of St Irenaeus, the episcopate is not a power over the Church, but the expression of her very nature. The sacramental identity and charism of the truth of the bishops is not a personal infallibility but that of the local church, identified with the Church in her entirety.

Since Pentecost, the Church, led by the Holy Spirit and the apostolic council of Jerusalem, without making itself the word of Christ, has nevertheless formulated its principle of life: "It seems good to the Holy Spirit and to us" (Acts 15:28). However, in the Church, "everything follows good order," and the bishop is responsible for correct teaching and the pastoral direction of the community. The universal *consensus* is the *sign* of the truth in the matter of faith, for the only supreme authority within the Church is the Holy Spirit. The bringing to birth of the "new creature" liberates and allows the Church to be seen as the place of the "glorious freedom of the children of God" (Rom 8:21). Our real skepticism is opposed to external authority and seeks the interior principle, finding in the mystery of the Church not authority but the Spirit of Truth.

The knowledge of the truth that makes us free is not knowledge about God but the knowledge of the Truth which is God, as St Simeon the New Theologian says well at the feast of the Meeting of Christ in the Temple: "I give thanks that without confusion or separation You have made yourself one Spirit with me" (*Hymns of Divine Love*). The divine fire makes the Creator and the creature inseparable, eliminates all distance, every objectification, every exteriorizing of authority between them. For Sartre, it is the thirst for formal freedom that dominates, but this freedom is empty, without an object. In the words of Simone Weil, it is the object, the content which dominates, the water of life, the Holy Spirit given without measure.

St Peter's sermon on the day of Pentecost cites the prophecy of Joel: "In the last days it will be, God declares, that I will pour out my Spirit upon all flesh, and your sons and your daughters shall prophesy, and your young men shall see visions, and your old men dream dreams" (Acts 2:17). The descent of the Holy Spirit signifies that the last days, the final times, have already qualitatively begun and that the gifts of the Spirit have begun to shower upon us even more abundantly than we suspect. After Vatican II, the new movements in the Church have activated the Body of Christ. Often we see a tentative, clumsy groping, yet a positive search, cutting through the historical towards the authentic relationship among the different parts of the one People of God: the bishops and the laity together and with the same identity as servants, in the image of the Lord. The Holy Spirit is able to slake the impatience and thirst of those who are seeking and to help them advance the Kingdom.

In the memoirs of his adolescence (*The Words*), Sartre had something quite profound to say: "I was waiting for the Creator (the Father), they gave me instead a great Master to please." The Church has to pay great attention to such waiting, to such a seeking, and respond to it. By this response, one would see in a bishop not an executive, a patron, a power who constrains, but the image of the father, and one who thirsts for freedom, the prodigal son who searches not for authority but for the father's heart. It is the joy and freedom of the children of God that is found in the Church, through all the rules and activities, it is the Holy Spirit whom we find.

Our interiorized obedience to God makes us contemplate that which we sing in the Liturgy: "One is holy, One is Lord, Jesus Christ, in the glory of God the Father. Amen." This is because the only lordship, the only authority revealed by God himself is that of Christ who knocks at the door of every human heart (Rev 3:20). And with Christ there is the Pentecostal lordship of the Holy Spirit, his freedom breathed into us as we wait for the lordship of the Father in the Kingdom. But can we call this lordship authority? This would be absurd. The Kingdom is the lordship of the Trinity of love for all, freed finally and completely by the One who is truth and joy without end. The Church, as St John the Baptist, must "decrease" so that she reveals only the presence of Christ, the Bridegroom and the Beloved, who already offers eucharistic communion with himself as a communion of marriage, with every human soul.

10

THE CHARISMS OF
WOMAN[1]

Our reflection here is inspired by anthropological concepts drawn from the Bible, from patristic thought and the spirituality of the East, of the Orthodox Church. In the luminous imagery of St Paul, the Church "...the whole body, joined and knit together by every ligament with which it is equipped, as each part is working properly, promotes the body's growth in building itself up in love" (Eph 4:16). The context of this verse clearly speaks of charisms, gifts which each receives in order to be of service to the ecclesial whole, where every person is complementary to the other. It is therefore the charismatic reality of the human being that is essential to our subject here.

In history, the shattered equilibrium of humanity all too easily leads to the formulation of false questions. Thus we have the "question" or the "problem" of woman. When men pose this without raising also the question of themselves, themselves as "problem," they thereby isolate themselves, cutting themselves off from the limpid sources of life, actually putting into question their own creativity and showing themselves lacking in reality.

In a male-dominated world where everything is marked by the patriarchal system, man, armed with his reason, his being, and existence, loses his cosmic connection with heaven and nature, also with the feminine as a mystery complementary to his own being. Eliminating the metaphysical and the mystical which generate him, sliding toward cerebral

---

1 "The Charisms of Woman," originally "La Femme et La Parole," published in *CATECHESE, Centre National de l'Enseignment Religieux* 16 (1964), pp. 265-276, and reprinted as "Les Charismes de la Femme," in *La nouveauté de l'Esprit*, pp. 237-254.

abstraction, man sees the deeper dimension closing before him, that of the Holy Spirit. He reviews the great avenues of civilization, well measured, where woman's place seems to be a minor one. Through an egocentric and self-defensive instinct, man imprisons woman as a maleficent power, a permanent menace to his freedom. She will be submissive to the supreme power of a leader, to the indisputable authority of man. According to the solar principle, that around which everything revolves, the only brilliance is man. A Pythagorean saying goes, "The principle of good creates order, light, and it is man. The principle of evil created chaos, the darkness, and that is woman."

Man seeks to affirm himself in surpassing everything that limits him. Every woman is such a limit, for she is "other," she presents him with "otherness." Here man sees a prison which shrinks his horizons and confines his spirit.

Collective conscience veils false myths. And it is Christian women who today apply to themselves again the ritual prescriptions defined in the rabbinical period in which resounded this prayer: "Blessed are You, Adonai, Lord, who did not make me a woman." The complex of Adam, masculine to be sure, takes refuge in these words: "It was the woman who gave me the fruit from the tree."

The revolution put into action by the Gospel will take a very long time, and even the disciples of the Lord were astonished by the simple fact that He, Christ, spoke with a woman (Jn 4:27).

The charisms of woman

Woman has her own manner of being, her own mode of existence, the gift of weaving her being in its own relationship to God, to others, and to herself. Despite so many historical distortions of which woman is the victim, she protects all the more profoundly in herself the mystery of her being and her charisms, or gifts which St Paul describes in the amazingly rich symbol of the "veil" (1 Cor 11), an evident sign of the sacred. Over against this, the great whore of Babylon (Rev 17) profanes and degrades her femininity insofar as it has a religious essence. She strips off her "veil," makes herself naked, disincarnates herself of the mystery of the feminine, of the *fiat* pronounced by her eternal motherhood. And this is the mystery which every woman must discern in order to read there her destiny, her vocation, her gifts.

The biblical narrative of the first human couple, Adam and Eve, reveals the original, the archetype of the consubstantiality, of the *complementarity* of principles. The Fall polarized man and woman and ever since they are either beings opposed and struggling against one another or else beings who accept each other's "otherness" and complement each other in order to make a "new creature" in Christ.

Man overflows his own being, more external to himself, his charism of expansion directs his vision constantly outside of himself. He constantly fills the world with his creative energies, imposing his mastery upon it and conquering it as engineer and constructor. Man receives at his side woman, who is to be his companion and helper. She is at one and the same time beloved, spouse, and mother. Far more interiorized than man, woman is completely at ease within the limits of her being by which she fills the world with her radiant presence. "The glory of man," (1 Cor 11:7) in her luminous purity, woman is like a mirror in which the face of man is reflected and revealed to himself and by which he is corrected. Thus she assists man in understanding himself and in realizing the meaning of his own being. Woman accomplishes this by discerning her destiny, for it is only through woman that man becomes what and who he really is.

St Peter's words (1 Pet 3:4) are addressed to every woman and contain a whole Gospel of her spiritual motherhood. This text defines most precisely woman's fundamental charism: the bringing to birth of man hidden in his own heart, *homo cordis absconditus*.

Man is more inclined to be indifferent to his own situation. On the contrary, the maternal instinct of woman, as at the marriage feast of Cana (Jn 2:1-10) immediately discovers the thirst for the spirit even of men and finds the eucharistic source to quench it. The ontological relationship of mother and child makes woman like Eve, "the source of life." She watches over every being, protects life and the world. Her interiorized and universalized charism of "motherhood" bears every woman toward the famished and needy and makes admirably precise her feminine essence: married or not, every woman is *mother in aeternum*. This is the "sacramental character" inscribed in her very being. The elements of her soul predispose her to "protect" everyone who crosses her path, to discover even in the most aggressive and strong being the child who is weak and defenseless.

If we define masculine love as "to love is to need," then the love of a woman means "to fulfill the need," not only to take care of it but to even foresee the need.

"Jesus, seeing his mother and near her the disciple whom he loved, said to his mother: 'Woman, there is your son'" (Jn 19:26-27). These words of the Lord make the Virgin Mary, the figure of Mother Church and of every woman, a truly ecclesial being. The eternal virgin and eternal feminine and the eternal mother from whom we derive the archetype of the *Magna Mater*.

The religious meaning of the feminine

Conqueror, adventurer, builder, man is not fatherly in his being. An ancient liturgical text projects upon the motherhood of the Virgin the light of the divine fatherhood: "You have given birth to the Son without a father, the Son whom the Father brought forth before the ages without a mother." The virgin Mary's motherhood is thus a human figure or image of the fatherhood of God.

Here we have an explanation of why the religious principle of dependence on the beyond, of receptivity, of communion is expressed so immediately by woman. The particular sensibility to pure spirituality resides far more in the *anima* than in the *animus*. It is the feminine soul which is nearest to the sources, to the origins, to birth. The Bible presents woman as the quintessential image of human nature's spiritual receptivity. In actuality, the promise of salvation was given to woman, for a woman received the Annunciation of the birth of Christ and it was a woman who first saw the Risen Lord, and it is a woman "clothed in the sun" who is the image of the Church and of the heavenly city in the Book of Revelation. Further, it is in the images of the beloved and the bride that God chose to express his love for us and the marital nature of his communion with us. Finally, the most important fact is that the Incarnation was accomplished in the Virgin's feminine nature. It is she who gave the Word of God her flesh and blood.

To divine fatherhood as a specific feature of God's very being directly corresponds the motherhood of woman, her receptive capacity for the divine. The whole goal of Christian life is to make of every human being a mother, a being predestined for the mystery of birth, "so that Christ may be formed in you" (Gal 4:19).

Sanctification is precisely the action of the Spirit who makes possible the miraculous birth of Jesus in the depths of the soul. This is why the Nativity symbolizes and expresses the charism of every woman, that of bringing God to birth in destitute souls: "The Word is constantly born anew in our hearts," says the Letter to Diognetus. For St Maximus the Confessor, the mystic is the one in whom the birth of Christ is manifest. In order to describe his spiritual fatherhood, even St Paul used the image of motherhood: "I undergo the sufferings of childbirth" (Gal 4:19).

The being of woman and her vocation

The Bible puts before us woman as the predestined point of encounter between God and mankind.

If the masculine participates in the Incarnation by his silence, in the person of St Joseph, on the contrary, it is woman who says *fiat* for us all. To the creative *fiat*, "Let it be," of the Father corresponds the humble *fiat* of the "handmaid of God." Christ could not take upon himself human flesh and blood unless humanity through Mary had not freely given it to him. The Virgin is therefore the point of encounter, the place of convergence of the two *fiats*.

As the figure of the Church, the Virgin personalizes the Church through her own motherly protection and through prayer. She is the Church's prayer of intercession.

In Greek the word for chastity means integrity and integration, the very power of unifying. An ancient liturgical prayer is directed to the *most pure Theotokos*: "By your love, bind my soul," free it from all psychic imprisonment, make unity spring up within me. Such integration is the only force capable of halting the enterprise of demolition to which modern male-dominated culture seems committed. In truth, the very salvation of civilization depends on the "eternal-motherhood" of woman.

On can grasp her salvific power if one understands that it is not at all because she was the "weaker sex" that Eve was tempted. On the contrary, she was lured precisely because she represented the principle of religious integration of human nature. Attentive in her heart, she immediately succumbed and docile Adam followed behind, claiming, that "the woman offered me the fruit," putting up no resistance whatsoever, not even asking the most basic of questions about what he was offered.

Left to himself, man would be lost in the infinity of his abstractions, in the perfected techniques of humiliating others. Degrading the other, he becomes degraded himself, creating a world corresponding to his own dehumanized vision. Man places himself in agony.

Man establishes himself in the world by his tools. Woman however does this by the gift of herself. In her very being she is intimately connected to the rhythms of nature. If the masculine quality is to do, that of woman is to be, and this is the religious dimension par excellence. Man creates science, philosophy, art but distorts all of these by his fearful objectification of "organized truth." Woman on the other hand, is opposed to all objectification, for her strength lies not so much in creation but in giving birth. It is by her being that she is herself the criterion which corrects every abstraction in order to bring values back to the center, to manifest correctly what the masculine creativity intends. Instinctively, woman always defends the primacy of being over theory, of the operative over the speculative, of the intuitive over the discursive. She possesses the gift of being able to directly penetrate the existence of another, the innate faculty of grasping the imponderable, of discerning the destiny of another person. To protect the world set up by men, as a virgin to purify it by giving to the world a soul, her own soul—such is the vocation of every woman, whether monastic, single, or married.

Man is ecstatic, going out of himself in the projection of his own genius beyond himself in mastering the world. Woman is enstatic in being turned in toward her own being, towards being itself. Woman operates on the ontological level. Hers is not to be a verb but *esse*, the essence, the very heart of a creature. This is the manifestation of sanctity, this sanctity of being that the demons cannot endure. It is not by fierce action but by her purity and sanctity that woman wounds the head of the dragon.

According to Heraclitus, "War is the father of all things, harmony and peace the mother." The father-warrior is symbolized by the bow, the mother-symphony by the lyre. But the lyre, we might say, is nothing but the sublimated bow, a bow with several strings. Rather than death, woman sings of life. Thus the masculine warrior and killer can be brought into harmony by woman and changed into a bearer of life, culture, worship, a celebrant of the Liturgy of praise.

Symbols and history

The *Didascalion,* or *Teaching of the Twelve Apostles*, ontologically links the feminine to the mystery of the Holy Spirit. "The deacon has the place of Christ and you must love him. You should honor the deaconesses as having the place of the Holy Spirit." This is why in the symbolism of the liturgical assembly the woman is called the "altar" and represents prayer. The image of the soul in adoration, woman is the human being who has become prayer. In the well-known fresco of the basilica of St Callixtus, man extends his hand over the bread of offering and it is the one who offers sacrifice, the bishop who does this, who presides at the Liturgy. Behind him we see the praying one, the woman in prayer, a pure and total self-offering. In her charism of protection she raise all of life, the world, all people up to God. She does this in the sign of the Spirit who "broods over" or covers all creation as the Hebrew word in the creation narrative of the book of Genesis suggests, the sign of the Paraclete, the Advocate and Consoler.

The ordained ministry, that of the priesthood and episcopacy, is a masculine function of witness. The bishop attests to the saving validity of the sacraments and has the power of celebrating them. He has the charism of watching over the purity of the deposit of faith and exercising the pastoral authority. The ministry of woman belongs to that of the royal priesthood, not that of attributed functions, as with the ordained episcopacy and priesthood, but that of her very nature. The ordained ministry is not to be found in such charisms. This would be to go against its own very being. However the vocation of woman, as personalized by the Virgin Mary, is not inferior to that of the ordained ministry. It is simply other, different, and here we come to the very heart of our discussion.

Monastic spirituality helps to clarify this idea. If, despite everything, woman was apparently a being inferior to man, on the contrary, when it comes to charisms, the equality between men and women is perfect. Clement of Alexandria observes: "The virtue of man and of woman is one and the same, one same nature of leading" (PG 8:260 C). Theodoret says that women "have struggled not less but even more than men...and with a weaker constitution they have nevertheless displayed the same resolve as men" (PG 82, 1489 B). The strength of women is "divine charity" and a particular grace for being captive by Christ. No one, therefore, should consider women to be inferior but esteem them capable of giving spiritual direction just as men. A woman of charisms, *theophotistos*, that is, one bearing the light of God, received the title of *amma,* or spiritual mother (*Vitae Patrum,* V, 19, 19). Such women were the mothers of their communities, their monasteries, as Pachomius was the father of his. And people came to such women for counsel as to the fathers, for example Ss Euphrosyne and Irene.

Abba Isaiah composed a book of the sayings of the mothers, the *Materikon*, comparable to the *Paterikon,* the sayings of the fathers. Except for the sacramental power and the preaching at the services, (reserved to the bishops and priests) the mothers had exactly the same prerogatives and responsibilities as the fathers among the male monastics. They are not called "Mothers of the Church," a title proper only to bishops and teachers, but they are surely spiritual mothers and share in the spreading of the gospel. Liturgical texts celebrate as "equal to the apostles" the women who proclaimed the gospel to those ignorant of it, by catechetical instruction and other forms of active evangelizing. We think here of Ss Helen and Nina as well as Mary Magdalen.

We should also mention here the institution of deaconesses. The *Didascalion* (III, 8) gives them the power of laying hands upon the sick. The *Apostolic Constitutions* (VIII, 19, 20) speak of their ordination with the laying on of hands and the invocation of the Holy Spirit, thus designating a minor order. The *Testament of Our Lord* (I, 40, 43) defines the tasks of the deaconesses and mentions that of the instruction of female catechumens, which the *Apostolic Constitutions* (II, 26) affirm, namely that the they "impart to these women catechumens the elements of doctrine." In the Nestorian or Pre-Chalcedonian Church the deaconesses read the Gospel in assemblies of women. In another ancient text we read: *Vidua sedit...*"she sits," an allusion to the *cathedra*, the seat or place for catechizing and exhortation. Among those who have offered glorious service in the Church can be mentioned Olympias the friend and disciple of St John Chrysostom, Procula and Pentadia, Anastasia the correspondent of Severus of Antioch, Macrina sister of St Basil, Lampadia his friend, Theosobia wife of St Gregory of Nyssa, as well as many others both known and unknown.

Woman and the word today

Christian consciousness has evolved. If in the times of rabbinical literature, a teacher in Israel would have declared it preferable to burn the Torah rather than to give its books to women to read, today again some repeat the words of St Paul, that the woman must be silent in the assembly.

The story of Martha and Mary shows that the gospel raised woman to the spiritual summit where access was opened to the "one thing necessary." St Paul, in proclaiming that "in Christ there is neither male nor female," inspired the practice of the Church and he himself was associated with a number of women whom he named in his apostolic ministry. It is sufficient to recall Phoebe and Priscilla (whom Harnack thought may have been the author of the *Letter to the Hebrews!*) among those who exercised a truly apostolic ministry. Other women were seized by the Spirit and spoke as prophets (Acts 21:9). If St Paul, so careful of maintaining order, ruled certain conditions and in certain circumstances forbade women to speak, the great truth he preached still remains: "Do not quench the Spirit, do not despise the words of prophets" (1 Thess. 5:19-20). Alongside 1 Corinthians 14 another passage from the same letter (11:3-16) attests to the legitimacy of prophecy and of proclamation by women, just as that of men. It had only to do with speech that disturbed the good order of the Church and truly prophetic speech. Certainly the task of preaching during the liturgical services was and remains the work of the bishop. Woman is predestined by her charisms to the tasks which best correspond to her own nature and to the priesthood of the laity. In the ministry of the laity all, men and women alike, are equal and serve in their own manner in the "frontline" in the struggle for the Kingdom of God in the world.

This is above all the service of the faith by word and by living witness. The first task of teaching is in the home and in school. But woman also has the keyrgmatic role in the parish, in catechesis. Perhaps more by prayerful silence than by speech she shares in the liturgical action of the communion of saints.

"Never in the course of history have events demanded more heroism of women than the events of our times," Pope Pius XII would say.

"There is a diversity of gifts...of ministries...of work. All is the work of one and the same Spirit, who gives these gifts to each in particular as he wishes," says St Paul (1 Cor 12). Married or single or monastic life represent very different and personal forms of *diakonia*, of service. The original image of the pure feminine essence eclipses the empirical boundaries and frontiers, revealing the grace of being a "spiritual mother" and "deaconess."

In this century Russia has been given a unique historical destiny, an experience charged with prophetic meaning for those who know how to read the book of the signs of the times.

The great spiritual masters, the *startzy* or elders, showed great and deep interest in the *diakonia* of women. The elders Ss Macarius and Ambrose of Optina, following the example of St Seraphim of Sarov, consecrated themselves to the mission of women, to apostolic formation, all of which witnessed to their astonishing clairvoyance, their lucid vision of the future.

Woman has an intuitive apprehension, in her very body, of the Spirit. She is endowed as no one else with a religious sense, *anima naturaliter christiana*, "a soul naturally Christian." The Communists realized this very well. The emancipation of women and the equality of the sexes were among the first of their preoccupations. The masculinization of woman required the modification of her anthropological type, her being rendered identical with man in psychic terms. This leveling project concealed a bitter revolt against God and his law and led to the annihiliation of woman's charismatic state. But the witness against this is unanimous. The safeguarding and passing on of the faith in Soviet Russia was done by Russian women. Religious renewal, just as the continuity of the tradition, is also the work of the wife and the mother. Women, even young Russian girls, aspire most often to the striking interiorizing and living of the truth which they see in the icons of the Theotokos. Their discrete femininity seems inspired by the icons of *Umilenie*, of the Virgin of tenderness, rather than the regime's ideals. It is the women of Soviet Russia, who by their charisms of compassion and not by violence, are keeping alive the eternal truths and from within are refashioning Russian Christianity.

After uttering her *fiat*, woman can no longer say: *Non, non sic futurum esse, non possumus*: No, not this way will the future be, we are not capable. It is not in vain that the great spiritual teachers were unanimously attentive to and hopeful about deepening the charismatic ministry of women.

It is from the heart of woman that spontaneously, instinctively springs up the invincible resistance to materialism and to all demonic elements which threaten the destruction of our modern world.

The salvation of the world will only come from holiness and holiness is more interior to woman in the conditions of modern life. According to the spiritual teachers, in silence there is great power. Active silence is full of presence. "The one who knows how to listen to the Word knows how to listen to silence." In a certain sense, even the Liturgy is the silence of the spirit which listens in singing and in that silence which is an organic part of all liturgical worship, as it is of a symphony. Thus the Virgin "held all the words of the Son in her heart" (Lk 2:51). Every woman has an innate intimacy, almost a complicity with Tradition, with the continuity of life. "The words kept in her heart" are those which a woman is able to recount, just as Mary Magdalene "went and told the disciples that she had seen the Lord and that he had said these things to her"; just as the myrrhbearing women "announced all these things to the eleven and to all the others." These women are called "Equal-to-the-Apostles." Woman has her charismatic ministry of witness and of being a servant of the Word in her own way, in the manner of the Holy Spirit who manifests, who reveals the Word and then hides himself behind the figure of the dove and the fiery tongues of Pentecost.

The "veil" which St Paul saw as a sign of the sacred and of mystery has given way, in these preapocalyptic times, to the image of the woman clothed in the sun, of the woman clothed in the Word. She preaches in and with and by all of her being, by an ontological brilliance. She brings to birth, to life, from the depths of her very body, from her heart, she extends the Word to the world.

The Eucharist—
Mystery of the Church [1]

Liturgy and sacrament

Each sacrament is always an event *within* the Church, *by* the Church and *for* the Church. Any fragmentation which isolates the action and the recipient is excluded. Every sacrament has repercussions for the entire Body and for all the faithful. Baptism is a birth in the Church and her enrichment by a new member. Sacramental absolution returns the penitent to the Church. Those who are married come first to the eucharistic assembly, garbed in the vesture, as it were, of their marital priesthood. The consecration of a bishop witnesses to the Eucharist and finally, in the Eucharist all are united in the communion of one and the same Spirit. Thus, each sacrament transcends its particularity and leads to a resounding catholicity. The gifts conferred are made manifest for all for it is in the Eucharist that the Church witnesses the descent of the Holy Spirit and all his gifts. This is why in the practice of the ancient Church every sacrament was an organic part of the eucharistic Liturgy which set a definitive seal upon that which was received and was conferred.

The Church of the first centuries united in one action baptism, chrismation and the Eucharist, which the Fathers called the "great initiation." The neophyte would pass successively through the three phases of the single action which made him or her a member of the "people of God," now recapitulated in Christ, and which raised the new Christian to the dignity of "priest, prophet, and king." The Eucharist, which came at the end of this gradual initiation, was at the

---

1 Originally published in *La pensée orthodoxe* 14 (1968), pp. 53-69.

same time its perfect accomplishment. According to the *Ecclesiastical Hierarchy* (III, 424) of Pseudo-Dionysius, which passed on a tradition already well established, the Eucharist is not one sacrament among others but is the *Sacrament of sacraments*.

This fundamental definition resides at the heart of Orthodox ecclesiology. It means that the Eucharist is not a sacrament *in* the Church but the sacrament *of* the Church herself. The Eucharist constitutes the Church, manifests and fully expresses her essence. This is why in the Eastern Church the word "liturgy, " *leitourgia: ergon tou laou*, literally "the common work of the people," is the designation for the entire eucharistic service.

Sacramental and doxological, constitutive and expressive, it is completely natural that down through the centuries the Liturgy has had a most refined pedagogical character and great formative power. Above all it makes us liturgical beings. The human person is a liturgist par excellence, the "new creature" who says with the psalmist, "I will sing to my God as long as I live." Such a person has become a *living eucharist*. The Liturgy responds, in St Paul's words, to God's own desires. The faithful are "destined according to the purpose of him who accomplishes all things, according to his counsel and will, so that we, who were the first to set our hope on Christ, might live for the praise of his glory...this is the pledge of our inheritance toward redemption as God's own people, to the praise of his glory" (Eph 1:11, 14). These doxological texts from the New Testament epistles contain numerous liturgical fragments. The Book of Revelation throughout, witnesses to a Liturgy which has evolved and which is especially rich in doxology. This praise forms the "memorial" of the marvelous things done by God in the past as well as those to come, both of which are made present in the liturgical *anamnesis,* or remembrance. Among developing liturgies, that of St James hearkens back to the ancient eucharistic formulary of Jerusalem and provides a gripping image of the heavenly world which Christ opened by his Ascension. It describes the "heaven of heavens" as an immense liturgical city, a temple and sanctuary where Christ, according to the Epistle to the Hebrews (9 and 12) is the great High Priest. The *Sanctus* hymn of the angels resounds day and night (Rev 4 and 5), the creatures and all the cosmos give thanks and the twenty-fours "elders" representing the universal priesthood of all the baptized, echo the praise of the angels around the throne. This is the iconographic image of the "Divine Liturgy," of the "divine Eucharist" celebrated in heaven by Christ. This image then teaches that every earthly Liturgy is nothing else but a participation in the heavenly, eternal Liturgy (Heb 9:24), the immense doxology that the Son renders to the Father. The Liturgy embraces heaven and earth and retains the blessing of the Father from age to age.

In light of this, the "one thing necessary" of which the Gospel speaks is nothing else but this act of adoration, doxology, and eucharistic thanksgiving. Indeed, the world was created for the messianic banquet. "The angel showed me the river of the water of life...and on the two banks of the river were found the tree of life" (Rev 22:1-2). In commenting on this passage from Revelation, the Fathers saw in it the image of the Kingdom in the form of the eucharistic Liturgy of the age to come.

This is why the birth of the Church on the day of Pentecost is immediately followed by its full revelation in the Apostles' breaking of the bread (Acts 2:46) the point at which the life of the faithful even takes on a eucharistic style: "They were together and had all things in common" (Acts 2:44). Through the "bread of life," Christ, his disciples were made into the same bread, the same love, a fragment of the "Body of God," in the words of St John Chrysostom. There we can say is the essence of Christianity. The Triune mystery of the life of God becomes the mystery of human life. "That they may be one, as we are one" (Jn 17:22). It is in the Eucharist that this high priestly prayer is experienced by the Church. It is during the Liturgy that the apostolic Church proclaimed the *kerygma* or message of salvation and it is during the Liturgy that all breathed the Name of God, his real coming and shining presence. The Liturgy thus constitutes a doxological reception of the Word made flesh. As the Cherubic Hymn sung during the lenten Liturgy of the Presanctified Gifts in the Orthodox Church says: "Now the powers of heaven do serve invisibly with us. Lo, the King of glory enters. Lo, the mystical sacrifice is upborne, fulfilled. Let us draw near with faith and love and become communicants of life eternal. Alleluia, Alleluia, Alleluia." Everything is here, the fullness is such that as the fourteenth century lay theologian Nicholas Cabasilas said: "one cannot go any further or add anything to it." The biblical sap and strength of the Word, the dogmatic definitions of the Councils, all the contemplative theology of the Fathers, all is marvelously synthesized and presented on the sacred stage of the temple: "the recapitulation of the entire economy of salvation," according to St Theodore the Studite,[2] "the cup of synthesis," in the beautiful words of St Irenaeus.[3]

The Eucharistic miracle

Through her mystical sense of veneration pushed to the extreme, the Eastern Church never asks the questions of "why" or "how" about the miracle of the Eucharist. The very first dogmatic reflection upon these questions came in the West from the ninth to the eleventh centuries (See *Concilium*, 24). In order to understand and express what a being is and how it exists, scholastic thought set up the opposition of the hidden substance to the visible appearance or *species*. St Thomas Aquinas introduced a more precise philosophical definition, namely Aristotelian teaching with its two categories of *substance* and *accident*. *Substance* can be translated as "that which stands by itself,"or "that which underlies something." *Accident* is "that which accompanies," or "the manner of being concomitantly."

According to St Thomas, substance and accidents are distinguished at the point where they are able to be separated. The Council of Constance expressed this point of view in condemning John Wycliffe. It is however, an interpretation tied to a specific historical period. The Fathers of the Council of Trent merely inherited the perspective of Constance. They were not disposed to employ any other category in affirming the change of the bread in the Eucharist. Their decree said: "In the consecration there takes place a change of all of the substance of the bread into all of the substance of the Body of Christ." The substance is therefore totally changed, despite the persistence of the appearances, that is the species, or accidents.

The encyclical *Humani generis* of Pope Pius XII in 1950 affirmed that the mystery of the Eucharist defies all efforts to understand it and thus it would be better to preserve the use of the Church's traditional

2   *Antirh.* 8, 99, 340 C.
3   *Adv. Haeres.* III, 16, 7.

terminology. The doctrine, however, is not tied to any one school of thought and therefore new interpretations are always possible.

The encyclical *Mysterium fidei* of Pope Paul VI in 1965 said that "The species acquire a new signification and a new end so that they are no longer ordinary food and drink...but a new ontological reality. Under these species one finds something completely different."

The term "transsignification" is composed of the word "sign" with a distinction between the sign which informs and the sign that contains and communicates what it signifies. Thus on the one hand, it signifies unity and love and on the other, the body and blood of the Lord. It is this ensemble which enters into the concept of the eucharistic sign which communicates the realities and implies therefore the real presence of the Lord. In the encyclical's meaning, one should be able to deduce from the Aristotelian-Thomistic perspectives a doctrine as wide as possible under the condition that in addition to the notions of "transsignification" and "transfinalization" is safeguarded the sense of an *ontological conversion* of the bread and wine.

Calvin's eucharistic teaching is often called "spiritualistic," the presence of Christ being in virtue of the Holy Spirit (*in virtute Spiritus Sancti*). Such a doctrine is opposed to that of the ubiquity of the body of Christ affirmed in Lutheranism. For Calvin, Christ is bodily present in heaven and it is the Holy Spirit who effects the "conjunction," or coming together of Christ's body and the sacramental signs. The Spirit here appears as the "channel" or "conduit" through which Christ descends to us.[4] For Calvin, in his understanding of the *epiclesis*, it is through the power of the Holy Spirit that the faithful are raised to heaven and this occurs when they receive and consume the eucharistic elements, communion with the body and blood of the heavenly Christ, which Calvin calls in his own realism "the food that saves our souls."[5] Nevertheless, he still shows himself to be more reticent when it comes to any guarantee of salvation through sacramental signs.

In order to keep things clear and precise here, it is important not to forget that for Calvin as for Luther, the kerygmatic message of the

4   *Inst. Chr.*, IV, p. 24.
5   *Letter to Bullinger*, 27, XII, 1562.

words of institution and the accent on the subjective aspect of the reality of salvation—"the blood of Christ shed for you"—surpass the objective or substantial aspects of the sacrament and the consecration of the elements. This is not so much a suppression of the objective nature of the sacrament as simply the primacy of a subjective interest on the part of the reformers. One can still see the explicit understanding of the objective reality of Christ and his presence in the Eucharist among liturgical, confessional Lutherans and for example in the Taizé community's Liturgy, which is in the Reformed Church tradition.

The Reformed thus stressed the *epiclesis*, the coming down of the Spirit upon all the faithful but diverted attention from the consecration of the elements, which seemed to make the presence of Christ conditioned by the faith of the communicant. On the contrary, the liturgical realism of Lutheranism confessed the presence of Christ very concretely, while the Holy Spirit for Luther, was in the service of Christ, pneumatology subordinated to Christology.

Luther completely rejected Zwingli's noetic-symbolist conception of the Eucharist, the bread signifying the body of Christ, stressing the absolutely correct concept of identity: "This is my body." But in wishing to explain this identity, Luther formulated a theory of "impanation," namely the presence of Christ *in pane, sub pane, cum pane*, that is, in, with and under the appearance of bread. This also came to be known as the "consubstantiation" of two realities which is no longer an identity but the coexistence of non-transubstantiated material of this world with the heavenly, transfigured body of Christ. There is no longer the persistence of the accidents attached to another substance but the penetration of the bread by the presence of the Lord.

But already much earlier St Thomas Aquinas would argue that it is not really correct to say that the bread is the body of Christ. The more precise expression would be *ex pane fit corpus Christi*, from the bread the body of Christ is made. This formula leads to a categorical rejection of identity between the sign and what is signified according to Jacques Maritain, who makes complete and explicit the Thomistic conception: "The sacred words, 'This is my body,' do not at all constitute an identity, but effect (as an instrumental cause) a change [transubstantiation]. Rather than creating an identity between the sign and that which it signifies, the sacrament of the Eucharist adds to the relationship of the sign to the signified that of cause to effect and presupposes the intervention of the First Cause producing the most radical change imaginable, a change of being as being."[6] Here we have the most remote position from that of the Eastern Church. According to Maritain, the relationship of cause and effect is added to the relationship of sign and signified. In place of posing an absolute identity between a signifying material and an immaterial reality signified (the essence of a miracle) the immediate and direct meaning of the words "This is my body" is strained, changing it to "This bread will become my body." This is a philosophical analysis which, for the Eastern Orthodox ear, makes the miracle too rational and material.

If we turn then, to the Eastern Church's stance, in the Eucharist we find ourselves before a mystery which cannot be discussed as though it were a problem to be solved or explained. One sees, from the beginning, a difference in attitude and of theological positions and a reaction conditioned by rather different presuppositions. Over against Western theories, the Eastern Church retains a certain cosmological immanentism which risks reifying the mystery by placing it within the cosmology and physics of this world. (One should consult the magisterial study of Fr Sergius Bulgakov.)[7]

In actuality, the transcendent reality of Christ's deified human nature, which is near the Father, and, on the other hand, the immanent and cosmic reality of the bread, are on the same ontological plane, for they both submit to the same law which pertains to the relationships between substance and accidents. Now is it right, is it even possible to speak of the substance and the accidents of the heavenly, resurrected and totally transfigured body of the Lord? "At the right hand of the Father"—this is not a place but a symbol of the proximity of Christ to

6 "Signe et symbole," in *Quatre essais* (1956), p. 80, cited by W. Weidlé, "La présence réelle," *La pensée orthodoxe* 1, 1966, p. 135.
7 "The eucharistic dogma," *Put'*, 20-21 (1930) [in Russian] and Constantine Andronikoff's French translation in *La pensée orthodoxe*, vol. 4 (1987), pp. 40-90. Also see the English translation in Fr Sergius Bulgakov, *The Holy Grail and the Eucharist,* Boris Jakim, ed. and trans., (Hudson NY: Lindisfarne, 1997), pp. 63-138.

the Father. When Bishop John A.T. Robinson, with all his naiveté, replaces "on high" and "below" with "depth," he remains precisely within the same spatial categories. "Heavenly" is not a cosmological idea. The "heavenly" state of the humanity of Christ is a transcensus which prohibits us from applying cosmic ontology and its laws to him. This state is not at all a disincarnation but a dematerialization. According to the fathers, after the Fall material is a condensation, a thickening of the spiritual and this is why, even after the Fall, "in sensible things, all is intelligible," according to St John Chrysostom, the assumption of the sensible into intelligibility is normative.[8]

The "glorified" body of Christ is beyond the still material world (1 Cor 15:40-49). It is a state in which the soul possess the energies of corporeality. It is not that there is no more any *ubiquitas* or omnipresence, for the heavenly body transcends every place, it is not everywhere because it is outside of, beyond space, all in keeping the power of manifesting itself in a given place and anywhere else in space for, "All power is given to me in heaven and on earth" (Mt 28:18).

Another difficulty noted by the Eastern Church is that of a certain doubling of the mystery. On the one hand, the body is offered for consumption, and on the other, the complete presence of Christ in the Host seems almost to lead necessarily to the extra-liturgical cult of adoration of the Eucharist. Christ having ascended to heaven is once again returned to a precise location, namely that of the eucharistic bread. Such a like quasi-reincarnation, by the grandeur of the event, risks becoming autonomous, thus distracting from the eating of the eucharistic meal and the nuptial, marital communion of God and mankind in the sacrament.

Even though Greek philosophy was familiar to the Fathers, they did not attempt any philosophical explanation or analysis of the Eucharist. Rather than going to Plato or Aristotle, they went directly to the Gospel. Rather than physical evidence, they chose the evidence of the Word. They read the text of the Scriptures and confessed the identity: "This is my body, this is my blood."

This is a confession which, though radical, is neither simplistic nor naive. The essential position of the Fathers is to see in the word of the

8   *In Matth. hom.* 84:4, PG 58, 743.

Lord a miracle which is not physical but metaphysical. "Metaphysics" is used here in the absolute sense of the term, beyond the limits of this world, a meta-cosmic miracle, one that is also meta-empirical. In reality, the heavenly body of the Lord no longer belongs to the reality of this world. Its transcendence poses a difference in nature between the eucharistic miracle and, for example, the miracle at the wedding in Cana, where one material, water, became another material, wine, on the same ontological plane and within the same cosmic limits.

The eucharistic miracle presents the most radical antinomy imaginable. In the spirit of the Fathers, the term *metabolé*, taken from *meta* and *ballo*, means "thrown and projected beyond." The eucharistic prayer or *anaphora* in chapter 13 of the Apostolic Constitution, in speaking of Enoch uses the same word, *metabolé* (Gen 5:24: "Enoch walked with God and was then no more, because God took him"). Enoch, taken by God, is "thrown or projected beyond," into the transcendence of heaven. It is evident that one cannot explain or define the subject of a cosmic material being projected, that is, raised "beyond" itself and assimilated into the transcendent. The entire action is meta-empirical, meta-logical and antinomic, for it expresses the identity of the different and the difference of the identical. Into this identity enters a signifying material reality and an immaterial reality that is signified. The one is not absorbed nor destroyed by the other. Their identification is dynamic, *in actu*. It leaves each in its own reality, in its own status quo. The antinomy here signifies that a reality is that which it is not and that it is not that which it is. The bread and the wine are the body and the blood, and the body and the blood are the bread and the wine. ("What would be the testimony of the senses...the bread which is seen is not bread, even if it seems so to the taste, but the body of Christ and the wine which is seen is not wine even if tasted but the blood of Christ.")[9] The Eucharist, then, is not a physical transformation, where the *terminus a quo* passes to the *terminus ad quem*, as the water turned completely into wine at the marriage feast at Cana.

It is also evident that the *metabolé* cannot be other than an object of faith, a vision of the invisible. It rejects every visible manifestation,

9 St Cyril of Jerusalem, *Cat.* 22, 9; PG 33, 110.4.

which would be contrary to its nature as a mystery. The introduction to the classic priest's handbook, published in Russia, makes it very clear that in the extraordinary case in which the eucharistic gifts would take on the physical and material appearance of the body and the blood, it would be necessary to wait until the end of such an unusual phenomenon for Communion, for such a vision is not normal and contradicts the very nature of the miracle of the Eucharist. For the Eucharist is not a physical conversion but a metaphysical transcensus which identifies the two different ontological realities. It is not "the one in the other," nor "the one and the other," physically, but the one is the other metaphysically. This places the miraculous reality outside all sensible perception inherent in things of this world, such as the taste of the wine at Cana.

Before Communion each one of the faithful prays: "I believe O Lord and I confess..that this is your own pure body and that this is your own true blood..." Above and beyond the experience of the senses, faith affirms absolutely and categorically, neither the transubstantiated bread nor the body, nor the bread coexisting beneath the form of bread. Faith rather confesses the bread by the power of the Holy Spirit identified with the body of the Lord. "This is my body" does not mean: "this bread will become my body in ceasing to be bread." But without abolishing the sign which signifies, the eucharistic miracle absorbs the contradiction, and in this a miracle remains.

"Take, eat...drink all of you..." "The heavenly bread and the cup of life" are given for our nourishment. The theology of the Fathers understands the Eucharist as a meal: "Whoever eats me will live through me." Thus St Irenaeus,[10] St Gregory of Nyssa,[11] St John of Damascus[12] explore the depths of analogy between heavenly and earthly eating and nourishment. During his life on earth, the bread and wine consumed by the Lord were integrated and assimilated into his corporeality. During the Last Supper, Christ extended the reality of his body beyond physical limits. He identified it with the bread and the wine and he gave them to the disciples, saying, "Eat and drink." "The bread," says St Gregory of Nyssa, "is no longer assimilated to the body of the Word

10   *Adv. Haer.* 4, 34.
11   *Orat. catech.* 37.
12   *De fide Orth.* 4, 13.

by eating but it is instantaneously the body of the Word."[13] Here is something infinitely greater than a simple physical change.

The things of this world are not able to exchange with each other or be transformed into each other. The eucharistic miracle, without any physical transformation, identifies earthly nourishment with the heavenly corporeality of Christ. It is precisely the corporeality, even if heavenly, which makes possible Communion in which each member of the faithful is united to Christ, both spiritually and corporally. The prayer of St Simeon Metaphrastes, read in thanksgiving after Communion, expresses this with great realism. "Freely, you have given your body for my food, you who are a fire consuming the unworthy. Do not consume me, O my Creator, but instead enter into my members, my veins, my heart. Consume the thorns of my transgressions. Cleanse my soul and sanctify my reasoning. Make firm my knees and my body. Illumine my five senses. Nail me to fear of you...Cleanse me, purify me and adorn me...Show me to be a temple of your one Spirit...as I become your tabernacle through Communion." And the prayer of the same saint, in preparation for Communion, asks for the healing of soul and body.

The eucharistic miracle does not make Christ descend from heaven to the altar. "It is not the body which ascended to heaven which descends," says St John of Damascus, "but the bread and wine which are one with the body and blood of the Lord."[14] *The Encyclical of the Patriarchs of the East* says the same thing: "The bread is identified with the heavenly body." The miracle does not abolish the reality of the Ascension, but expresses a completely new relationship between this world and the heavenly body of the Lord. Already between the Resurrection and the Ascension, Christ was not with the disciples as in the past. His apparitions were of a different nature. Visibly, the laws of physics no longer had a hold on him. His body attained the summit of spiritualization and deification and was going toward the beyond, the transcendent, where the disciples were not able to come. Yet, "All power is given to me in heaven and on earth." By this power Christ

13 *Orat. catech.* 37; PG 45, 96–97.
14 *De fide orth.* 4, 13.

retains a living connection with the world and is able to appropriate bread and wine as his own body and blood. For the Jews, blood is the soul of the flesh. The shedding of blood on the cross signified death. The reunion of the body and the blood signified the Resurrection. With the blood, the faithful commune with the living body of the Lord.

In summarizing the teaching of the Fathers, beyond any physical conversion, for the eyes of faith after the *epiclesis*, quite simply there is nothing else on the diskos and in the chalice except the body and blood of Christ. Fr Jugie, in his study *The Sacrament of the Eucharist in St Irenaeus*, observes: "The Bishop of Lyons, thought to be the greatest realist among the Greek Fathers, saw in the Eucharist, after the consecration, just one thing alone: the body and blood of Jesus Christ." Here we see the ultra-realism of the act of faith. This realism remains the central and unchanging point of the Fathers' teaching; e.g., Ss Sophronius, Maximus the Confessor, Germanus. They faithfully echo the tradition which, for St John of Damascus, is that "the bread and wine are not a figure." The miracle is in the immediate and total identification of the body and blood with the eucharistic gifts.[15] He also says, "We commune of the two natures, of the body corporally and of the divinity spiritually."[16] By the *metabolé* the gifts are projected beyond, into divine Transcendence, in the heavenly body.[17] Supported by the authority of God, the Fathers affirm this, but every analysis of the modalities is excluded. "The *epiclesis* effects that which is accessible only by faith." "The mode of the miracle is not susceptible to any investigation." In this assertion, St John of Damascus affirms and synthesizes the tradition. The identity is sacramental, a mystery, miraculous, for it does not abolish the signs that signify. We hear Christ himself saying: "This is my body." We receive him and we venerate the miracle in the silence of our worshipping souls.

The presence of Christ in the Eucharist has a very specific purpose which defines and conditions it. It is that Christ be united with the faithful in giving himself as food. Communion with Christ who is present is not fulfilled except in the very act of eating and drinking.

15 *De fide orth.* 4, 13.
16 *De imag.* 3, 26.
17 St Cyril of Jerusalem, *Cat.* 23, 7.

During the Last Supper, Christ was visibly present in his earthly form. He was also present in another manner, in a manner already heavenly by anticipation. He was present in the bread and wine he broke and blessed. No confusion of the two states is possible. The Ascension took away the historical and earthly presence, making possible only Christ's liturgical presence, in the eucharistic dimension. Thus the eucharistic gifts are not the localizing of an extra-eucharistic presence. Their full reality is exactly limited to the eucharistic consumption in which Christ offers himself mysteriously but also most really, for he unites himself to us substantially, in a nuptial, marital way.

The Communion of the sick shares in the same liturgical act as the rest of the assembly. The Eucharist extends even to their homes in order to nourish with the bread and wine the person who is ill. The eucharistic gifts reserved for the communion of the sick are always objectively the body and blood of the Lord, but they are kept hidden, never exposed, for the act of adoration is never detached from the mystery of the eucharistic meal. One profoundly venerates the sacred reality of the eucharistic gifts, but in the Eastern Church, no cult of veneration or adoration outside the Divine Liturgy is possible. At the historical moment when in the West the adoration of the blessed sacrament appeared, in the churches of the East the icon of the Savior was placed over the altar during Communion. An ancient iconographic composition shows Christ giving his body and blood to the apostles and this icon was placed at the center of the altar area. The eucharistic gifts are destined to be consumed and veneration directed toward the icon.

Epiclesis

In speaking of the relationship between the Word and the Holy Spirit during the earthly mission of Christ, the Fathers saw, in a certain way in Christ the great precursor or forerunner of the Holy Spirit. Thus for St Athanasius, "The Word took on flesh so that we could receive the Holy Spirit...God became a bearer of flesh (*sarcophore*) so that we might become bearers of the Spirit (*pneumatophores*)."[18] For St Simeon the New Theologian, "Such was the end and destiny of the whole work

18 *De incarn.* 8; PG 26, 996 C.

of our salvation by Christ, that those who believe receive the Holy Spirit."[19] Nicholas Cabasilas, the fourteenth-century Byzantine lay theologian said, "What is the effect and result of the actions of Christ?...it is nothing else but the descent of the Holy Spirit upon the Church."[20] The Lord himself said: "It would be better for you that I leave...I will pray the Father and he will give you another Paraclete."

Therefore, the Ascension of the Lord is the *epiclesis* or calling down of the Spirit par excellence because it is divine. The Son asks the Father to give the Spirit and, in response to this prayer, the Father sends the Spirit and inaugurates Pentecost. This action opens the final part of the economy of salvation and places the Spirit, after his hypostatic descent, into a completely new relationship with the world. After the Fall, the action of the Holy Spirit had become external to human nature. This is why, during the earthly mission of Christ and before Pentecost, *the relationship of a person to the Spirit could not occur except through and in Christ.* Conversely, on the day of Pentecost the Holy Spirit was restored to us, becoming an "internal fact" of our nature and becoming more intimate to us than we are to ourselves. This is why since the Ascension, *it is the relationship to Christ which takes place only through and in the Holy Spirit.* During his earthly life, Christ was historically visible, he was there *right in front* of his disciples. The Ascension took away this historical visibility of the Lord: "The world will see me no longer." Thus the Lord's departure is real, but Pentecost gives back to the world the interiorized presence of Christ and reveals this now not in front of the disciples but within them: "I will come to you...I am with you always even to the end of the age." The presence of the Lord is just as real as his departure. "On that day [Pentecost] you will know that I am in you." This interiorization occurs precisely through and in the Holy Spirit. As St Paul says, "The love of God has been poured into our hearts by the Holy Spirit, who is given to us" (Rom 5:5). It is by the Spirit that we say "Abba, Father," and pronounce the Name of Jesus. St John of Damascus said: "The Holy Spirit is the image of the Son. This is why it is through the Spirit that we know Christ." The Spirit is the place of the nuptial encounter of mankind and Jesus, the wedding feast of God and man....

19 *Discours.* 38.
20 *Commentary on the Divine Liturgy,* chap. 37.

This is all the mystery of Christ: his being raised to the Father and at the same time his return to the world but now under a hidden form in the Holy Spirit. Since the Epiphany, the Spirit rests upon the humanity of Christ and every manifestation of the Spirit is inseparable from the manifestation of Christ. According to St Gregory of Cyprus, the Spirit proceeds from the Father but his very *raison d'être* is in the Son. It is this copresence that explains the expression "another Advocate," and in which one can discern the identification Christ makes between the coming of the Holy Spirit and his own return. This "other Advocate," correctly *allos* not *heteros*, is not a "new" Advocate but the same one, only manifested differently. Now he is "bi-unique," because the saying concerning the Holy Spirit is realized: "For he will remain with you always." So too the other saying concerning Christ is fulfilled: "And behold, I am with you always." The Paraclete is Christ, upon whom the Spirit rests, and he is the Spirit who rests upon Christ, revealing and manifesting him.

If then, after the Ascension, it is in and through the Spirit alone that Christ is present, the manifestation of the eucharistic presence of Christ can only occur through the intervention of the Holy Spirit. This underscores the importance of the *epiclesis.* The *metabolé* or change is the projection of the gifts beyond the world into the theandric (divine-human) reality of Christ. The Spirit rests there, receives the gifts and identifies them by his power with the body and blood of Christ.

The prayer for the gifts essentially says all this: "That our God, who loves mankind, who has received them upon his holy, heavenly and invisible altar, will send down on us in return the gift of the Holy Spirit." Through the *epiclesis* the eucharistic gifts "are placed on the heavenly altar" and it is the body and the blood of Christ which are offered to the faithful.

The priest pronounces the words of institution as a *typos* or type of Christ without attributing to them any divine power. St John Chrysostom, called the "Eucharistic Doctor," stresses this: "The priest who pronounces the holy words is only the figure of the True Priest but the grace and power of these words come from God alone.[21] For the

---

21 PG 49, 380.

Eastern Church the only true priest is Christ. "Grant that we be given the grace to receive your most pure body from your powerful hand," is what the celebrant prays. "For you are the Offerer and the Offered, the Receiver and the Received, O Christ our God...." St John Chrysostom says, "It is not the priest who accomplishes what happens. We only have the role of servants. The one who sanctifies and acts, it is he...."[22]

Thus the priest does not pronounce the words of institution *in persona Christi*, in the person of Christ, but *in nomine Christi*, in the name of Christ. In order that the word of Christ commemorated by the priest may be effective, the priest invokes the Holy Spirit. The Spirit then makes an epiphanic *anamnesis* or commemoration, identifying the "memorial" with the very words of Christ which perform the miracle: "This is my body." The rite of the *zeon*, the pouring of the hot water into the chalice, emphasizes the Pentecostal character of the Eucharist. At the beginning in the preparation rite (*proskomedia*), the "holy union" of water and wine is a Christological rite symbolizing the union of the two natures in Christ. The rite of the *zeon* after the Christ's words of institution and the calling down of the Spirit is pneumatological. We commune in the warm, living blood of the crucified and glorified Christ, "full of the Holy Spirit." Placing the consecrated part of the host marked with *IC*, Jesus, into the chalice, the priest says, "The fullness of the Holy Spirit," and the hot water is poured in with the words, "The warmth of faith, full of the Holy Spirit." St Ephrem the Syrian comments: "The one who eats the body of the Lord with faith consumes with this the fire of the Holy Spirit."[23]

For the Fathers, if there is no access to the Father except through the Son, then there is no access to the Son except through the Spirit. This is why the *epiclesis* is the threshold of every relationship and of communion with Christ and the Father. The theology of the Holy Spirit, "the giver of life and the source of all grace," who is hypostasized or personalized holiness and who is the sanctifier in his very essence, defines the active principle of every divine action. If the *anaphora* or eucharistic

22 In *Matth. Hom.* 82; *De Pentec. Hom.* 1, 4.
23 Cited in Hamman, *La Messe*, Paris, 1964, p. 34.

prayer of the Eastern Church is striking in its Trinitarian structure, it is because it is addressed to the Father in order that the Holy Spirit manifest Christ. Its Trinitarian theology requires that we call down the Spirit, in the *epiclesis*. In ecumenical dialogue, the question of the *epiclesis* is methodologically more important than that of the *Filioque*, for it is in light of the *epiclesis* that one is able to correctly state the *Filioque*, two aspects of the same fundamental problem. The *epiclesis* makes precise the relationships between the Father and the Spirit and by invocation addressed to the Father, expresses authentic Trinitarian theology. The three-fold relationships of the persons of the Trinity are always reciprocal and do not establish the persons but rather are the result of the persons. Only relationships of opposition (or the opposition of relationships) are negative and are not sufficient. But such relationships of opposition are only one aspect of the positive relationships which are infinitely richer, those of communion, of manifestation, of reciprocity, and of love. Without reducing the economy of salvation to only the economy of the Son or that of the Spirit, it is necessary to open the one to the other, to the ultimate economy of the Father, and of the Trinity, and of the Kingdom. It is also necessary to distinguish the hypostatic procession of the Spirit from the Father and the procession *per Filium*, through the Son, of the divine energies of which the Spirit is the receptacle and the agent.

The sacrificial aspect of the Eucharist

The saving action of Christ offers the unique sacrifice which suffices one time for all: "Christ has ascended to heaven with his sacrifice," says St John Chrysostom.[24] Christian worship is the perpetual reception of this through the act of giving thanks, the Eucharist.

The Gospel narratives of the Holy Supper define different aspects of the sacrifice of Christ as a sacrificial meal. Exegesis distinguishes two traditions of the Old Testament culminating in their New Testament synthesis and their messianic fulfillment in the person of Jesus Christ.

According to Matthew 26:26-29 and Mark 14:22-25, the Lord says, "This is my blood, the blood of the new covenant." This expression

---

24 *In Hebr. Hom*, 17.

comes from the Torah, Exodus 24:8. It evokes the theology of the covenant and the sacrifice confirmed in public worship. Further, it shows the
fulfillment of the covenant of Sinai in the Supper and the reunion of the
people of God in Christ. It is Jesus who offers the "blood of the covenant." Thus, the sacrifice is made present in the Supper and confers on it
the meaning and value of a Liturgy of sacrifice and of the covenant.

According to Luke 22:15-20 and Paul (1 Cor 11:23-26), the word is
connected not to the books of the Law but to the theology of the
prophets: "This cup is the new covenant in my blood." Here the reference is to Jeremiah 31 and to the controversy with the priestly tradition.
"I want mercy not sacrifice" (Hos 6:6). The ancient cult, now broken
down, gives way to the Supper of the Lord which looks forward to the
complete offering of himself and ultimate mercy and forgiveness.

On the cross, the servant of Yahweh unites the blood of the sacrifice
and the new covenant, thereby fulfilling the Law and the prophets. In
place of the old rite, now powerless, and of mankind, incapable of
giving itself and replacing itself with a victim, it is Christ who is the
true worship and the sacrifice "for many" and "for us" and we receive
him in the liturgical action of thanksgiving.

Christ's action, accomplished once and for all, enters the Liturgy, is
present and alive through the epiphanic *anamnesis*. We experience him
in the communal as well as personal reception of Communion, not as a
connection to the past but as a very real gift. It is in this sense that we
can speak of the Eucharist as sacrifice. The sacrifice of Christ which
happened uniquely is present here and now. The words, "for many"
expresses the universal dimension of the Eucharist and "for you," the
reunited community of the people of God.

In the Old Testament in the rite of "remembrance," Israel commemorated the covenant of salvation, received it as present and effective and
participated in its blessings and power. The Christian action of remembrance, the *anamnesis* is a re-presentation which makes present the totality of salvation. There is a connection to the past: "In the night in which
he was given over..." as well as to the present: "Do this in memory of
me," and also in the sense of the offering which means " to bear before"
the face of the Father. Thus there is also the appeal to God to make the
Parousia, the Second Coming, take place: "until he comes again."

"Each time...you proclaim..." This sacramental proclamation brings about the presence of the reality it announces. The sacrifice of salvation and the giving of thanks both call and attract reciprocally. Every eucharistic "proclamation" extends the action of salvation "here, now and everywhere" and enables each of us to appropriate this ourselves. The sacrificial aspect of the Eucharist can only be understood in this interaction of time and eternity.

Through the power of the liturgical mystery we are projected to the point where eternity and time intersect. There we become contemporaries of the biblical events, we live in them and are witnesses to them. Each liturgical reading of the Gospel places us in the events related there. "At that time...," the formula which precedes each reading refers to sacred time, *in illo tempore*, "the former" enters and becomes the "now," the "contemporary." At Christmas we really are there at the nativity of Christ and the risen Lord truly appears before us in the night of the Paschal vigil.

There is no trace here of the dead time of repetition. Everything remains and is present once and for all. Eternity touches time in the liturgical celebration in which a remembrance, a souvenir, a "memorial" is accompanied by the event itself. "It is the same sacrifice that we offer, not one today and another tomorrow," says St John Chrysostom.[25] "It is just Christ, completely present here and there, forming only one and the same body, and this one and the same body is offered in different places, yet there is only one sacrifice...and the victim offered today is the same one offered on the day of redemption and cannot be consumed...we only offer this one victim as the priest of the old law and it is always the same... Believe that what is celebrated today is the very same feast that Christ celebrated when he was at table and none other."[26] Theodore of Mopsuestia says the same thing: "It is not something new but it is the Liturgy which takes place in heaven and we are the ones who are celebrating it in heaven." To be at one and the same time in heaven and on earth is being introduced into eternity and eternity is breaking in upon time. In the Presanctified Liturgy we hear

---

25 *2 Tim. Hom.* 45.
26 *Hom.* 12 on Heb 3, PG 63:131 C; *Hom.* 27 on 1 Cor, 4, PG 61, 228.

this: "Here in reality is his most pure body and his life-giving blood which are about to be placed at this very hour on the mystical table...."

The *epiclesis* over the faithful means that the faithful enter into communion with the Holy Spirit and that they are thus one with Christ. Christ connects us with his offering. Integrated into him we offer to the Father our life, the lives of all the faithful and of the whole world as part of this, Christ's one offering. The offertory prayer makes this clear: "Lord God...make us worthy of offering these gifts and spiritual sacrifices...so that our sacrifice may be acceptable and that the Holy Spirit may descend upon us, upon these gifts and upon all the people." Thus it is Christ alone who offers and is offered: "Your own of your own we offer unto you, on behalf of all and for all."

According to the Fathers, after the Ascension Christ does not intercede again, anew. Glorified, he is at the Father's right hand but the Church through the *anaphora*, the eucharistic prayer, intercedes in Christ insofar as he is the Head. The Church is integrated into his unique action which establishes an opening between heaven and earth through which the Spirit never ceases to be poured out in a Pentecost.

Christ the High Priest has offered his unique sacrifice for all time and for all people. The Liturgy actualizes this here and now. The sacrifice of the Cross, sacramentally represented, is not repeated because it remains beyond all time and because its mystery is "deciphered" in the always present reality of the Ascension.

In the acts of the Council of Trent, the discussion of the Eucharist is separated from that of sacrifice. A certain primacy of the doctrine of sacrifice, even its separation from worship, led to the cult or adoration of the eucharistic gifts apart from communion. For the Eastern Church to over accentuate the aspect of sacrifice is to risk fragmenting the unity of the mystery and separating the sacrifice from the Supper of the Lord.

It is characteristic of the Eastern Church's Liturgy that it is not possible to isolate the precise moment when the miracle of the Eucharist takes place. From the beginning to the very end the Liturgy is just one single action in which the *epiclesis* appears as final affirmation of the unique sacramental symphony. It is for communion that the assembly is reunited and it is after the meal that the celebrant proclaims: "As far as it is in our power, Christ our God, we have here accomplished the mystery of our salvation and the Church sings: "We have seen the true Light, we have received the heavenly Spirit, we have found the true faith, worshipping the undivided Trinity who has saved us," and the Kingdom has thus come among us in an immense Pentecost of the age to come.

All theologies culminate in this Epiphany of the Trinity, shining from the Light that has no end. Here we find illumined the ultimate meaning of the coming of Christ which is the descent of the Holy Spirit upon the faithful. Members of Christ, coinheritors with the Son and thus adopted children, they are brought into communion with the Father.

Eucharistic ecclesiology

According to the Fathers the liturgical norm is the participation in the Holy Meal by the totality of the Body on every Lord's Day. Fr Nicholas Afanasiev draws attention to Acts 2:47:"The Lord added every day to the Church those who were saved," and he underscores that the translation of the Greek, *epi to auto* by "Church," is an excellent interpretation and adequate eucharistic definition of the very essence of the Church—the ensemble of the faithful, gathered in the same place and for the same thing, Eucharist—Church.[27] After Pentecost, the Church is where the eucharistic *koinonia,* or communion, takes place.

Eucharistic ecclesiology teaches that every local church with a bishop as its eucharistic head, possesses the fullness of the Church of God. Thus it is evident that the Church is indivisible, she never is the sum of her parts, for there cannot exist any "part" of the Church. "Where Christ is, there is the Church." All local churches are equivalent members, consubstantial to the image of the Trinity. Their communion expresses the overflowing love of the Body and also the dynamism of missionary expansion. The *una sancta* is the communion of different places where she is manifest, always equal to herself. A council is rightly the place where mutual love is expressed and it is this quality of love for all that God reveals. It is why the council or assembly of the Church is the organ for dogmatic proclamations. The churches are not complete for they are, each and every one of them the one holy,

27 Also see Acts 1:15; 2:1; Ignatius of Antioch, *Eph* 13:1; *Magn.* 7:1.

catholic and apostolic Church. A council witnesses to the unity of the churches. A council does not have power over the Church for it does not speak *to* the Church but *in* the Church. The principle of power has given way to that of accord, of love.

A parallel order can be seen in the mystery of the Trinity. For the Fathers, ecclesiology sketches out a magnificent icon of the "Three Divine Persons, united not to confound each other but to mutually contain each other" (St John of Damascus). The Father assures unity without undermining the perfect equality of the three. This excludes any subordinant submission and incidentally shows the patristic understanding of the "monarchy" of the Father as *the one who presides in Trinitarian love*. To this "leading image," in the communion of the churches which are perfectly equal in their ultimate reality, where each is the "Church of God," is the "one whose presides in love." Before the schism, the Church of Rome enjoyed the charism of honorary authority. The Pope was the image of the heavenly Father, but quite rightly, without any jurisdictional power over the other churches. The three great churches, that of Rome, the Orthodox, and the one stemming from the Reformation, joined in the concord of faith, could reflect the communion of the Three Divine Persons of the Trinity in their own communion as perfectly equal churches, united in the one who presides in love, in the image of the Father.

The Eucharist: source of the priestly hierarchy

Oscar Cullman has very clearly shown the place of the sacraments in the New Testament and Emil Brunner rightly affirms that the appearance of a new hierarchical Church takes its origin in the institution of the sacraments.[28] In reality the sacraments constitute the Church. It is by baptism that one enters the Church, and the canons give order to the sacramental structure. It is in the Eucharist that Christ is present completely and that the Church manifests her fullness.

Certain scholastic treatises consider the sacrament of the priesthood as the "mother of all the sacraments" and thereby deform the most

---

28 Emil Brunner, *The Misunderstanding of the Church,* trs. Harold Knight (Philadelphia: Westminster Press, 1953).

ancient and firm tradition of the Church. Ecclesiastical functions have their origin in those actions which they accomplish. The bishop possesses sacramental, doctrinal, and pastoral power because he presides at the Eucharist. Upon being consecrated, a bishop, before any other task, immediately presides at the Eucharist.

The Lord instituted the Eucharist as the very sacrament of the Church herself and the episcopacy is included as its condition. This is why every definition of the priesthood, in the Eastern Church, is always in reference to the Eucharist. A bishop is, above all, the witness to the eucharistic feast, the one who presides and witnesses to its authenticity: "Only the Eucharist celebrated by the bishop is true," affirms St Ignatius of Antioch.[29] The priest is the one to whom the bishop delegates the liturgical power of celebrating, and the deacon assists both in their liturgical functions.

In Old Testament times, the Church, locus of the divine presence, was defined in terms of institutional forms of worship: "I will consecrate the tent of assembly and the altar and I will consecrate Aaron and his sons so that they will act as priests. I then will abide in the midst of the children of Israel and will be their God" (Ex 29:44-45). But there is another passage: "So since the Law contains no more than a reflection of the good things which were still to come, and no true image of them" (Heb 10:1), now Christ "is abolishing the first sort to establish the second"(Heb 10:9). Thus the New Testament reverses the order. The sacramental institution does not precede but follows and flows from the presence and the "fullness of the One who fills all in all," "who is the head by whom is the whole body is fitted and joined together... (Eph 4:16). Thus all of the sacraments are organic parts of the eucharistic Liturgy.

The bishop, according to St Ignatius, "takes the place of God in presiding over the community." The presbyters who surround him are the images of the apostles.[30] Every celebration of the Eucharist reproduces the Holy Supper. This determines the place of the bishop and his liturgical function, for "the Church is where the Eucharist is celebrated." St Ignatius is very clear on this point: "Our teaching is in accord with

29 *Smyrn.* 5:8.
30 *Magn.* 6:1.

the Eucharist and the Eucharist confirms our teaching." The ministry of teaching flows from his presiding at the Liturgy, when the bishop proclaims the Word and celebrates its ultimate fulfillment in the Eucharist. "The certain charism of truth" comes from the sacramental order, which prolongs in history the action of salvation and the historical visibility of Christ. This is why it is vital that the Eucharist be identified with the time of Christ, the apostles and every moment of history. The ordination of a bishop by other bishops during the eucharistic Liturgy assures this identification, the Truth of the *una sancta*. (Luther clearly defines the marks of the Church: the proclamation of the Word and the administration of the sacraments.) This is absolutely true but the ancient tradition adds that it is the bishop who possesses the charism of guaranteeing the purity of preaching and the authenticity of the Eucharist. It is the mark or note of apostolicity which teaches that "the Church is in the bishop and the bishop in the Church." Einar Mollard, professor in the Lutheran theological faculty in Oslo, cites the study of Von Campenhausen (*Kirchliches Amt und geistliche Vollmacht in der ersten drei Jahrhunderten*, 1963) which found, already at the end of the first century, three regional accents of the episcopal role: "In Rome the bishop is the privileged celebrant of the Liturgy of the community, in Syria his model is a that of a spiritual father, in Asia Minor the preacher charged with apostolic teaching."

Since the time of St Ignatius of Antioch, the liturgical presidency by a bishop was normative and canon law assigns the Eucharist to episcopal function. This is the fundamental affirmation of the inseparable character of sacramental and jurisdictional powers and explains why the jurisdictional power of a bishop may never be extended nor exercised beyond the borders of the sacramental community of his own church.

The unity of the bishops does not come from their submission to an "extra-eucharistic" center but from the identity of the faith and the Eucharist which make them but one. The Orthodox Church does not operate with a concept of validity per se, it is not "valid orders" which give the power to preside at the Eucharist but the inseparability of doctrine and liturgical life. One cannot separate Christ from dogmatic truth, Christ from the sacramental life. The one who presides at the Eucharist possesses the full doctrinal authority. The Second Vatican

Council affirmed the sacramental validity of the episcopacy of the Eastern Church and for this reason authorized local intercommunion while at the same time was obliged to restrict its doctrinal authority, the episcopacy of the Eastern Church not being in communion with the see of Rome.

The words of St Irenaeus already cited show that the celebration of the Eucharist is the peak experience of the faith of the Church and the sign of a complete communion which includes Trinitarian doctrine, Christology, the Holy Spirit, ecclesiology, the ministry of the priesthood and the principle of apostolic succession. Therefore it must be seen that the Eastern Churches' opposition to intercommunion is not a mere conservatism. Where there is no unity of the faith, an open celebration would risk making of eucharistic unity a lie. Dogmatic unity with the Church of Rome can be achieved, given the immense diversity of traditions before the schism. The major obstacle resides in papal infallibility and universal jurisdiction. For the Eastern Church the place of the pope insofar as bishop of Rome and of his prerogatives is not a matter of dogma but a question of canon law, which determines the dimensions and the limits of the episcopal power of dioceses, of metropolitanates and of patriarchates. In accepting the priority of honor of Rome, the Eastern Church is able to consider the Roman "dogma" as a local tradition limited to the West which cannot be imposed upon the East or upon her ecclesiology and conciliar structure.

The experience of the Eucharist

To the ontological relationship of the Word to his humanity corresponds the dynamic relationship, the energy of the Holy Spirit. The Spirit deifies the humanity of Jesus and dwells there as anointing and dove. Commenting upon the *epiclesis* of the faithful, St Maximus the Confessor places himself in this same dynamism: "All of us who share in the same bread and cup are made one with each other in the communion of the unique Holy Spirit." Communion with God is projected immediately into the human dimension, into what the spiritual teachers call the "sacrament of the brother." St Cyril of Alexandria emphasizes the physical unity that the "mystical or sacramental blessing" produces in us the faithful.[31] One can even say that the Eucharist is like a transcendent support for every social action when it is directed toward the qualitative unity of all.

The faithful are "christified," "made into the Word," and according to St John Chrysostom, become like lions, figures of invincible power.[32] "By a veritable transfer of deifying energy," writes Nicholas Cabasilas, the clay is transformed into the substance of its Maker, the King of all."[33] This sharing of nature between Christ and those who partake of his "sacred flesh" constitutes the universal effect of the Eucharist. The bodily is rightly joined to the spiritual. Those who commune become "one in the flesh and blood" of Christ, sharing in his divine nature, according to St Cyril of Jerusalem.[34] St Maximus emphasizes this divinizing or *theosis*: "The Eucharist transforms a person making him or her very much like God, so much so that the faithful could be called 'gods' because God has completely become one with them and filled them."[35]

The Eastern Church's prayers are very clear: "I know that neither the immensity of my faults nor the great number of my transgressions can surpass the infinite tenderness and immense love of my God for men...at the same time joyously and trembling I receive the fire...as from the burning bush which was not consumed" (*Prayer of St Simeon the New Theologian*). The best act of thanksgiving is that of the martyr St Ignatius of Antioch himself "ground by the teeth of the beasts," transformed into the "bread of Christ," acceptable to the Lord (*Letter to Romans* 4:1). "The heart absorbs the Lord and the Lord absorbs the heart" (*Philokalia*). "In consuming the flesh of the Bridegroom and his blood, we enter the communion of marriage with him," writes St Theodore of Cyrus.[36] Here one can understand the words of St John of Kronstadt describing his own experience of the Eucharist in his book, *My Life in Christ*: "The days I did not celebrate the Eucharist, I felt as though I were dying."

31 *In Joannem XI*, PG 74:557.
32 *Hom. 46* on St. John.
33 *The Life in Christ*, p. 97.
34 *Cat.* 22:3.
35 *Myst.* 21.
36 See "Eucharistie du Cantique du Cantiques," *Irénikon* (1950), p. 274.

The Eucharist and eschatology

The Liturgy of the catechumens, or the first part of the Liturgy, is that of the Word. The Gospel is placed at the center of the altar. The liturgy of the faithful is that of the Eucharist when the bread and the cup are placed there. "He commanded and they were created," (Psalm 148:5) and thus what is announced by the Word is accomplished in the eucharistic bread and cup.

One cannot imagine any separation or opposition. The first part, the Liturgy of the catechumens, with its roots in the Liturgy of the synagogue, deepens the theology of time, of history. The Liturgy of the faithful is centered on the theology of the Kingdom, introducing history into the age to come. The prayer of *anamnesis*, or commemoration, says this: "Remembering this saving commandment and all those things which have come to pass for us: the Cross, the tomb, the Resurrection on the third day, the Ascension into heaven, the sitting on the right hand and the second and glorious coming."

When, in the early church, the penitents and catechumens were dismissed, the doors of the temple, of the church, were shut. Even today the deacon or the priest recalls this, singing: "The doors, the doors, in wisdom, let us attend!" just before the Creed. According to Ss Maximus the Confessor and Simeon of Thessalonica, the exclamation, "The doors" really has nothing to do with those of the church building. Rather, we are here at the threshold of the "fearful and ineffable mystery." It is the doors of history which are closed. "The catechumens are sent out and the faithful remain, and this moment reveals the end of time," St Simeon says. The one who remains in the temple enters into eschatology, the last things where the doors are opened. Therefore the faithful are judged, proclaim their faith in saying the Creed and at the moment of Communion "consume the fire of the age to come" and by anticipation are raised from death and actually see the coming of the Kingdom. It is the "second *Parousia*" and the "entrance into the marriage chamber of Christ,"[37] the brilliant feast and direct encounter.

After having assumed all the earthly coming of Christ, the Eucharist is the taste of final Communion: "Taste and see that the Lord is good"

---

37 St Maximus, *Myst.* 15 and 25.

(Psalm 33:8). It is at the "table without the veil" that the faithful will fully see that they really are "gods and the children of God." While arranging the eucharistic vessels after Communion, the deacon or priest prays: "O Christ, great and most holy Pascha, O Wisdom, Word and Power of God, grant that we may more perfectly partake of you in the never-ending day of your Kingdom."

In the preparation rite of the *proskomedia*, the priest mentioned the names of the living and the dead to be remembered and places particles of bread for each of them on the *diskos,* or paten. After Communion, they are immersed in the chalice, in the blood of Christ. At the conclusion of the Liturgy, the deacon or priest joins together the living and the dead in the great mystery of death conquered, saying: "Wash away O Lord, the sins of all those remembered here by your precious blood, through the prayers of your saints."

The Eucharist establishes communion with the totality of the Body. In the case of those who have died, it involves the participation of souls separated momentarily from their bodies. We cannot be more precise about this mystery except to cite the words of Nicholas Cabasilas: "It is then not surprising that Christ should grant to those departed souls, who are innocent of such faults, a share in this sacred banquet. It is amazing and supernatural that a man living in corruption can nourish himself on incorruptible flesh, but what is strange in the idea of an immortal soul nourishing itself on immortal food as is its nature? And if the first thing, which is marvelous and beyond nature, has been accomplished by God in his ineffable love and hidden wisdom, why should he not accomplish the other, which is both logical and likely?"[38]

Thus eucharistic communion embraces the divine and the human, the living and the dead, the historical age in which we live as well as the Eighth Day of the age of the Kingdom to come. The Eucharist points the destiny of this world towards the glorious reentry of the Spouse of the Lamb, the Church, into the communion of the love of the Holy Trinity, the Eucharist of the Kingdom which will go on forever.

---

38 *A Commentary on the Divine Liturgy*, J.M. Hussey and P.A. McNulty, trans, Crestwood NY: St Vladimir's Seminary Press (1983), p. 98.

Select Bibliography

Paul Evdokimov

1942 *Dostoievsky et le problème du mal.* Lyon: Ed. du Livre français.

1947 "La culture et l'eschatologie," *Le Semeur*, 50: 358-369.

1950 "Message aux Églises," *Dieu vivant*, 15:31-42.

1958 *La femme et le salut du monde.* Paris-Tournai: Casterman. [*Woman and the Salvation of the World*, trans., Anthony P. Gythiel, Crestwood, NY: SVS Press, 1994].

1959 *L'orthodoxie.* Neuchatel-Paris: Delachaux et Niestle.

1961 *Gogol et Dostoievski.* Paris: Desclée de Brouwer.

1962 *Le sacrament de l'amour.* Paris: Ed. de l'Epi. [*The Sacrament of Love*, trans., Anthony P. Gythiel and Victoria Steadman, Crestwood, NY: SVS Press, 1985].

1963 "Communicatio in sacris: une possibilité?" *Le messager orthodoxe*, 14, 25: 17-31.

1964 *Les âges de la vie spirituelle.* Paris: Desclée de Brouwer. [*The Ages of Spirituality*, rev. trans., Michael Plekon and Alexis Vinogradov, Crestwood, NY: SVS Press, 1998].

1966 *La prière de l'Eglise d'Orient.* Éditions Salvator, Mulhouse.

1968 *La connaissance de Dieu selon la tradition orientale.* Lyon: Xavier-Mappus.

1969 *L'Esprit Saint dans la tradition orthodoxe.* Paris: Ed. du Cerf.

1970 *Art de l'icône: Théologie de la beauté.* Tournai: Desclée de Brouwer.[*The Art of the Icon, A Theology of Beauty*, trans., Steven Bigham, Torrance CA: Oakwood, 1990].

1970 *Le Christ dans la penseé russe.* Paris: Ed. du Cerf.

1972 *L'amour fou de Dieu.* Paris: ed. du Seuil. [anthology]

1977 *La nouveauté de l'esprit.* Begrolles: Abbaye de Bellefontaine. [anthology]

1977 *Le buisson ardent.* Paris: Ed. P.Lathielleux. [anthology]

Elisabeth Behr-Sigel

1977 *Alexandre Boukharev. Un théologien de l'Église orthodoxe russe en dialogue avec le monde moderne.* Paris: Beauchesne.

1982   *Prière et sainteté dans l'Église russe.* Begrolles: Abbaye de Bellefontaine.

1991   *The Ministry of Women in the Church.* Torrance, CA: Oakwood.

1992   *The Place of the Heart: An Introduction to Orthodox Spirituality.* Torrance, CA: Oakwood.

1993   *Lev Gillet, un moine de l'Église d'Orient.* Paris: Ed. du Cerf.

Olivier Clément

1971   "Paul Evdokimov: Temoin de la beauté de Dieu," *Contacts* 73-74 [Special commemorative issue with biography, bibliography, remembrances, unpublished works.]

1985   *Orient-Occident, Deux Passeurs: Vladimir Lossky, Paul Evdokimov.* Geneva: Labor et Fides.

1995   "Paul Evdokimov, Témoin de la beauté de Dieu," Contacts, 172, special 25th anniversary number with essays on him.

Alexander Kniazeff

1979   *L'institut Saint-Serge.* Paris: Ed. Beauchesne.

Aidan Nichols, O.P.

1989   *Theology in the Russian Diaspora.* NY: Cambridge University Press.

1995   *Light from the East: Authors and Themes in Orthodox Theology.* London: Sheed & Ward.

Peter C. Phan

1979   "Mariage, monachisme et eschatologie: Contribution de Paul Evdokimov à la spiritualité chrétienne." *Ephemerides Liturgicae,* 93:352-380.

1981   "Evdokimov and the monk within." *Sobornost* 3, 1:53-61.

1985   *Culture and Eschatology: The Iconographical Vision of Paul Evdokimov.* NY: Peter Lang. [Contains the most exhaustive bibliography of and about Paul Evdokimov thus compiled].

Marc Raeff

1990   *Russia Abroad: A Cultural History of the Russian Emigration, 1919-1939.* NY: Oxford University Press.

Lewis Shaw

1996   "John Meyendorff and the Heritage of the Russian Theological Tradition." in *New Perspectives on Historical Theology: Essays in Memory of John Meyendorff,* Bradley Nassif, ed. Grand Rapids: Eerdmans, 10-35.

Nikita Struve

1996   *70 ans de l'emigration russe: 1919-1989.* Paris: Fayard.

Rowan Williams

1976   "Bread in the Wilderness: The Monastic Ideal in Thomas Merton and Paul Evdokimov." M. Basil Pennington, ed., *Monastic Tradition, East and West, One Yet Two.* Kalamazoo MI: Cistercian Publications.

Nicholas Zernov

1963   *The Russian Religious Renaissance of the Twentieth Century.* London: Darton, Longman & Todd.

Michael Plekon

1999   "Monasticism in the Marketplace, the Monastery, the World, and Within: An Eastern Church Perspective." *Cistercian Studies Quarterly,* 34:3, 339-368.

1998   "Open in Faith, Open to the World: The Work and Witness of Alexander Men." *Eastern Churches Journal,* 5: 2, 105-130.

1997   "'Always Everyone and Always Together': The Eucharistic Ecclesiology of Nicholas Afanasiev's *The Lord's Supper* Revisited." *St Vladimir's Theological Quarterly,* 41:2/3, 141-174.

1997   "Interiorized Monasticism: Paul Evdokimov on the Spiritual Life." *The American Benedictine Review,* 48: 3, September, 227-253.

1996   "The Church, the Eucharist and the Kingdom: Towards an Assessment of Alexander Schmemann's Theological Legacy." *St Vladimir's Theological Quarterly,* 40:3, 119-144.

1996   "Paul Evdokimov: Theologian of the Church and the World." *Modern Theology,* 12:1, 85-107.

1995   "Le Visage du Père en la Mère de Dieu: Marie dans les écrits théologiques de Paul Evdokimov." ["The Face of the Father in the Mother of God: Mary in Paul Evdokimov's Theology."] *Contacts,* 172, 270-286.

1995   "The God Whose Power is Weakness, Whose Love is Foolish: Divine Philanthropy, the Heart of Paul Evdokimov's Theology." *Sourozh,* 60, May, 15-26.

1995   "A Liturgical Being, A Life of Service: Paul Evdokimov's Gift and Witness to the Church." *Sobornost,* 17: 2, 28-37.

1995   "Alexander Schmemann: Father and Teacher of the Church." *Pro Ecclesia,* 3:3, 275-288.